Don't Disturb the Neighbors

Don't Disturb the Neighbors

The United States and Democracy in Mexico, 1980–1995

Jacqueline Mazza

Routledge

New York and London

Published in 2001 by
Routledge
29 West 35th Street
New York, NY 10001

Published in Great Britain in 2001 by
Routledge
11 New Fetter Lane
London EC4P 4EE

Printed in the United States of America on acid-free paper
Design and typography: Jack Donner

Library of Congress Cataloging-in-Publication Data

Mazza, Jacqueline.
    Don't disturb the neighbors : the United States and democracy in Mexico,
    1980–1995 / by Jacqueline Mazza.
          p.   cm.
    Includes bibliographical references.
    ISBN 0–415–92304–2 — ISBN 0–415–92305–0 (pbk.)
    1. United States—Foreign relations—Mexico. 2. Mexico—Foreign relations—
United States. 3. United States—Foreign relations—1989-   . 4. Democracy—
Mexico—History—20th century. 5. Mexico—Politics and government—1988–
I. Title.

E183.8.M6 .M39 2000
327.73072—dc21
                                                        00–032834

To my parents,
Frank and Constance Mazza

Contents

Preface

Today it is commonplace to hear that the promotion of democracy abroad is one of the fundamental principles of U.S. post–Cold War foreign policy. Supporting democracy has become the explicit rationale behind key diplomatic and military actions and an extensive program of international assistance. Much of what has been written about U.S. policy looks at those instances when the United States has been explicit about its pro-democracy objectives: for example, when the United States publicly condemns fraudulent elections (e.g., in the Philippines and Panama), leads a multilateral force to reinstall a democratically elected leader (e.g., Haiti), or supports a pro-democracy referendum (e.g., Chile). What interested me, however, were those cases when U.S. policy has not been so explicit. How does this universal U.S. goal apply more broadly in practice? How, or does it, apply to countries in which the United States has compelling economic, political, and security interests, interests that might not always coincide with greater democracy.

This is a book about one such case. For most of the contemporary history between the United States and Mexico, democracy has been a relatively minor issue in bilateral relations. Mexico has long been considered a country where inherent sensitivities to U.S. influence and a complex range of interests, including concern for internal stability, have rendered U.S. support for democracy in Mexico difficult to detect.

Trying to understand how U.S. policy functions without the standard pieces of evidence—a big aid program, a major foreign policy action, or even major speeches—is a bit like being a blindfolded detective. It is much harder to decipher a policy for which the written record is sparse and about which policymakers are reticent to discuss. Change is more likely in the near future with the inauguration of Mexico's first opposition president in more than seventy years, but sensitivity regarding Mexico's internal politics clearly dominated recent bilateral relations. My hope is to progress from broad generalizations and taboos of the recent past to a better understanding of how this increasingly important aspect of bilateral relations functions.

This book contains the first review of what was said and done by the United States regarding evolving democracy in Mexico during the Reagan administration in 1980 until the peso crisis in 1995, a period during which the United States developed a broad-based policy to support democracy abroad. In addition to a comprehensive review of the public record, this book relies on over sixty interviews of principally American, but also Mexican, officials who were generous with their time and insights when this work was a doctoral dissertation for the Johns Hopkins University, School of Advanced International Studies (SAIS).

My initial review of the public record revealed that the theme of democracy in Mexico arose in the United States largely during periods of key bilateral controversies or events, such as the North American Free Trade Agreement (NAFTA). Outside of such contexts of heightened bilateral controversy, democracy often faded from the bilateral agenda. The book thus provides focused consideration of four periods in which there was a greater spotlight on the issue of democracy in Mexico: (1) the period of high bilateral tension and open criticism of Mexico during the Reagan administration, 1982–1986; (2) negotiations surrounding the passage of NAFTA, 1989–1992; (3) the 1994 Mexican presidential elections; and (4) the peso crisis, 1994–1995. These case studies are presented chronologically within chapters covering each U.S. administration and are linked to the broader evolution of U.S. policy.

There have been many challenges to this topic. First, what is to be studied? What actions, statements, and activities are relevant to a study of democratization policy toward a single country? The book utilizes a list of policy instruments to support democracy developed by Samuel Huntington.[1] He provides six categories of instruments: statements of U.S. officials, economic pressures, diplomatic actions, material support for rebel forces and opposition parties, military actions, and multilateral diplomacy. It is only the instruments of public statements, diplomatic actions, and, in specific instances, political assistance that are relevant to the Mexican case.

More difficult still was deciding to stick narrowly to U.S.-understood terms of promoting democracy—democratic institution-building, free and fair elections, respect for human rights. There are many policies that intersect and are affected by the nature of internal politics—drugs, corruption, and stability, just to start. There are also indirect U.S. pro-democracy influences through the U.S.

media and culture. But to address each of these influences comprehensively would require separate volumes. The book thus sticks more narrowly to explicit U.S. pro-democracy efforts and addresses intersecting policies and influences only as public officials made direct links to Mexican democracy.

A second challenge encountered was examining U.S. policy toward a subject—Mexican democratic development—that defies easy classification and was advancing during the time period under consideration. To nearly all observers, the Mexican political system during the 1980s and 1990s was liberalizing in important directions and operating with both democratic and anti-democratic elements. Larry Diamond developed a special category, "semi-democracy," to classify countries like Mexico, which he saw as largely democratic in structure but authoritarian in practice.[2] During the time period covered by this book, the non-partisan New York-based Freedom House rated Mexico as "partly free," receiving a rating of 4 for political liberties and 4 for civil liberties (on a scale of 1 to 10) in 1995.[3] This book does not attempt to track the evolution of the Mexican political system or evaluate its political changes; this too is a study in itself. Rather, the book keeps more narrowly to the subject of U.S. policy and public response as the Mexican system evolved.

A third challenge was that, as an examination of recent U.S. policy, this study had to rely largely on public sources and interviews. Access to classified materials was limited to those documents that have been obtained by various sources under the Freedom of Information Act (FOIA) or disclosed in the press. Efforts were made in interviews to probe the distinction between public and private, behind-the-scenes activities of the various administrations, and these observations have been incorporated into the volume. FOIA requests would literally take decades to provide a complete, if there ever could be one, record of private communications. But it must be remembered that it is the public portion of U.S. policy that is the fundamental core of any U.S. policy to support democracy overseas. It is the public policy that constitutes the U.S. government's communication to the opposition and civil society of foreign nations as well as to its own bureaucracy and Congress, which are not privy to private communications. A behind-the-scenes policy can only be so effective if it is not backed up by a credible public policy. Furthermore, the public face of U.S. policy creates a framework from which any private dialogue is duly constrained. As Richard Neustadt explains, "The tendency of bureaucratic language to create in private the same images presented to the public should never be underrated. Further, public statements force the policymaker to work with the goals and expectations established by those statements because Congressmen and various aid constituencies do not forget the rhetoric even if the official may want to."[4]

I would like to thank sincerely the American and Mexican officials who con-tributed so importantly to this work by agreeing to be interviewed. Any infer-ences, analyses, and mistakes are my own. But it is only with their contribution that this record could be compiled at all. They might not all agree with the con-clusions or even the subject matter, but they displayed the utmost profession-alism and generosity of spirit. I appreciated more and more the heavy demands they faced in managing such a complex bilateral relationship and such a sensi-tive subject of bilateral relations. This is neither a simple story nor a simple relationship.

I also want to particularly thank my three principal academic advisors while this work was a doctoral dissertation. Drs. Riordan Roett and Carol Wise of SAIS and John Bailey of Georgetown University each contributed their sage counsel and guidance through each chapter. I also benefited from the support of family and friends: my parents, Frank and Constance Mazza, whose support has been deep and heartfelt and to whom I dedicate this book, my encourag-ing pack of siblings, brothers and sisters-in-law, and friends: Susan, Carmela, Patti, and Jana. And to my son Daniel, who provided a daily source of laugh-ter, joy, and perspective.

1.

Introduction

The United States has grappled with the question of promoting democracy abroad, in some fashion, from the very beginning of the Republic. America's founding fathers weighed whether the new democratic nation was to lead the world by example or by action. Should the United States to be the model or the modeler? Supporting democracy overseas was largely promoted as a moral imperative, and, as such, it rarely became the dominant focus of a U.S. foreign policy based on national interests. Important, but controversial exceptions were during the Wilson presidency and just after World War II. The historic record of U.S. support for democracy overseas has been a mixed one, with great variability in the countries targeted, instruments employed, and results achieved—from wholesale successes to devastating failures.

The Cold War brought a larger foreign policy context to any U.S. predisposition to support democratic government. Containment of the Soviet Union, first articulated by George Kennan, expanded quickly to the broader containment of communist influence worldwide. This placed emphasis on building alliances with strong anti-communist states in the Third World, even if it meant explicitly sacrificing democratic principles. Not only security but also economic and other interests could be seen to dominate over a preference for democratic government.

In the midst of the Cold War, Ronald Reagan began to shift the rhetoric, at least, for supporting democracy overseas. In 1982, he announced that the United States would openly support the worldwide democratic revolution and directly foster "the infrastructure of democracy."[1] In contrast to its predecessors, the Reagan administration argued that support for democracy abroad was more than just in U.S. moral interests—it was in U.S. national security interests as well. Dubbed "idealpolitik," the administration envisioned the fusion of realism and idealism where the state can increase its security by promoting its values and ideals.[2] How far this policy went in real terms is widely debated. U.S. policy toward Central America, for example, was largely cast as a pro-democracy policy, but there, Thomas Carothers argues, Reagan administration policy was still fundamentally anti-communism with a pro-democracy veneer.[3]

In the post–Cold War era, both Presidents Bush and Clinton elevated support for democracy abroad to one of three fundamental principles of U.S. foreign policy. The Clinton administration tested, with incomplete success, whether "democratic enlargement" might be the organizing framework for all of U.S. foreign policy. With the rapid embrace of democracy worldwide following the fall of the Berlin wall, democracy has come to characterize the post–Cold War era as the baseline political system. Not only national governments but also multilateral institutions have embraced active support for promoting democracy overseas as never before. The end of communism created new opportunities and freed policymakers from the traditional constraints of earlier years, according to Lars Schoultz, who called it the "end of the era of strategic denial."[4]

Despite the prominent international position now occupied by democracy promotion, much less is known about how this new sweeping normative goal is applied in practice. As in the past, scholars still find substantial variability in how and where this universal principle is applied. In some countries, U.S. support for a democratic transition is prominent and vocal; in others, it is hardly noticeable. Contrast Haiti to China, Poland to Russia. Often when U.S. support for democracy abroad is examined today, scholars look at the most prominent cases, countries in which U.S. efforts have been most explicit. But what explains the cases when it is not? What constrains this policy from being universally applied? One can jump to many quick conclusions about why the United States might not openly advocate democratic change in particular nations—the threat or impact on critical U.S. interests, foreign resistance to American influence, for example—but these explanations are rarely articulated by U.S. officials, nor are they probed for their validity.

Democracy Policy Toward Geostrategic States

One can quickly surmise that it seems to be important Third World states with close strategic, political, or economic relations with the United States where American support for democracy seems less prominent. Towards these geostrategic nations, pro-democracy assistance and political support are highly constrained, in contrast to more active and vocal assistance toward other nations.

Mexico fits the bill of a geostrategic state, but other examples might include Russia, China, Indonesia, Turkey, Kuwait, and Saudi Arabia. These countries have widely varying political systems and different sets of interests with the United States, yet they are similar in the constrained nature of relations with the United States over their internal political systems. These are countries in which active support for democracy might be seen to conflict with other more pressing goals. Some of these countries may also be viewed as particularly resistant to U.S. influence.

The Case of Mexico

Mexico clearly fits the profile of a geostrategic country in which the promotion of democracy has been less evident. It is a country with deep historic sensitivities to U.S. intervention in its internal affairs. Foreign and domestic policies intermingle in one of the United States' most complex bilateral relationships. An explicit dialogue or open support for pro-democracy forces as seen toward other countries is not as apparent in past relations with Mexico. Scholars have argued that U.S. interests in stability in Mexico have traditionally dominated over interest in supporting democracy.[5] Mexican scholar Lorenzo Meyer confirms that "historically, the non-democratic nature of the Mexican political system has not been a significant factor in Mexican-U.S. relations."[6] He argues that the only exception has been during the Wilsonian period, when an anti-authoritarian revolt during the Mexican revolution coincided with Wilson's democratic reform movement; even this period, however, was brief and conflictive.[7] In an era when democracy promotion is touted as at the top of the U.S. agenda, how did U.S. officials think about and treat the question of democracy in Mexico? Did the United States make explicit tradeoffs between stability and economic and other interests in deciding whether to pursue support for democracy? Or did the U.S. simply "exempt" geostrategic states like Mexico from its policy of promoting democracy abroad?

This book seeks to understand recent U.S. relations with Mexico over democracy by first trying to identify and document whether there is a discernible pattern to these relations over time. It starts in 1980 at the beginning of the Reagan administration as a broader U.S. policy to promote democracy abroad was emerging. It follows U.S. policy through to the end of the peso crisis in 1995. This is a very dynamic fifteen-year period in which Mexico embarked on sweeping economic reforms and, to a lesser extent, political reform. The book compiles the public record over this time period, looking at who was publicly raising the question of democracy in Mexico in what way and what specific pro-democracy support was given. An initially detected pattern was that democracy in Mexico was typically raised publicly and critically by only a minority within U.S. policy circles. The majority seemed aloof, rarely criticizing anti-democratic events in Mexico publicly or pushing for change. The minority, on the other hand, appears to raise the question of the lack of full democracy in Mexico only as it coincided and reinforced another more pressing issue—be it the passage of NAFTA, anti-drug policy, or the peso crisis. These periods of greater attention to the question of democracy in Mexico form case studies within each of the chapters.

Through each U.S. administration in the post–Cold War period, the book seeks to verify this initially-observed majority-minority pattern of U.S. relations with Mexico over democracy and track its evolution. With each administration and case study period, the book tries to probe a bit deeper into why this particular pattern of relations occurred. Why is the subject of democracy in Mexico raised typically by an often-outcast minority? Why did most U.S. policymakers feel that they should be silent about anti-democratic events in Mexico when they do not feel the same toward other nations? How are decisions made about particular pro-democratic actions or statements, and how have relations evolved over time?

It was first thought that U.S. policy could be explained from a rational actor–realist perspective. This theory maintains that nations, behaving as single actors, make policy decisions based on a rational assessment of national interests. In this case, one could envision U.S. policymakers actively weighing democracy promotion against other pressing interests with Mexico—internal stability, trade, drug policy, for example—and explicitly deciding on a minimal course of action on democracy that does not harm these other interests. A minority, least affected by the weight of the bilateral agenda, would be the most likely to explicitly advocate political change in Mexico. What could have developed over time, it was first thought, was a realist consensus that active U.S. promotion of democracy in Mexico was counter to specific U.S. interests.

After a series of interviews, however, there simply wasn't enough evidence that realist calculations were being actively made. A consensus requires extensive internal debate, evidence of alternative policies being considered, and a public and private airing of opinion to arrive at a policy course. Policy discussion was actually highly limited. Nor were there substantial policy differences found among various U.S. bureaucracies that could have explained policy working based on the bureaucratic politics model. What was more common was not the weighing of policy alternatives over promoting democracy in Mexico, but simply the unspoken agreement of "non-action" among U.S. officials. U.S. officials had already prejudged how they should handle the question of democracy in Mexico even as Mexico was undergoing substantial political and economic change itself.

Understanding Implicit Policymaking

If U.S. policymaking was more implicit, it might be better explained as operating on a set of internalized beliefs, beliefs so embedded and shared that they do not require frequent discussion or provoke bureaucratic conflict. Alexander George and Ole Holsti's work on "operational codes," which builds on the work of Nathan Leites, offers some interesting insights.[8] George explains that operational code refers to a general set of beliefs about fundamental issues of history and politics that relate specifically to the problem of action—how policy should operate. These beliefs influence the perception and diagnoses of events and importantly constitute the rules of conduct and norms of behavior of decision making. Operational code, George admits, is a bit of a misnomer because it seems to imply that there is a mechanical set of recipes that a policymaker applies.[9] George, in fact, thinks a better name than operational code would be "approaches to political calculation."[10] George, Leites, Holsti, and others were all talking about a series of more fundamental beliefs constituting a policymaker's operational code. But, more broadly, their work illuminates how beliefs can frame and restrict policy responses. In the case of promoting democracy in Mexico, one can ask whether it was more implicit "operational" beliefs about *how* democracy policy should operate toward a country like Mexico that shaped U.S. official thinking.

While chronicling the record of U.S. policy toward democracy in Mexico then, this book explores through interviews with U.S. officials one particular operational or policy belief: that the United States should not openly criticize Mexican politics. Observers of United States–Mexican relations will say they see this regularly. While the United States may clumsily criticize the Mexican government on a host of policies, it is relatively quiet on Mexico's internal politics. And if it did criticize Mexican lack of full democracy, the Mexican government made a point of challenging any such U.S. criticism as illegitimate and tantamount to interference in its internal affairs.

What is explored here is how widespread and internalized such a ban on public criticism of Mexican internal politics may be, and how and whether it serves to shape how the United States approaches democratic development toward Mexico. It is not that avoiding public criticism is a "bad" idea per se. What is being investigated is whether a self-imposed ban on public criticism may have had a broader impact in limiting, de facto, the range of pro-democracy political options considered and the pro-democracy policy pursued.

The identification of a belief against criticizing Mexican internal politics would not mean that it is the only belief at work. Nor would it mean that other determinants, such as assessments of U.S. national interests, were not also influencing U.S. decision making toward democracy in Mexico. Alexander

George is careful to point out that even the larger concept of the operational code refers to an important influence on decision making, not the sole determinant. In the case of U.S. policy toward democracy in Mexico, it simply means that one part of U.S. relations can be more often explained as operating on a "default" setting, stemming from a given belief or assumptions than from day-to-day political calculations of national interests. Implicit policymaking seems even more likely in the case of geostrategic states for which policymakers must manage a complex relationship and may find bilateral relations more manageable if one part of the relationship operates without question.

Origins of a Presumed Ban on Public Criticism

If such a belief against public criticism of Mexican politics operates, where might it likely have come from? It is not supposed that such a belief is ideological, although it may seem that way. Rather, the origin of such a belief likely comes from earlier assessments of U.S. interests that are simply so embedded and accepted that they are not revisited. While the book explores with U.S. officials the reasons why they may believe they should not criticize Mexican politics publicly, it is helpful to discuss at the outset where these early assessments of U.S. interests may have come from.

A belief against public criticism is likely to arise from a widening of the foreign policy importance of a particular country and the perceived need to balance competing interests. In the case of Mexico and other geostrategic states, this is likely to stem from the broadening foreign policy context of World War II and the subsequent building of anti-communist alliances during the Cold War. Most analysts note an important shift in the troubled United States–Mexican relationship during World War II and under Franklin Delano Roosevelt's Good Neighbor policy. Lorenzo Meyer and Josefina Zoraida Vázquez maintain that, while not free from friction, the World War II period was one in which the national interests of the two countries coincided more closely than ever before.[11]

After initial sympathies with the Axis powers, the Mexican government became an important and needed ally in World War II. Mexico accelerated the production of raw materials and became an important supplier of metals; it lent workers to the United States under the *bracero* program and, while not sending soldiers to battle, served as a reserve of manpower if needed. While becoming more needed, the Mexican government was also becoming more reliable and moderate in U.S. eyes.

After World War II, Mexico's broader foreign policy utility continued. Mexican President Alemán supported the common Western defense along the lines of the Truman Doctrine. While Mexican anti-communism had its limitations and confrontations with the United States,[12] the Mexican government led a strong, stable anti-communist state that had many advantages for the United States. Mexico's position permitted the United States to deploy an "economy of military force" in the Mexican/Caribbean region, as Sergio Aguayo argues.[13] The Mexican government ensured that the United States didn't have to worry about communism within their borders; the United States gave Mexico more leeway in foreign policy in return. Jorge Domínguez has described this earlier as a set of political bargains between the United States and Mexico.[14]

Implicit in the widening foreign policy importance of Mexico was the lessening of interest in the internal makeup of such a successful regime, particularly as it was delivering on the higher priority interests of stability and anti-communism. Not only did the lack of democracy in Mexico likely become dwarfed by other, more pressing interests, but it also became questionable itself, as political change might affect Mexican internal stability or the growth of the left.

The geostrategic rationale for keeping quiet on internal political events in Mexico was highly reinforced by the particular history of U.S. relations with Mexico. Any question of U.S. interference in Mexican internal affairs evokes a painful past and certain conflict between the two nations. After provoking war with Mexico in 1848, the United States annexed one half of Mexican territory. The United States directly meddled in the Mexican revolution of 1910, and President Wilson sent U.S. troops to occupy the port city of Veracruz in 1914. The strong stance the Mexican government has maintained regarding foreign interference in any nation's internal affairs results directly from its past relationship with the United States. As Robert Pastor sums up, "[T]here is no country in the world which is more sensitive to U.S. efforts to influence it than Mexico, and no country as successful in resisting American influence."[15] Even as the Mexican political system began to slowly open up in the 1980s, both the more general foreign policy rationale and the more specific history of U.S.–Mexican relations were powerful subcurrents underlying the restraint on public criticism, as each of the following chapters explores further.

The Reagan administration provides an important starting point to begin this fifteen-year investigation of U.S. treatment of democracy in Mexico. By 1982, the administration had begun to articulate a universal policy to foster democracy overseas, arguing that such a policy was in U.S. strategic interests. Yet, from the outset, a different set of dynamics appeared to be shaping U.S. policy toward Mexico. Little was said about democracy in Mexico as this major policy was unfolding. Slowly and fitfully, the actions of a small, emerging minority within the administration and Congress came to overshadow a broader predisposition to keep quiet on Mexican internal politics.

2.

The First Reagan Administration: Public Criticism Emerges Slowly

The Reagan administration started its tenure with the stated intention of developing a new, more positive relationship with Mexico than its predecessor, the Carter administration. Within two years, however, the administration's initial desire to rejuvenate bilateral relations was overwhelmed by a series of bilateral tensions encompassing financial crisis, Mexican foreign policy toward Central America, drugs, and immigration. The treatment of the question of democracy in Mexico must be seen in the context of first calmed, then rising bilateral tensions. It is within the context of this greater stress on the bilateral relationship that a minority of policy officials tried to link their particular policy concerns with the undemocratic nature of the Mexican political system.

A period of more open criticism of Mexican politics can be identified from late 1982 to its unforeseen end in August 1986 in the second term. The case study period is divided here between the first administration with its continued escalation into a second phase in the second administration. To a number of observers, the 1982–1986 period reflects a deliberate administration policy to openly criticize the Mexican ruling party for its anti-democratic practices and favor the right-wing National Action Party (PAN in Spanish), a policy whose underlying intent was to get Mexico to change its foreign policy toward Central America.[1] Others have argued that criticism of Mexico during this period was motivated largely by concern about Mexican instability rather than by any ideological agenda of right-wing conservatives.[2] Far from a concerted, administration-wide policy, public criticism can be seen to come from only a small minority of officials, often considered the far right of the Reagan policy team. This minority raised the issue of democracy in Mexico mainly as it coincided with other pressing policy concerns of instability, Mexican foreign policy, and the drug trade. It is this vocal minority contingent, at times uncontradicted by the administration, that appears to present a collective image of Reagan administration–directed criticism of Mexican politics. The broader foreign policy direction, though, still favored and was driven by an operational belief against openly criticizing Mexican politics. This is the policy line that reasserts itself by mid-way in the second term.

Early Administration Years: 1981–1982

United States–Mexican relations under the Carter administration had deteriorated markedly, from policy disagreements over oil, trade, and asylum for the Shah of Iran to personal animosity between the two presidents. "Conventional wisdom has it that relations between Mexico and the United States went from bad to worse during the Carter administration,"[3] argues Susan Kaufman Purcell. Improving relations with Mexico was put explicitly at the top of the Reagan administration's Latin America agenda. Thomas Enders, appointed as Assistant Secretary of State for Inter-American Affairs, emphasized this priority in one of his first speeches. He identified three main tasks for U.S. policy in the hemisphere: to improve relations with Mexico, to counter Cuban influence in the Caribbean and Central America, and to revitalize alliances with the major South American countries.[4]

Early relations under the Reagan administration improved noticeably with a closer personal affinity between Reagan and Mexican President López Portillo.[5] According to Philip Hughes, who first handled Latin American Affairs for Vice President Bush and then joined the National Security Council (NSC) in 1985, "We did some extraordinary things to try and be nice to the Mexicans in the early years of the Reagan administration ... [My] sense in those years, late López Portillo, early De la Madrid, was that both governments were groping for ways to better relations."[6] Among these efforts he includes the pre-inaugural meeting of López Portillo and Reagan in January 1981, President Reagan's agreement to attend the 1981 Third World Summit in Cancun at the persistent urging of President López Portillo, and the financial bailout package later provided by the United States as the debt crisis broke in 1982.

There was a desire not only to keep Mexican relations on an even keel, but also to keep the subject off the radar screen completely. The administration sought to forge ahead on what it considered to be more pressing concerns in Central America, specifically the civil war in El Salvador and Sandinista control of the Nicaraguan government. Diplomat T. Frank Crigler recalls he was asked by Enders to move back to Washington to take the top job of Mexico

Country Director at the State Department. "Tom Enders called me up in Bogota to take it, to partly get it out of his hair, not because it was so troublesome at the time, but because there was so much more important stuff going on south of there." He remarked that Enders's attitude regarding Mexican relations was "to keep things calm; don't involve the 6th floor,"[7] referring to the floor where the top level State Department officials worked.

Official U.S. Statements: 1981–1982

Outwardly, in terms of its public statements about Mexican politics or democracy, the new administration was relatively silent. Nor did Mexico receive any special attention in congressional legislation or notable mention in the *Congressional Record*,[8] apart from the usual mention during hearings on the appointment of the U.S. ambassador to Mexico. What little was said about Mexico's internal politics by the administration was far from critical and never referred to the undemocratic nature of the system. For example, in a speech to the Organization of American States (OAS) General Assembly in 1982, Secretary of State George Shultz included Mexico in a list of countries where "democratic institutions have functioned without interruption for a generation or more."[9] In confirmation hearings for ambassador-designate John Gavin there is also little reference to democracy, save a statement by Gavin that "I am firmly dedicated to the proposition that nothing could be better for our nation than a free, viable and prosperous Mexico."[10] The repetition of this phrase "a free, viable and prosperous Mexico," particularly the "free" portion, was, in later years, to draw criticism when he repeated it in Mexico, but this raised no concerns at the initial hearing in Washington.

This noncritical public characterization of the Mexican political system contrasted with some privately-held views within the administration. A 1981 secret State Department memorandum, for example, called Mexico a "unique quasi-authoritarian government" and continued: "[A]lthough elections are held regularly and a new President assumes power every six years, the choice in fact is made by the elite of the all-encompassing Institutional Revolutionary Party (PRI)."[11]

While the official public record of this period reveals little conflict or concern regarding the nature of the Mexican political system, policy disagreements over Mexico were brewing both within the administration and with Mexico in a number of key areas. A small faction of political appointees were voicing preoccupations with Mexico's susceptibility to leftist influence and its activist Central America policy. Besides these two concerns, budding contacts between Republican activists and the right-wing PAN party fed Mexican government preoccupations. These three emerging areas of conflict during the honeymoon period of 1980–1982 would ultimately affect the motivations of a small cadre of Republican officials who later engaged in open criticism of the Mexican regime.

Mexico: Potential Instability

At the outset of the Reagan administration, key advisors—and the president himself—expressed concern that Soviet and perceived communist activism in Central America could spread to Mexico. In a campaign speech in March 1980, candidate Reagan asked: "Must we let Grenada, Nicaragua, El Salvador all become additional 'Cubas,' new outposts for Soviet combat brigades? Will the next push of the Moscow–Havana axis be northward to Guatemala, then to Mexico, south to Costa Rica and Panama?"[12]

The concern that Mexico could be destabilized by outside forces came from those who believed that communist-inspired violence could take root in Mexico. While one of the most politically stable of all developing countries, Mexico was seen as vulnerable, by adherents of this view, because of its penchant for corruption, authoritarian political institutions, and the strength of nationalist, left-wing political forces. One adherent who published this view widely before joining the Reagan administration was Constantine Menges. Menges was hired by Central Intelligence Agency (CIA) Director William Casey to lead the National Intelligence Office for Latin America at the CIA in the first years of the administration. He later moved to be Special Assistant for Latin American affairs in the National Security Council from 1983 to 1986. He warned in 1980:

> The Sandinista victory in Nicaragua last July encouraged leftist terrorists' assaults against the Governments of El Salvador and Guatemala; these continue to gain force and might succeed soon. That in turn would open Mexico to the politics of polarization through leftist terror and to possible destabilization by a coalition of reformist, radical and Communist groups opposed to the current regime. Mexico might then become an Iran-next-door.[13]

John Sammis, a Special Assistant to the U.S. Ambassador in Mexico City in the early 1980s remembers that Iran was a "cottage industry" within the U.S. government: "[E]veryone was trying to pick the next Iran."[14] Director Casey heard that Mexico could be this next Iran principally from two sources: Menges and Defense Intelligence Agency (DIA) Chief Eugene Tighe. Tighe warned Casey that Mexico was a big concern, with an insurgency in the countryside where local police, not the central government, controlled some areas. This was a place where a Khomeini-type leader could arise from instability he warned.[15] Most did not agree with this Iran-on-our-doorstep interpretation. CIA analyst Frank Horton explains how it worked for the few people who held this view:

> In the first years of the Reagan administration a powerful image of Mexico was of another Iran ... Mexico as Iran: superficially stable, rotting inside; a corrupt ruling institution that was losing or had already lost its grip on politics as well as ignorant of what was going on in its own country—complacency in Mexico City, complacency about Mexico in Washington. This was the sand on which the intellectual edifice was built.[16]

Throughout Mexico's history, stability has been a preeminent concern of the United States. But this more extreme view that instability would come from leftist contagion from Central America appears to have been held by a minority of political appointees at the CIA and State Department, a handful of military leaders, and perhaps a few Senators, notably Senator Jesse Helms (R-NC), then Chairman of the Senate Foreign Relations Committee. General Gordon Sumner, appointed as special advisor to Tom Enders at Helms's behest, was one of the political appointees in the State Department known to be concerned with corruption and leftist political instability in Mexico. For the most part, the careerists in the State Department continued to view the ruling PRI as "an agent of stability."[17] As Crigler describes it, this early view of growing instability "wasn't common. It was the nut group, strongly convinced people."[18] Menges confirms as well that "many in the State Department were reluctant to admit it, reluctant to think that that might happen."[19] CIA analyst Horton explains: "This doomsday view of Mexico led to differences of opinion between those in the administration who held it and the professional, career people in the places that mattered, State and the CIA."[20] Crigler explains further the internal dynamic: "Careerists [career foreign service and civil service personnel] recognized that these were politically important people that you had to tolerate ... and yet you never take them as seriously as they might have wished."[21]

Jesse Helms raised the issue of potential Mexican instability in the confirmation hearings for the ambassador-designate to Mexico, John Gavin. Gavin was a close friend of President Reagan's, a fellow actor with a degree in Latin American affairs and close business ties to Mexico. Both Helms and Gavin would later become identified as principal critics of Mexico. At the confirmation hearings, however, they showed some of their differences. Helms was known to have supported Gavin as a fellow conservative, but he could see that Gavin did not see the danger of Mexican instability: "Would you agree that the political situation in Mexico is not all that stable?"[22] Gavin responded: "I believe, on balance, that we need not fear for the security of the Mexican republic."[23]

The internal debate over the leftist virus was kept largely in house in the early phase, occasionally spilling out in a press statement or speech. Constantine Menges indicated, "Much of this debate and discussion would happen at NSC meetings."[24] Assistant Secretary of State Elliot Abrams described the concern about Mexican instability as localized around Director Casey. "With the exception of Casey," he argued, "the whole administration—Treasury, Commerce, State, NSC—was not worried about stability in Mexico."[25] While the concern with leftist-inspired instability was relatively narrowly based, concern for Mexican policy toward Central America was much more widespread and was later to color much of the political relations between the two countries.

Mexico's Activist Central America Policy

The independence of Mexican foreign policy, even its anti-American nature, has long been considered an acceptable *modus vivendi* between the two countries. As long as Mexican policy did not directly undermine U.S. interests, Mexican support for left-wing governments and anti-American rhetoric had been perceived as helping the Mexican government solidify its support on the left and maintain a strong, anti-communist state. This informal understanding showed great signs of strain during the Reagan years, as many in the administration perceived Mexico's Central American activism to work against its policy of emphasizing military solutions to the conflicts in Nicaragua and El Salvador. The Mexican government openly supported the Sandinista government in Nicaragua, communist Cuba, and the leftist rebels in El Salvador. This support was more than just rhetorical. It included financial assistance to Nicaragua, permission to allow leftist rebels to meet freely on Mexican territory, and, beginning in January 1983, leadership in seeking a negotiated, solution to the Central America conflict through the Contadora group (Panama, Colombia, Venezuela, and Mexico). But to many in the Reagan administration, the Mexican government showed its contempt for U.S. policy all too overtly. The Mexican government defiantly took issue with U.S. foreign policy in the region by warning against a U.S. invasion of Cuba or Nicaragua, by denying the importance of U.S.-backed elections in El Salvador in 1982, and by finding unacceptable the administration's Caribbean Basin Initiative (July 1982) because it excluded Cuba and Nicaragua. An act that early on particularly incensed the administration occurred in August 1981 when Mexico and France announced joint recognition of the Salvadoran rebels and their political affiliate, the FDR (Democratic Revolutionary Front). With this declaration, the administration saw the Mexicans as "playing with fire."[26]

Mexico Country Director Crigler explains the early dominance given to the Central American issue in United States–Mexico relations: "They [Enders and the Interamerican Affairs Bureau] were far more concerned about this sort of meddlesome Mexican role in Central America than they were anything else about Mexico. This issue continuously intruded to color all the others."[27]

Republican Affinity for the PAN Opposition Party

A final seed of discord being sown in this honeymoon period was a new ideological affinity between the center-right PAN in Mexico and Republican activists. Meetings with opposition parties were considered relatively routine diplomacy in other countries. But previous U.S. administrations had clearly steered away from antagonizing the Mexican government by avoiding public contact with any of Mexico's small and nascent opposition parties. This began to change in the early 1980s. The relationships and contacts between members of the PAN, the administration, and Republican activists in the early 1980s had impetus in both the United States and Mexico.

The origin of these links in the United States, recalls Howard Wiarda, was in 1979–1980, largely from activists associated with the president's Foreign Policy Advisory Group.[28] These activists were establishing contacts with like-minded political parties around the globe in order to build a stronger community of conservative, anti-communist parties. There was a natural attraction between the pro-democracy, business-based PAN and Republican activists in think tanks around Washington. The Heritage Foundation and the Inter-American Defense Council were the most prominent institutions helping facilitate PAN trips to Washington during the 1980s to participate in various seminars and meetings. On one occasion, PAN leaders made a presentation at a weekly meeting of the White House Office of Public Diplomacy.[29]

A similar drive came from a number of PAN activists in Mexico. PAN leaders were both responding to this new ideological opening by Reagan activists and shifting their own strategy to build international networks and support to pressure for political change in Mexico. This included approaching U.S. politicians and interest groups and filing human rights cases in international forums for the first time. In 1982, the PAN named its first foreign affairs secretary, Jesus Gonzales Schmall. These external activities of the PAN were a dramatic break from the age-old tradition of keeping foreigners, particularly the United States, out of domestic matters. They were to cause great controversy both within the PAN and between the PAN and the Mexican government.

While the PAN fit the profile of a conservative, pro-democracy party committed to liberal economic reforms, reception within the administration was mixed. The Reagan administration officials interviewed argued that the administration saw the PAN as a limited, regional party with little chance of governing. "We liked the PAN but we didn't take them seriously," recalls NSC staffer Kim Flower.[30] In the 1990s, the PAN was to have much greater national reach, but administration officials argued that they did not see this at the time. A classified 1981 cable from the U.S. consul in Monterrey describes the PAN as "a fly biting the rump of the state."[31] Elliot Abrams remembers an early meeting with the PAN in 1981–1982, facilitated by Republican activists, when he was Assistant Secretary of State for Human Rights. Abrams recalls that PAN visitors requested three things: some sort of association with the United States that would help legitimize them as a party, help in getting Republican financial support for their party, and U.S. assistance in pushing for a more open and competitive political system. Abrams recalls, "[T]heir view was the louder you [the United States] are, the better off we're all going to be."[32] This was an explicit calling for the breaking of the operational belief against public criticism, and it is what the administration was accused of doing within a few short years. But Abrams and many other administration officials say they did not want to do this in the case of Mexico. The administration did permit the initiation of contacts with the PAN as they had with other conservative parties, but contacts were fewer and more limited than with other nations. By the mid-1980s, a number of contacts in Mexico were to become more explicit between the PAN and administration officials, but administration officials continued to argue that this did not constitute a political or pro-democracy strategy. While the administration did agree to visits with the PAN, there seems to have been little concrete results from them, save an irritant to the Mexican government.

These three emerging sources of tensions—questions over instability in Mexico, Mexican policy toward Central America, contacts with the PAN—would surface more notably in the next two years. But during this early period, they were largely on the sidelines. It was extremely rare for officials to make publicly any direct link to the Mexican political system. At no point did the administration ever publicly call for greater democracy in the country. Mexico Country Director T. Frank Crigler explains that U.S. officials did not question or probe Mexico's electoral or political systems in these early years: "The only political issue that mattered was Central America."[33]

Case Study, Phase I:
August 1982–December 1984

No event was to shift the relative calm of the first years of the Reagan administration's relations with Mexico more than the growing economic crisis in Mexico. The crisis culminated in a dramatic financial rescue package engineered by the United States in late 1982. Mexican debt had tripled since 1976 to over $87 billion. U.S. officials were clearly taken aback by Mexico's nationalization of the banks, its suspension of debt payments, and the potential ruin to the international financial system if the crisis was not resolved. As the economic crisis continued to unfold, more vocal characterizations of the Mexican political system emanated from the U.S. Embassy in Mexico City. Washington was intensely preoccupied with Mexico during the financial crisis, but when the crisis subsided, the administration returned to being only tangentially involved with Mexico, principally as Mexico intersected with its Central America policy. This then left the lead to the independent-minded ambassador, John Gavin.

Economic Crisis Raises the Specter of Instability

In August 1982, Mexico surprised the world by announcing it had run out of foreign-exchange reserves and was suspending its foreign debt payments. Mexico had borrowed heavily based on promising oil revenues; interest rates, however, were very high. When oil prices fell sharply in 1981, Mexico was stuck with mountains of debt it could not repay. The prospect of the second lead debtor in the Third World defaulting was monumental for the Reagan administration, for both Mexico's stability, and for the viability of the international financial system overall. George High, Deputy Chief of Mission at the U.S. Embassy in Mexico City from August 1982 to June 1983, then Country Director for Mexico from 1983–1985, recalls: "In 1982, the overriding issue clearly was economic; the banking crisis, that was almost the entire focus of Washington and the embassy."[34]

As High confirms, however, the political dimensions of the banking crisis received less attention. The 1982 package was largely handled by the Treasury Department and Federal Reserve Board (FED) Chairman Paul Volker and within the NSC. Georges Fauriol of the Center for Strategic and International Studies (CSIS) explains that this produced a "clean" package that did not expand to political conditions or the political context of the crisis, as would be the case a decade later in the 1994–1995 peso crisis.[35]

As the 1982 banking crisis raised the fear that economic instability and falling income could also lead to political instability, the ideas of the small cadre of political appointees began to reemerge. Constantine Menges argues that with the financial crisis, the "sense of Mexico's potential vulnerability was enhanced.... Now even some in the State Department were saying, 'Ah, Mexico's pretty brittle.' "[36] Crigler explains:

> The [1982 banking crisis] crisis was when the nut group was resurrected.... When the peso went belly-up then these people came to the fore again and said, look, what's happening there is not just that López Portillo has stolen all the

wealth of the country. Unless we take a more active interest in the country's internal problems we risk having internal collapse on our borders. People were beginning to pay more attention.[37]

He adds: "It took us a while to recognize the whole polity was in crisis. We had a belief in a kind of permanence of the PRI, that the PRI was able to remake itself for any crisis that came down the pike.[38] This concern regarding Mexico's potential instability and the capacity of its internal political institutions was short-lived. Mexico's decisive concessions during the crisis helped overcome the preoccupations of some regarding its potential vulnerability. Mexico made a series of politically difficult decisions to obtain the U.S. bridge financing necessary to cover the period until International Monetary Fund (IMF) and commercial bank negotiations could be completed. Mexico's major concessions—reducing its fiscal deficit, lowering real wages, and correcting for an overvalued peso—were to bind even more U.S. policymakers to the incoming De la Madrid administration. Instability went back to being the concern of a minority, albeit vocal.

Washington Relatively Quiet as New Mexican President Takes Over

Whatever the internal preoccupations of some U.S. policymakers, Washington officials continued to speak very rarely of the Mexican political system, and when they did, it was cast predominantly in positive, democratic terms reflecting a continued adherence to an operational belief against open criticism. Deputy Treasury Secretary Robert T. McNamara, for example, portrayed Mexico in a press conference as a "Western, democratic, politically stable country" that was a good friend and ally of the United States.[39]

Hopes for this friendship were tied to the newly elected president, Miguel De la Madrid, inaugurated on December 1, 1982. De la Madrid laid promise to a somewhat different presidency than his predecessor. He was from the new "technocrat" class, schooled in U.S.-style management and economics. He took over with promises of "moral renovation," implying a crackdown on the corruption of his predecessor's regime. There was also the glint of a political opening, as the PRI permitted a series of PAN opposition victories at a very local level in 1983.

U.S. Embassy Takes a Prominent Role

As the Washington spotlight on Mexico was fading by late 1982, Ambassador Gavin was assuming a more active role in commenting on Mexican society within Mexico. Gavin had assumed the ambassadorship in May 1981 and had expressed his disapproval of Mexican policies only in private during his first year. After the 1982 crisis, his comments appeared more openly.[40] He appeared, for example, on an ABC television report, "Mexico: Times of Crisis," saying that many Mexicans wondered whether the country's institutions were strong enough to withstand economic collapse.[41]

Ambassador Gavin's style was in sharp contrast to his predecessor, Julian Nava, who did not utter public criticisms. With family ties in northern Mexico and flawless erudite Mexican Spanish, Gavin criticized what he called Mexican hypersensitivity to U.S. actions, repeating his belief that Mexico needed to "grow up," stop blaming the United States for all its difficulties, and take responsibility for its own problems. "At times he [Gavin] was very critical of things that were said, more likely from PRI. . . . He felt the United States was turning the other cheek for generations."[42] This was his personal conviction, one that fed his motivation to speak out publicly, but it was not what particularly motivated others in Washington who occasionally spoke out during the same period. With Gavin's outspoken comments and under siege with a host of economic problems, López Portillo had threatened to declare Gavin *persona non grata.*

But with Reagan's friendship, Gavin had a lot of leeway. He did not trust the State Department and dealt directly with the White House, often through NSC Director William Clark, with whom he had gone to prep school. This strategy produced results. It also meant that Gavin was less likely to be taken on for not adhering to unspoken assumptions about not speaking out publicly. "Gavin's access to the White House had advantages and high level attention, but [it] meant he was less likely to be moderated by State career bureaucrats."[43] The Mexican government was also acutely aware that Gavin wielded substantial power. "He had to be treated with great respect, hell, he was the guy who was orchestrating things in Mexico and they [the Mexican government] knew it. If there was a Mexican official who wanted to see somebody in the White House, John Gavin knew about it before it happened."[44]

Embassy Contacts with the PAN

Under Gavin's tenure, U.S. embassy officials did hold a number of meetings and social events inviting Mexican opposition officials, predominantly those from the right-wing PAN party. While Gavin saw this as standard diplomatic practice in any other country, he was aware that it marked a change in Mexican relations.[45] Meetings between the PAN and the U.S. Embassy were still rather rare, and most took place at lower levels between embassy political officers and PAN officials. PAN leader Schmall recalls that Gavin was always "very polite" but "very cautious."[46] Gavin did meet with Manuel Cloutier, a prominent businessman and the PAN 1982 presidential candidate. Embassy officials say they also met sporadically with Mexican political figures on the left. There was little or no contact with the nascent Mexican human rights community.[47] "Gavin himself went out of his way to demonstrate his moral support for the PAN. I don't think it went beyond that," explained Crigler,[48] a noted critic of Gavin's style. The sum of these contacts was enough to convey preference. The U.S. Embassy became perceived by many as sympathetic to the PAN, a party closer to the policy preferences of the Reagan administration and more decidedly democratic.

April 1983 Meeting in Hermosillo

One particular meeting of U.S. embassy and PAN officials in Hermosillo, Sonora in April 1983, received widespread Mexican press attention and was often cited as a key example of a U.S. government strategy to support the PAN at the expense of the PRI. As the new number two officer in the Embassy in August 1982, George High was making his rounds to each of the consulates to get to know the country and U.S. Embassy operations. The PAN had recently scored some regional victories in municipal elections in the North. High remembers that the local U.S. consul set up his meetings (as was common practice). In this case, he describes the consul [Anthony Arrendono] as "young, and not-so-politically astute." The consul set up a series of meetings with the PAN and the PRI. Most notably, it included a dinner party:

> The dinner party, which was a mistake, had people from PAN and the local bishop and that got in the newspapers. I, a high official from the U.S. Embassy, meet with the opposition and the bishop. No one from PRI was invited to the dinner, they were invited to lunch, I believe.[49]

Gavin was reportedly "livid" at the Mexican press, accusing it of cheap Mexican politics.[50] As High recalled, Embassy officials had met previously with the PAN in Mexico City. What caused the most conflict, he noted, was "the where [Sonora] and the bishop. If the bishop hadn't been there it would have been a different story. . . . It was the Americans mixing the opposition and the Church," particularly in an area of PAN strength.[51] The Mexican press reported that Ambassador Gavin was present at the dinner, although he was not in the country at the time. "The story of 'Gavin's dinner,' states Mexican political scientist Jorge Castañeda, "was covered widely because the PRI wanted to use it to discredit the PAN for conspiring with the United States ambassador."[52] Awkward as it was, U.S. officials say the meeting had little to do with any deliberate administration policy or intention to pressure the PRI for political change.

Sporadic Criticism from Washington: Central America Focus

With Gavin playing a prominent role in United States–Mexico relations, there appears to be little evidence of significant public statements from Washington-based State Department or NSC officials, from the Secretary of State down, regarding Mexico and its political system. What does appear from Washington are attempts to recast Mexican politics to coincide and support administration policy in Central America, in particular in support of the Nicaraguan contra rebels.

A minor stir was caused by statements made in February 1984 by General Paul Gorman, Chief of the Southern Military Command. In a question-and-answer session following his testimony before the Senate Armed Services Committee, Gorman called Mexico "the most corrupt government and society of Central America, a one-party state that has pursued a policy of accommodation with international leftists." He continued that Mexico City was becoming a "center of subversion throughout Central America." He concluded that Mexico could become the United States' "number one security risk."[53] The comments were isolated and not backed up by any other administration official. Clearly distancing itself from this interpretation, the Latin American Bureau at the State Department sent a cable to all its Latin American posts providing them with the key statements made by Gorman but instructing them to respond to any questions on the matter as follows:

> While we have not seen a transcript of General Gorman's remarks in his capacity as Chief of the Southern Command, it is our understanding that he was answering questions on the security of Central America and the administration's legislative package for implementing the report of the National Bipartisan Commission on Central America. He was asked for his personal views on Mexico, a matter beyond the principal focus of the hearing. Mexico is fully capable of handling its domestic affairs.[54]

This isolated public criticism was quickly refuted and papered over. Washington's primary interest continued to be Central America. Two particular events that demonstrate how Central America colored the way some Washington officials depicted Mexico were the 1984 CIA intelligence estimate for Mexico and plans for a persuasion campaign against Mexico. Both events spilled out onto the front pages and fed the impression of an administration-orchestrated campaign against Mexico. They reveal, in hindsight, rather deep disputes within the administration on how to conduct Central America policy.

1984 CIA Estimate on Mexico: Fitting with Central America Policy Objectives.[55]

Within the intelligence community, a battle was brewing between the so-called Mexico alarmists (Casey, Menges, Tighe), Defense Secretary Weinberger (to a lesser extent), and the rank-and-file moderates who saw little basis for claiming instability in Mexico. In 1983–84, Director Casey had ordered stepped-up intelligence reporting on Mexico; no intelligence estimate had been done on Mexico for a number of years. Casey had received a top-secret report from the President's Foreign Intelligence Advisory Board (PFIAB), a group of outside advisors and presidential friends. While not based on intelligence sources, the five-page report claimed that the CIA was hiding its head in the sand and forecast leftist activity and grave political instability in Mexico. Horton describes the nature of the allegations:

> These allegations—as distinct from evidence—questioned the effectiveness or even the existence of the traditional political and cultural props to stability in Mexico. They ranged the spectrum of Mexican society, the examples following being purposely stated in general terms: the weakness or the actual demise of the political system, leaked rumors of significant corruption in the new Mexican administration, the power of the right opposition, the subversive work of the radical left, the clandestine influence in Mexico of Soviets and Cubans, restless and subversive squatters in the cities, sullen and Marxist students, a desperate middle class withdrawing its support from the system, radical labor unions, angry *campesinos*. And so on: shadows in the dark, distant lightning, far-off thunder.[56]

As Bob Woodward tells it, "Horton knew that Casey wanted a frightening document to get the White House and the PFIAB off his back. He wanted to show that Mexico was weak."[57] He argues, "The overriding policy concern for Casey was the Nicaraguan operation. Trouble in Mexico fit neatly. A forecast that did not promise trouble did not fit into Casey's scenario. If a wave of communism and consequent immigration was only a remote concern, it gave less urgency to the contra cause."[58]

A first draft of the intelligence estimate, "Mexico under De la Madrid," was done by Brian Latelle, a CIA analyst who was closer to Casey's views. Latelle's draft warned of potential instability; hinted that there could be rioting which the Mexican Army would have to suppress; and warned that the Soviets and Cubans were quietly organizing in Mexico. Horton, Latelle's boss, rewrote the draft and Casey and Horton reportedly battled daily over it. Horton received two long memos from Casey with material to be reinserted, including points on rural dissatisfaction and urban unrest. Horton was sure the second memo came from Menges.

The interagency meeting of the National Foreign Intelligence Board was held in April 1984. Casey made it clear that he felt that Mexico was on the verge of collapse and he wanted to insert a mathematical probability for collapse of 50 percent into the estimate. Only three agencies, the FBI, Commerce, and Treasury, that is, those least involved in foreign intelligence, agreed. The military intelligence agencies—the National Security Agency (NSA), DIA, the Air Force, and the Marine Corps—all expressed only moderate concern for Mexico. Casey fumed at his defeat and ordered the intelligence estimate be rewritten with a lower probability of 20 percent. The final document, hardly a doomsday scenario, made few waves internally. The text, later disclosed publicly, reads as follows:

> But the majority of the intelligence-community principals also judge there is roughly a one-in-five chance that during the period of this estimate—Centrifugal forces now at work within the system, combined with internal political opposition and perhaps external pressure, will result in the political destabilization of Mexico.[59]

The military intelligence agencies still noted their disagreement in a prominent footnote. Horton, knowing he and Casey no longer trusted each other, decided he would leave in May when his contract was up. Three weeks later, to the CIA's surprise, Horton's comments to a *New York Times* reporter appeared on the front page. The article quotes administration sources as saying that Casey wanted a tougher report, in part to help persuade the White House to approve a program of covert and economic pressures on Mexico that would help gather support for U.S. policies in Central America.[60] That program, dubbed a persuasion campaign, was to reveal again how one faction was trying to rally against Mexico's policy toward Central America drawing on the nature of their internal politics, but without widespread administration agreement.

Persuasion Campaign against Mexico

Following a January 1984 NSC meeting, President Reagan signed a secret presidential directive ordering a persuasion campaign against Mexico. Events had heated up in the region: evidence surfaced linking the CIA to the mining of Nicaraguan harbors in January 1984; the "two-track" approach of Enders (using negotiations as a tactic to gain political support for the administration's Central America policy) had been abandoned with his ouster; and, the Contadora countries were continuing to push for a mediated solution to the conflict in Central America. The administration viewed the Contadora process as undermining its policy of military pressure and was concerned that Contadora's progress would erode support in Congress for military aid to the contras.

Following the January NSC meeting, Constantine Menges drew up a draft memorandum of a persuasion campaign to be launched toward Mexico. According to later press disclosures, the memorandum authorized U.S. officials to "intensify diplomatic efforts with the Mexican government to reduce its material and diplomatic support for the communist guerrillas and its economic and diplomatic support for the Nicaraguan government."[61] The directive reportedly authorized, among permissible actions, the possibility of economic sanctions against Mexico. These sanctions, if used, were to be directed at changing not Mexican internal politics, but its external policy toward Central America. The directive ordered that these actions be taken so as to influence Mexican opinion for the upcoming May 1984 visit of De la Madrid to Washington. Menges recounts how State Department officials stalled for months on the campaign, and told him they hadn't acted on it because Ambassador Gavin was opposed to it.[62] After another meeting with Motley aides Craig Johnstone and James Michael at the State Department, Menges was told the campaign would go forward.

The following week, however, just before the De la Madrid meeting in early May, a *Newsweek* article reported a "Constantine Menges" plan to put economic pressure on Mexico to change its Central America policy, prompting angry reactions from the Mexican press. While the plan proposed the possibility of economic sanctions against Mexico, Menges said he wanted it made clear that no economic sanctions were ordered. "But in fact I knew that 'someone' had used the classic insider's weapon—the leak of distorted information in order to kill an idea. When I returned to Washington, McFarlane [NSC Advisor] refused to put any pressure on State, and there was no Mexican persuasion campaign."[63]

May 1984 De la Madrid Trip to Washington

The presidential visit to Washington in early May 1984 was marred not only by the bombshell revelation of the aborted "Menges persuasion plan" but also by an equally explosive report by Jack Anderson charging President De la Madrid with massive corruption, published in Anderson's nationally syndicated column.[64] Anderson cited as his sources a senior administration official and another source with access to CIA and NSA documents. He charged that De la Madrid had funneled a minimum of $162 million into a secret foreign bank account. The shockwaves from the report were louder in Mexico than in the United States, where the report was widely circulated and cited as further evidence of a U.S. conspiracy against the government.

Noting that Anderson cited U.S. government sources, the Mexican government lodged, for the first time in memory, a formal complaint about a foreign press report. George High, who by this time had moved back to Washington to direct the Mexico Country Desk at the State Department, says his review of the intelligence record found nothing to substantiate such a charge. Namely, there were no intelligence reports with such information. The problem, High recalls, is that one high U.S. official argued that the United States could only make a denial based on what they currently knew, but suppose further information came out later? While this was not the majority opinion, High says they agreed to go with the more circumspect version.[65] The communiqué read: "The U.S. government applauds De la Madrid's commitment to addressing the issue of honesty in government. All information available to all United States government agencies leads us to the firm conclusion that De la Madrid has set both a high personal and official standard in keeping with this commitment."[66] To compensate further, Mexican government and U.S. Embassy officials let the press know that they thought the information was fabricated and planted by U.S. opponents of Mexican foreign policy to Central America.[67] The *Washington Post* also apologized. Mexico read lack of support into the less than total absolution. While the outcome was still troublesome for Mexico at home, it is still difficult to interpret this incident as an administration-wide desire to confront Mexico publicly on internal corruption. The few sources talking to Anderson had other motivations.

With these two bombshells, diplomatic slights over how high ranking a U.S. official met De la Madrid at his arrival in Washington, and sharp words over Central America, the meeting turned out to be "a disaster,"[68] as one participant labeled it. Participants say the Reagan–De la Madrid meeting did not touch on questions of democracy, human rights, or political reform. But Reagan was particularly outspoken on Central America. George High recalls, "They felt they had some success in getting De la Madrid to agree that Mexico perhaps should tone down its comments and statements and things it was doing."[69] President De la Madrid did not shrink from controversy while in Washington. In speaking to a joint session of the U.S. Congress, he said that Mexico could not accept Central America becoming "part of the East–West confrontation" and warned against militarization of Central America.[70] Despite press attention on Central America, the more burdensome issue discussed was economic troubles. President De la Madrid had instituted a tough austerity program, but he argued that Mexico's burgeoning $85 billion debt was hard to service at continued high U.S. interest rates. Mexican products faced protectionist barriers in the United States. Inflation was down from 100 percent in 1982 but was still running at 50 to 60 percent.[71]

Renewed Spotlight on PAN Sympathies in Mid–1984

By the summer of 1984, the impression that the United States was favoring the PAN at the expense of the ruling party was given renewed impetus by two events: an invitation to the PAN to attend the Republican Party Convention in Dallas and yet another controversial meeting with the PAN, the Church, and U.S. officials in Hermosillo.

The 1984 Republican Convention

At first glance, it appeared to be a striking change in policy from the Mexican perspective: the American president's party issues an invitation to a Mexican opposition party to attend the Republican convention for the first time ever and refuses to invite a PRI representative for balance. Perhaps this was evidence, finally, that the Republican administration was seeking to favor the PAN, perhaps to even bring about a competitive two-party state. The actual course to arrive at this policy decision was less purposeful and, in practical terms, came down to just one person's decision.

The 1984 Convention marked another venue in the Republican strategy to build international solidarity among like-minded conservative parties. The ultimate aim was to support the development of a conservative International Democratic Union (IDU), akin to the Socialist International for left-wing parties. An outreach program was developed to bring foreign party leaders to the Republican Convention in 1984 for the first time. Richard Allen, former National Security Advisor to President Reagan in 1981–1982, was the organizer and fundraiser for the international outreach program. This was a privately-funded effort distinct from the traditional convention activities or the traditional invitations to ambassadors and foreign representatives. Richard Allen remembers: "I obviously wanted some Latin American parties, and the PRI, being a nondemocratic party, an anti-democratic party, was of course not welcome."[72] Allen explained that when word got out that he invited the PAN and not the PRI, Gavin and a number of other close friends of the president lobbied him to change his mind, arguing that "we have interests down there." "Jack Gavin, a good friend of mine, wanted to get the PRI in. . . . I said 'absolutely no way, period.' He [Gavin] thought they might be insulted but that's too bad."[73] Allen's knowledge and acquaintance with the PAN was not personal. In fact, he had never met with them as national security advisor. Allen recalls: "I thought I knew precisely what the president would or would not have wanted. Obviously I didn't take it up with him directly." Things got pretty nasty. Allen remembers: "As I recall there was some kind of idle threat made; the PRI made an idle threat."[74] Gavin lobbied hard for the PRI, taking unjustified criticism from the Mexican government for the diplomatic slight to the De la Madrid administration.

Allen got his way. His international organization raised its own funds and participants paid their own way. Four PAN members met with George Shultz, Casper Weinberger, and other U.S. officials and attended party functions.

While the invitation involved no explicit endorsement of the PAN, PAN attendee Schmall contends it was still an important and significant step for the party. "It gave us confidence that we could continue forward."[75] It was, however, also an appearance that had high political costs for the PAN back in Mexico. PAN attendees were criticized both within and outside the party, and Schmall remembers that the Mexican Congress even called to have his citizenship revoked over the legitimacy of such contacts. While administration officials did seek to overturn Allen's decision, it was simply not a large enough issue to involve the intervention of the highest levels of the government. The Mexican ambassador to Washington, Jorge Espinosa de los Reyes, was invited and did attend, but as a diplomat rather than a party representative. He did not attend any of the functions that included the PAN. The furor raised over the invitation in 1984, however, was to be absolutely muted and commonplace by the next convention in 1988.

A Second Meeting in Hermosillo

Around the same time, August 1984, Ambassador Gavin was making his rounds to each of the consulates and got caught in yet another snare in the politically sensitive Northern region when it came time again for meetings in Hermosillo, Sonora. There was greater political significance to a meeting at this time, as statewide elections were coming up in July 1985 and the PAN was thought to have a good chance at a governorship. The area's key political officials were the PRI governor, a PANista mayor, and the prominent archbishop.

One of Gavin's special assistants, John Sammis, explains that Ambassador Gavin "thought he would do it in an open fashion and invite them [the governor, mayor, and archbishop] to lunch together."[76] He explained that first the governor declined; then his deputy declined. Finally, the U.S. Embassy told the governor's office they were free to send whomever they wished. When Ambassador Gavin and his staff got to the luncheon, reporters were all over the place but no one showed up from the PRI. "Gavin invited them [the reporters] to join them for lunch so they could see nothing conspiratorial was going on."[77] This did not prevent, however, a barrage of criticism that once again the United States was directly siding with the PAN. Morris Busby, who was deputy chief of mission at the U.S. Embassy at the time, recalls, "They [the Mexican government] just had a fit." The Mexican complaint was paraphrased as: "The press follows you around and when you meet with our opposition you are basically supporting them."[78] Gavin's reply was that he was supposed to meet with the opposition. The "who set up whom" gets a little complicated as it was clear that the press, largely pro-government, was tipped off as to the whereabouts of the private lunch. Robert Pastor writes, "The real message of the dinner, however, was not that the United States was conspiring with the PAN, but that the PRI wanted it to appear that this was happening. The ambassador, once again, proved the unwitting accomplice."[79]

These meetings must be seen as distinct from evidence of direct administration support for the PAN within Mexico. Despite PAN urgings, the administration did not publicly support PAN charges of electoral fraud, or its calls for political reform in Mexico. There is no evidence of any public financial assistance to any opposition party during this period. These are precisely the kinds of pro-democracy support the Reagan administration provided conservative parties in other nations. Outside of a mention in the State Department's annual human rights report, no evidence was found of public statements supporting opposition claims at the time of the infraction. In November 1984, for example, just as the first Reagan administration was winding down, the PAN alleged major fraud in municipal elections in the city of Chemax on the Yucatán peninsula. There were protests, and the PAN refused to accept the municipal government installed by the PRI. There appears to have been no U.S. statement on these elections, and the State Department's *Country Report on Human Rights* gives little credence to the allegations of fraud.

First Administration Ends

In contrast to the quiet and calm of the 1981–1982 period, questions and conflicts over Mexico's political system and its undemocratic elements arose sporadically over time in the wake of the 1982 economic crisis and deepening U.S. involvement in Central America. While to some this gave the appearance of an overall administration policy to support a democratic alternative or opening in Mexico, the actual events and their origins do not bear this out in retrospect. Three principal trends from this period can be detected. First, there are actually few direct actions that can be found related to supporting democracy in Mexico. The second, more dominant trend is that the words of political criticism spoken during this time came from just a handful of political appointees with widely varying interests and concerns. The concerns of this minority centered on how Mexico's internal politics affected other more immediate interests, including political instability, Central America policy, corruption, and personal convictions about the immature United States–Mexico relationship. The concerns of this minority coincided with and would be bolstered by greater democracy in Mexico, but they were not the principle motivation.

A third trend of U.S. relations during the period was the initiation of contact between U.S. officials and the PAN opposition party. This was clearly a change. PAN leader Schmall confirms that prior to the Gavin-headed embassy it was "absolutely false" that any U.S. official, either in Washington or Mexico city, met with PAN party leaders, but even under Gavin, the PAN was still kept at arm's length.[80] There is little evidence that these meetings, promoted by a cadre of Republican and PAN activists, were part of a concerted policy from the top levels of the administration or that administration officials perceived their meetings or even implicit support as significant to bringing about democracy in Mexico. Elliot Abrams maintains, "There was a lot of doubt, even within the Reagan administration.... It is probably the conservative party in Latin America with which we had the least to do because of the tremendous sensitivities of the Mexican government."[81]

Striking during this period of more intense interest in Mexico's internal stability was the absence of extensive internal U.S. debates or discussions about Mexican domestic affairs. As Crigler describes it, the coordinating groups organized by the State Department's Mexico desk were "on everything but political issues.... This meant that we either might have done a better job privately of worrying about the political side of things or by neglect or default it didn't get attention."[82] This draws attention further to the absence of a policymaking process to direct a U.S. policy toward evolving democracy in Mexico. The mainstream of the Reagan administration largely stayed away from direct attacks on the De la Madrid administration in keeping with the internalized belief against openly criticizing the Mexican regime. The operation of this belief can be seen, in part, in the lack of support given the minority, and in the absence of criticism of Mexican politics in official U.S. documents.

It was the growing bilateral tensions with Mexico over a range of issues—Central America, economic policy, drugs—that began to create an environment in which the mainstream of the administration felt little motivation to restrain the vocal minority. Bilateral relations were to become even more strident as the second Reagan administration got underway rocked by the shocking murder of a U.S. drug agent in Mexico. The escalation of bilateral tensions in the second administration was to significantly change the tenor of public criticism and came to involve Washington policymakers, and the U.S. Congress, to a much greater extent.

3.

The Second Reagan Administration: Bilateral Tensions Peak and Recede

Bilateral tensions that had been mounting in the mid-1980s erupted dramatically early into the second Reagan administration. The catalyzing event was the torture and murder of U.S. drug agent Enrique Camarena in February 1985. The murder "drove U.S.–Mexican relations down to their blackest point in twenty to twenty-five years," one U.S. diplomat observed.[1] In this heightened acrimonious environment, the pool of minority voices criticizing Mexico widened, and the nature of the criticism became more direct.

This period of heightened public criticism continues from January 1985 to August 1986 in a second phase of the case study. This phase is characterized not only by sharper and more explicit criticism, but also by the widening of the range of critics to the U.S. Congress. The type of public criticism of Mexico's internal politics that arose in these short years was unprecedented, but this criticism can still be seen to come only from a small minority of officials. Some have argued that the administration abruptly changed a strategy of explicit pressure and criticism of Mexican politics when they saw the results of the 1988 Mexican presidential elections.[2] In this critical election, the administration fell silent to widespread allegations of fraud and warmly embraced the PRI victor, Carlos Salinas, who defeated the left-wing challenger.

The disappearance of U.S. government criticism toward Mexico by this minority, though, actually ends before these elections, by August 1986. Rather than a deliberate policy change, this shift is likely better explained by the convergence of a number of bureaucratic and policy trends and unprecedented U.S. media coverage of Mexican politics. These trends mask the more compelling evidence that the Reagan administration avoided the development of an explicit policy toward evolving Mexican democracy in favor of loose administration over a few minority voices. It is the operational belief against public criticism of Mexico held by the majority that reasserts itself as the dominant policy position in late 1986 and is reflected in the administration's response to the 1988 Mexican presidential elections.

Reagan Administration Case Study, Phase II: January 1985–August 1986

The Camarena Murder

U.S. Drug Enforcement Agency (DEA) agent Enrique "Kiki" Camarena had been investigating drug activities in northern Mexico and uncovered a vast drug ranch protected by local authorities. Its annual production was so large—eight thousand tons of marijuana—that it blew the lid off of U.S. figures for total annual marijuana consumption. The ranch was raided at Camarena's instigation. As the United States was to find out much later, Camarena was tortured and murdered to pay for the resulting loss of millions in profits to the local drug lord. "We knew within five to six days that he [Camarena] was dead. . . . He was set up and killed by the Mexican security forces he was working with."[3] Very slowly the Mexicans admitted to the participation of government forces, but they argued that the case's resolution was a local "police matter," and not for U.S. investigation or interference. In the American view, the Mexican government deliberately withheld information, misled U.S. officials, and stalled resolution of the case. Evidence and witnesses disappeared, raids were made without contacting U.S. authorities, mysterious bodies turned up planted in different locations. Even Secretary of State Shultz, whose public statements on Mexico were rare, told a Senate Committee, "Our level of tolerance has been exceeded."[4]

The U.S. government had, through its own sources, obtained the tapes of Camarena's sadistic and prolonged torture. Mexican officials had denied that these specific audiotapes existed. While kept close at hand, the tapes made the rounds among key officials in the White House, the U.S. Embassy, the State Department, the DEA, and Congress (the Intelligence Committees). On the tapes could be heard the voices of Mexican security officials present at the torture. This concrete display of the frightening reaches of Mexican corruption deeply affected U.S. officials, including many in the Embassy who remembered Camarena as a friend. Assistant Secretary of State Elliot Abrams recalls: "All of a sudden there was a psychological distancing. We had to say to ourselves, how bad is it down there?"[5]

Such blatant drug corruption from which even U.S. officials were not protected prompted a wider range of U.S. congressional and administration officials to look critically at Mexico. As the case dragged on, Customs Director Von Raab took the initiative to institute vehicle-by-vehicle searches at the border—to the consternation of the State Department and the attorney general—in an effort to pressure the Mexican government to pursue Camarena's murderers.[6] Congressmen and Senators who had not previously been deeply involved in United States–Mexico relations felt the need to legislate some U.S. response. Senator Dennis DeConcini (D-AZ) called for the foreclosure of Mexican loans or the imposition of other economic sanctions. Senator Paula Hawkins (R-FL) and Representative Larry Smith (D-FL) both accused Mexico of "massive corruption."[7] Their statements signaled a widening of the congressional circle concerned with Mexico. Following the robbery and murder of a number of U.S. tourists and Jehovah's Witnesses in Mexico, both Houses of Congress considered some form of travel advisory to publicly warn U.S. citizens against travel to Mexico. Travel advisories are typically a State Department prerogative. They are rarely invoked, as it can mean the loss of millions in tourist dollars to the affected country. In this case, it was Congress pressing to go further than the Reagan State Department. The House passed a travel advisory for Jalisco in May, sponsored by Bruce Vento (D-MI), whose constituent had been one of the American tourists killed. Reportedly "furious" over the Camarena affair and having heard the grisly tape of his torture, Senator Joseph Biden (D-DE) introduced a travel advisory in the Senate.[8] Despite their own frustrations, administration officials still made some efforts to contain public criticism of Mexico. With the assistance of Senator Phil Gramm (R-TX), the State Department successfully maneuvered to have Biden withdraw his travel measure.

Tenor of Criticism from Mexican Embassy

In the context of high tensions over the Camarena case and U.S. pressure for its resolution, Ambassador Gavin became more overt in his public comments on the Mexican political system. He told an American newspaper in February 1985, for example, "I believe that the PRI has to take into consideration the true aspirations of more and more Mexicans. Some attack the PRI not only for not being revolutionary, but for not being evolutionary."[9] The U.S. Ambassador's sharp criticisms of the Mexican press—that it was corrupt and funded by the Soviet Union—became more frequent in the 1985–1986 period.[10] He also criticized the treatment of opposition parties in Mexico.

Ambassador Gavin came under attack from various sectors of Mexican society, but he did not back down. He was censured by Foreign Minister Sepulveda, labor unionists asked for his expulsion, and he was vilified in the

Mexican Congress. He recalled publicly in January 1985 a conversation with Ronald Reagan, who told him that if he "wasn't criticized once a month, he wasn't doing his job."[11] By mid-1985, however, the press noted that both sides were trying to tone down their comments following the Camarena murder and that the Mexican government had instructed the Mexican media and government officials to soften their criticism of the ambassador.[12]

Reagan administration officials have indicated that there were private discussions between U.S. and Mexican officials about the lack of democracy in the Mexican political system, but no direct confrontations or extensive dialogue. Human rights were rarely, if ever, discussed.[13] A few U.S. officials mentioned that a typical forum for political commentary was in "cocktail party conversation" where comments were made in passing.[14] Direct discussions, however, were generally perceived by those interviewed to be counterproductive, sparking conflict with the Mexicans that could affect other aspects of the bilateral relationship. The Embassy's number two official at the time, Morris Busby, recalled: "We were constantly on them about their political system, but more in an anecdotal fashion." Reflecting the shared assumption that there should not be direct public criticism of Mexico, he continued: "We didn't go in making demarches and tell them that we think they are stealing the elections or anything like that."[15] Diplomat George High notes that comments on the preemptive side were made, for example, expressing the hope that elections would be clean.[16] Busby recalls one incident when a popular PAN candidate in a small town in the North (of about three to four hundred people) came in to talk to him, musing that he received not one vote in his town, according to official government tallies. The candidate pointed out to the U.S. Embassy the absurdity of results in which no one in his hometown had voted for him . . . not his mother, not himself. When Busby relayed this to his Mexican counterparts their response was, "well . . . he was not very popular." "What I did when I was there, I just sort of laughed at them," said Busby.[17]

According to a number of U.S. diplomats, the Mexican government's response to U.S. private comments about their political system during this time was often to defend that bipartisanship and democracy existed within the PRI. Busby explains, "They also would tell you privately, why don't you Americans shut up about this [criticism of the political system]?"[18] Busby paraphrased the Mexicans further: "It was a terrible, terrible civil war and the PRI has brought stability and peace to this country and revolution is scarcely beneath the surface and you ought not promote instability by trying to encourage opposition to the PRI."[19] Ambassador Gavin said that the Mexican government had handled his comments about corrupt governors at various times by telling him, "Elections are coming up soon, and they'll be out of office. That way we don't upset the system, and you don't want to disturb the system, do you?"[20]

While the Mexicans may have emphasized stability as a reason to discourage U.S. criticism, interviews with U.S. officials who served in the 1980s revealed few who felt that U.S. comments or pressure would destabilize the PRI. Private comments were looked on as a minor means of whittling away at the undemocratic system. U.S. officials never argued that this was extensive or directed toward any specific goal. This heavily constrained public and private dialogue, in which only a minority spoke publicly and loudly, continued to characterize the Reagan years, even as the U.S. media was reporting more extensively and critically on Mexican elections. In the wake of the Camarena murder and growing electoral base of the PAN in the North, the U.S. media began to focus more on Mexican internal politics and upcoming elections in Sonora and Nuevo Leon in mid-1985. In this period, the combination of greater U.S. press attention on Mexican politics and the vocal comments of a minority of U.S. officials fed the impression that the Reagan administration sought political change in Mexico.

1985 Elections: U.S. Press Spurs Focus on Electoral Fraud

The July 7, 1985, state and congressional elections were played up in the U.S. press as the first real challenge to the PRI from the underdog PAN. "An 'unprecedented' challenge, threatening to crack the 55-year old dominance of national and state politics by the Institutional Revolutionary Party,"[21] wrote the *Washington Post*. For the first time, the PAN was believed to have enough support for a shot at the governorships in Nuevo Leon and Sonora.

These elections came on the heels of previous electoral violence in late 1984. PAN leaders had cried fraud in elections in the northern town of Piedras Negras. In a New Year's Eve protest, PAN supporters burned the town hall and the army was called in. The PAN protest had led to brick and bottle throwing at local police, which erupted into a police shootout. One hundred demonstrators had fled across the U.S. border under the sound of gunfire. By the end of the week, all the protesters had returned to Mexico. The spillover from unresolved complaints of electoral fraud had literally touched the U.S. border, although without any U.S. commentary or acknowledgment.

The July 1985 regional elections were marred as well by violence and charges that the PRI had again engaged in widespread fraud. The PRI swept all 7 governorships, 295 of the 300 seats in the Chamber of Deputies, and most local and state offices. Despite indications that the popular PAN candidate and former mayor, Manuel Rosas, was favored in Sonora, the PRI candidate, Valdez, a career bureaucrat from Mexico City, was reported to have won in a 3 to 1 landslide. Even in Rosas's hometown, precincts were showing votes such as 400 to 0, 320 to 0. In Nuevo Leon, where the PRI also won by a healthy margin, PAN supporters scuffled with election officials at one polling place, demanding that the ballot box be inspected before the polls opened. In the scuffle, the box fell open and was found to be full of votes marked for the PRI. Lucy Conger, an American reporter present at the elections, recalls, "There was fraud and we did witness it. We actually saw PRIistas stuffing ballots." She also recalls the PRI press conference following the elections where American reporters more aggressively confronted PRI officials about fraud.[22] "The significance of these incidents is not just that they happened, but that they happened in full view of the foreign press," wrote the *Los Angeles Times*.[23]

Despite the perception that the United States was highly critical of Mexican democracy, there was no public administration comment on the elections. There was the perception that the Embassy was playing up the elections beforehand as important for the PAN.[24] In a records search, the only press statement found was one in which a U.S. official denied beforehand that the United States wanted to intervene or had any favorite in the election.[25] There were no statements on the results of the elections. The lone official U.S. comment at the time came from an unusual source, Congressman Barney Frank, a liberal Democrat from Massachusetts. Reading the press reports, Congressman Frank entered a *Washington Post* editorial into the *Congressional Record* with the following comment: "I believe it is important that those of us who believe in democracy let the Mexican government know how disappointed we are in their conduct in these recent elections.[26]

This was not a loud commentary. These words were never spoken on the House floor or before the media. They were inserted into the "Extension of Remarks" section of the official *Congressional Record*. Buried in the back, such insertions are rarely noticed on Capitol Hill. But no matter how quiet this lone remark, how unremarkable it was intended to be, or how common this was toward other nations, it represented a change in bilateral relations since no such statements had been made in public in recent memory.

The Mexican ambassador to the United States complained bitterly to Rep. Frank and sent his protest letter to other U.S. papers. He asked the Congressman to submit his rebuttal to two U.S. editorials in the *Congressional Record* in the interest of "free debate." The Congressman did so on September 4 and nothing further was heard from him, or the House of Representatives for that matter, on Mexican elections for the rest of the administration. A year later, PRI officials admitted to fraud, and conceded that their margin of victory in Sonora, in particular, was grossly inflated. They signaled at that time that such "excesses" would no longer be tolerated.[27]

Early 1986: Mexicali Summit and Focus on Central America

With the Camarena murder case still dragging on and bilateral tensions over Central America persisting, the Mexicali summit meeting in January 1986 demonstrated just how acrimonious the relationship between the two countries had become. George Shultz and James Baker were reportedly "mad as hell" at their meetings with Foreign Minister Sepulveda. While a number of press reports put a generally positive spin on the meeting,[28] NSC staffer Philip Hughes recalls that there was a lot of discord at the level of the ministers: "They stiffed us on every issue. . . . That's our sovereign policy," he recalls of the Mexican attitude.[29] The *Los Angeles Times* reported that Shultz "dressed down his opposite number, Bernardo Sepulveda, for Mexico's voting record in the United Nations."[30] A key issue at the summit was Mexico's exploding international debt. Oil prices had plummeted in January, making it clear that Mexico needed a massive infusion of capital and/or a drastic reduction in its interest payments to keep afloat. The United States pledged to obtain help for Mexico from international lenders (World Bank, IMF) under the auspices of the still-developing Baker Plan.

In Washington in early 1986, most officials working on Latin America continued to be preoccupied by the Central American crisis. With the emphasis on winning appropriations for the Nicaraguan contra rebels, Kim Flower, NSC staffer for Latin America from January 1986 to June 1987, reported: "I didn't spend more than five minutes a week on Mexico."[31] As throughout this period, official State Department releases did not hint at any differences over internal politics. The State Department's 1986 "Background on Mexico" brief from the Department of Public Affairs characterized Mexico as a "federal republic with a separation of powers into independent executive, legislative and judicial branches of government" and describes the PRI as the "dominant political force."[32]

The Helms Hearings: May–June 1986

The apex of this period of more open criticism was a series of hearings held by the Senate Foreign Relations Committee in mid-May, under the stewardship of Jesse Helms (R-NC), with follow-up hearings in mid-June. The hearings were widely criticized as unadulterated "Mexico-bashing" and a forum for right-wing senators to make racist remarks and scurrilous accusations against Mexican officials. Embarrassingly for the United States, the hearings engaged in direct, and not always accurate, character assassination. The level and kinds of U.S. official statements made about Mexican democracy and the political system during the hearings marked an extraordinary departure from the past, even for the most vocal critics of Mexico.

When Senator Helms's gavel pounded for order at 10:00 A.M. on May 13, it was clear that he intended to publicly question the very core of the Mexican political system. After reciting a litany of problems in Mexico, Helms stated:

> Indeed, I have a feeling that at the root of the problems we have been outlining is the failure of the democratic system in Mexico. Has the long-term political stability of Mexico been purchased at the price of political freedom? Has the dominance of one party for so long resulted in the breakdown of the checks and balances, which any political system must have if it is to counteract corruption, inefficiency, and despotism?[33]

The two most explosive charges from the hearings stemmed from specific allegations of drug corruption against Mexican officials and public charges of electoral fraud. Customs Director William Von Raab claimed that President De la Madrid's second cousin was involved in drug trafficking (in classified testimony), and said that corruption was so pervasive that he had to assume a Mexican official was dishonest until proven otherwise.[34] Senator Helms had directly accused the governor of Sonora of drug corruption; he later had to retract this, saying he meant to refer to the governor of Sinaloa. Ambassador Gavin, who had just recently announced his resignation, defended the integrity of the governor of Sonora, but did state that there were at least two other governors "up to their elbows in the drug trade."[35]

Departing Ambassador Gavin and Elliot Abrams mentioned charges of electoral fraud in the 1985 regional elections; this was the first such public recognition of the charges by U.S. officials outside of those made in the State Department's annual human rights reports. Both were careful to say they were repeating claims of the Mexican opposition, despite Helms's attempts to get them to more flatly accuse the Mexican government of fraud. The closest Abrams came to saying so was: "Effective opposition showings have been thwarted by nationwide PRI voting strength and organizational power, by maneuvers to divide the opposition, by extensive use of patronage, and, according to evidence presented by the opposition, by continuing electoral fraud."[36] In Mexico's defense, Abrams drew clear distinctions with the Soviet Union, pointing out that in Mexico there were opposition victories at the local level and a critical press.

The most sensational electoral claims made by Helms were based on two alleged sets of electoral statistics for the 1985 regional elections and De la Madrid's 1982 presidential election, which he produced and had placed in the official record. One set was the official results published by the Mexican Federal Election Commission. The other set, Helms claimed, was a top-secret set from the chief of staff of the Mexican military, purporting to be the actual election results. Helms said he got these figures from sources within the Mexican government. The figures read that President De la Madrid received only 39.78 percent of the national vote in 1982, not the 71.24 percent reported; and that the PRI had received only 48.02 percent of the regional vote in 1985, not the 71.10 percent officially reported. "I believe that this is a scandal sufficient to impeach the legitimacy of the government," charged Helms.[37]

Helms also made a connection between the growing financial crisis and the U.S. need to be concerned about the political system: "Mexico's debt stability should be evaluated on the basis of the viability of its political system."[38] For the first time in public as well, Helms raised the question of why there wasn't foreign electoral observation in Mexico. Both Gavin and Abrams, however, quickly disposed of this issue, saying it was simply unacceptable to the Mexican government.

The participants in the hearings realized that they were breaking with past tradition rooted in the U.S. government's shared operational belief against public criticism of Mexico. Abrams stated explicitly: "Helms was violating a taboo, which was you don't say nasty things in public about Mexico."[39] He stated as such at the hearing:

> So I think that the kind of speeches that Ambassador Gavin has made in Mexico City during his time there and this kind of hearing—and this is a novel hearing— I think if you were to go back and look over the last 10 years and ask how many hearings have there been in the House or Senate on a question like this, I think the answer is that there have not been any.[40]

Senator Pete Wilson (R-CA) explained the operational belief thusly:

> There is an historically understandable sensitivity on the part of our good neighbors in Mexico about what they have termed "interventionism." I think, very honestly, the time for that sensitivity is really past if we are going to deal with the monumental problems that are afflicting both nations.... [W]e really cannot accept the premise that what happens within Mexico is the purely internal concern of a sovereign nation that is our neighbor.[41]

While a taboo was clearly being broken, only a few senators and administration officials did so. There were significant disagreements as to how much and what type of political criticism U.S. officials deemed appropriate. Only Senator Helms made specific charges of electoral fraud. Democratic senators participated only minimally in the hearings, and when they did, none made any charges or implicated in any way the Mexican political system. Senator John Kerry (D-MA) spoke about drug trafficking problems, and Senator Chris Dodd

(D-CT) queried about Mexico's important role as a leader of the Contadora group. Senator Lloyd Bentsen (D-TX) remarked on the Senate floor, "No useful purpose is served by these strident attacks. Mexican officials, whose integrity or legitimacy have been questioned, are thrown on the defensive and embroiled in controversy, thus making it harder for them to make the courageous decisions which are necessary for Mexico's recovery."[42] Beyond the Democrats, Helms got little support from the rest of the Committee Republicans. Senators Kassenbaum (R-KA), Evans (R-WA), and Pell (D-RI) did not comment on Mexico's political system. This was Jesse Helms's show.

Reaction within Mexico to these hearings was loud and forceful, galvanizing Mexicans across the political spectrum. The Mexican press had a heyday attacking the United States. As Abrams describes it, the Mexicans "flipped out."[43] The government lodged a formal protest with the State Department and organized a massive demonstration of 60,000 people in Mexico City. Counterproductive to the intent of the hearings, the PRI appeared to be strengthened by a resurgence of nationalism and anti-U.S. sentiment. Wayne Cornelius maintains that the hearings allowed "the die-hard anti-democratic members of Mexico's political elite to wrap themselves in the flag and demand repression of the anti-patriotic domestic opposition, conveniently distracting the Mexican public from the need for fundamental political change."[44] Jorge Castañeda argues that the thrust of Mexican criticism was less on what was actually said in the hearings than on the illegitimacy of the United States speaking on Mexican internal matters.[45]

U.S. Government Apologizes for the Hearings

Reagan administration officials later tried to distance themselves from the views expressed at the hearings. They attempted to convince the Mexicans that Helms, and even some U.S. officials, did not represent administration views. Attorney General Edwin Meese made a formal apology, stating that Von Raab's views did not represent those of the "President, the U.S. government or the Department of Justice."[46] Meese was reportedly concerned that poor relations could affect his much-cultivated relationship with the Mexican attorney general and future cooperation in the war on drugs. The U.S. Embassy in Mexico apologized, in particular, to the governor of Sonora, saying there was no evidence against him. Secretary Shultz wrote a conciliatory letter to the Mexican government, stressing the desire for good relations. The State Department denied there was any evidence of electoral fraud in 1982.[47] Treasury Secretary Baker, who was known to think that the United States had much more important issues with Mexico than its internal politics,[48] was ironically quoted in summing up the charges that they "do not represent administration policy, even though they may be true."[49]

Participants differed on just how much the administration initially opposed the holding of the hearings. Elliot Abrams said it was clear beforehand that the administration opposed the hearings, although other accounts indicate that the administration was more supportive.[50] Abrams reflected that he was not trying to send a specific message from the administration: "I was trying to walk a straight rope between the administration-announced position and my own view that there was a lot of truth to what he [Helms] was saying."[51] The Mexico Desk at the State Department was known to oppose the hearings, and the State Department had first sought to bar Ambassador Gavin from testifying at the follow-on hearings in June.[52] The Mexican government also sought to have the hearings canceled. But William Perry, NSC staff person for Latin America at the time, says the White House never tried to stop the hearings, explaining, as did many other interviewees that there was "no way to stop hearings with a guy like Helms." Moreover, added Perry, "Sometimes it's OK. . . . The good cop/bad cop thing works sometime."[53]

To a large extent the Mexicans ultimately accepted that these were minority views, but there remained concern that the administration was still not forceful enough in its rebuttal or specific in just what the U.S. position was. Perry Shankle, Mexico Country Director at the time, explained that the Mexicans were still left in an ambiguous position:

> It was easy for Helms to make a shambles of U.S.–Mexico relations in the absence of a unified administration policy. The Mexicans took Helms seriously because they could never be sure they didn't have to. No one in the administration who had the authority to deny him would do so. I could assure the Mexican embassy that Helms didn't speak for the US government, and that's what they wanted to hear, but how could they be sure? Where was Reagan, Shultz, the voices of real authority? Why should they believe me? Or any one in ARA [Latin American Bureau], for that matter, including the Assistant Secretary?[54]

The Mexican response made much of the fact that the Americans were hitting them when they were down—at a time of great economic vulnerability when they were seeking massive infusions of international assistance to stave off burgeoning debt. But William Perry explains that the timing of the hearings was coincidental. Helms actually wanted to have the hearings in 1985, but Perry, then a staff member on Helms's committee, said he was persuaded that it would be too hardhearted to have such hearings right after the earthquake.[55]

Without a doubt, the hearings and their aftermath indicated that the administration was not speaking with one voice on Mexico and that minority views had surfaced loudly enough to involve top Cabinet officials. Cathryn Thorup explained:

The hearings highlighted monumental disorganization among the various U.S. agencies and a lack of cooperation between the executive and legislative branches. While one part of the Department of State attempted to have the hearings postponed or canceled, another wanted to use the opportunity to push Mexico on a variety of points. . . . While the motives for displeasure with Mexico—both within the administration and on Capitol Hill—would not have disappeared, it is unlikely that this would have caused quite as much damage to the bilateral relationship had there been a greater degree of coordination within the executive branch.[56]

The fallout from the hearings came at a time when the U.S. government needed to be coalescing toward a new standby financial assistance package for Mexico to stave off a serious financial crisis. President De la Madrid had threatened default on its $100 billion debt, a direct challenge to the Baker Plan. Treasury Secretary Baker, NSC Advisor John Poindexter, law enforcement agency heads, and other senior officials met to launch a coordination effort and review policy toward Mexico during the last week of May.

While the administration moved to smooth over the uproar caused by the hearings and concentrate on the new financial assistance package, a few lone voices in the Senate were to follow the line of the hearings for a short while longer. Speculation was building in Mexico over upcoming state and municipal elections, particularly in Chihuahua in July 1986, where the PAN had its next best chance of capturing a governorship. PAN officials visited with a number of U.S. officials in Washington in an effort to raise U.S. awareness and support prior to the elections. Administration officials largely turned a deaf ear to PAN requests for attention to these elections. Only a few in Congress showed any interest. A small minority in Congress was to respond for just a few months longer to emerging political developments in Mexico until more pressing issues took precedence.

Senate Resolution on 1986 Chihuahua Elections

It was from Senator DeConcini (D-AZ) that PAN officials received one of the few sympathetic responses to its request for U.S. attention on the upcoming elections. Senator DeConcini introduced a resolution calling on the government to conduct clean elections. Resolutions like this were common in the mid-1980s toward Central America, but this one broke all precedent in U.S. official comment toward politics in Mexico.

DeConcini's Senate Resolution 437 specifically cited alleged electoral fraud in December 1984 and July 1985 and made note of the violence surrounding recent electoral protests in January 1986. The resolution urged the Mexican president to "live up to his pledge to achieve morally renovated elections and open the one-party system of Mexico to greater democratic freedoms."[57] It further encouraged the Mexican government to appoint a special independent citizen body, representing all recognized political parties, to objectively evaluate and monitor the upcoming 1986 elections.

The elections were held before there was any Senate consideration of the resolution. The PRI candidate was again declared the winner in the governorship amidst violent protests and complaints of overt fraud. There were repeated massive protests, bridges were blocked between the United States and Mexico, and Catholic bishops publicly denounced the fraud. As Sidney Weintraub described it, "The events following this fraud were unprecedented in modern Mexican history."[58]

DeConcini revised the resolution (S.Con.Res 158). The text now encouraged President De la Madrid to "nullify the fraudulent elections in Chihuahua" and "schedule new elections monitored by a newly created internal nonpartisan committee to demonstrate his commitment to a free and fair vote." It also called for President Reagan to raise the elections as well as opening up the Mexican political system with President De la Madrid in the upcoming bilateral meeting in Washington in August.[59]

In the aftermath, PAN officials launched a wider effort to publicize the fraud of the Chihuahua elections within the United States. A group of activists hired a public relations firm, met with a group of U.S. congressional leaders at Washington's National Press Club, and reached out to the U.S. press. The reaction of U.S. congressional leaders to their complaints ranged from "indifference to concern," according to a PAN official.[60] NSC official Kim Flower remembers PAN leaders coming to talk with him about the fraud in Chihuahua. He recalled that his reaction was not affirmative: "Sounds probably right what you say, but we can't do anything about your political system."[61]

Despite the press coverage and meetings with U.S. officials, the only official U.S. reaction PAN officials got was from a small group of senators. The revised resolution had garnered only a handful of supporters. Senators DeConcini and Pete Wilson (R-CA) were the primary sponsors. The three other Senate cosponsors were either from border states or had key interests in anti-narcotics policy: Pete Domenici (D-NM), Paula Hawkins (R-FL), and Phil Gramm (R-TX). In introducing the revised resolution in the Senate, DeConcini notes, "American foreign policy must remain true, consistent and fair. When we discuss fair elections, we must encourage all our friends to be accountable."[62]

But the vast majority of DeConcini's Democratic colleagues were not persuaded by the consistency argument. Many Senate Democrats' views toward Mexico were shaped by what they saw as a more progressive foreign policy of Mexico toward Central America and a better-than-average record on political rights. Senate Democratic aide Janice O'Connell recalls: "Mexico was quite helpful on Central America. They tried to move toward a political solution on Central America, which is what the Democrats wanted."[63] "Mexico bashing" was negatively associated only with the far right. "I remember being uneasy about that [the DeConcini resolution]. Mexico's supposed to be a good guy."[64] Chief Democratic aide on the Senate Foreign Relations Committee Barry Sklar felt the association of the tenor of the resolution with the recent Helms hearings limited the interest among Democrats: "When someone like DeConcini comes out with this thing that mimics Helms, I said wait a minute, I can't go along with you."[65]

While the DeConcini resolution made a big splash in the Mexican press, it was a mere blip on the screen of Washington politics. While it was, technically, the first contemporary resolution on Mexican internal politics introduced in either House, it never went very far. The resolution was never considered by any Committee or on the Senate floor; no one in the House of Representatives introduced a companion bill. The resolution faded away after the August visit of President De la Madrid to Washington. During that visit, De la Madrid met personally with Senator DeConcini. He told the Senator that the elections were an internal Mexican matter, something for the state of Chihuahua to resolve. "Surely they have given you incomplete information. . . . [P]ersonally, it was regrettable that some Mexicans went abroad to solicit help from other governments,"[66] said De la Madrid. After the face-to-face meeting with the Mexican president, DeConcini said he would reevaluate the resolution and took no further action. A spokesman for DeConcini stated that the Senator didn't want to be associated with Senator Helms and feared that protest in Mexico would only provoke a stronger reaction in the Senate.[67]

Solicitation of PAN for Covert Funds for the Contras

Yet another subplot added intrigue to this unusual moment in United States–Mexican relations in the summer of 1986. Republican supporters of the Nicaraguan contra rebels were taking the initiative in various quarters to raise private money to compensate for uncertain U.S. congressional funding for the contras, fundraising that was soon to explode on the front pages with the Iran–Contra affair. That summer, contacts were initiated between Republican contra activists and PAN officials. There appear to have been at least two meetings. Just prior to President De la Madrid's visit to Washington, contra fundraiser Carl "Spitz" Channel met with Ricardo Villa, a former PAN congressman from Puebla, in a hotel in Washington.[68] Villa was considered more extreme among PANistas and was one of the PAN members sanctioned for meeting with Helms. Channel had agreed to finance television spots against De la Madrid and the Mexican government, building on his reputation for the pro-contra commercials he had financed in collaboration with Lieutenant Colonel Oliver North.

Press reports indicate a second PAN-Channel meeting right after De la Madrid returned to Mexico.[69] In this meeting, Channel offered U.S. support to the PAN in exchange for making a financial contribution to a series of U.S. television commercials meant to pressure Congress into funding the contras. In an extraordinary document unearthed under the Freedom of Information Act, a member of Channel's group, the National Endowment for the Preservation of Liberty, wrote to the PAN, confirming the limited role the PAN played within the Reagan administration:

> I think you would agree with me that you and your people do not have the closeness with President Reagan and the White House that you so richly deserve—in view of the fact that you represent the Freedom Fighters of Mexico. . . . If the President were to know that you and your people were actively supporting his policies in Nicaragua there is no doubt he and the White House would be far more attentive to your plight in Mexico and far more inclined to acknowledge your fight for democracy.[70]

No evidence has surfaced that either of these initiatives were carried out. The commercials, if made, never ran. Yet the tenor of the letter reinforces the growing impression that PAN officials had difficulty getting support from the mainstream of the administration and were often relegated to dealing with Republican party activists.

1986 Debt Package and August Meeting with De la Madrid

A significant shift in the tenor of relations was apparent by the August 1986 meeting of Presidents Reagan and De la Madrid in Washington. A cloud had pervaded U.S. financial relations with Mexico in 1986 as Mexico edged closer to total crisis. President De la Madrid had earlier announced that he might be forced to suspend payments on Mexico's $100 billion external debt. Mexico had borrowed heavily, in part on the assumption that oil prices would remain high. There were manifold causes and potential effects of the debt crisis in 1986. But U.S. officials clearly feared, in particular, the effect on international financial markets of Mexico's inability to service its debt and bring inflation under control.

By August 1986, De la Madrid was able to arrive on a triumphant note, having won approval of a major financial assistance package from the IMF and the World Bank. With U.S. support, the standby agreement provided $3.6 billion in assistance, with billions more to come from private banks. The package embraced the principle of the Baker Plan, in which a developing country was to be helped to grow out of its debt with further lending and concessions by private banks. Mexico had agreed again to a difficult economic reform program, including subsidy reductions, trade liberalization, privatization of state industries, tax reform, and tighter government spending. They had also recently joined the General Agreement on Tariffs and Trade (GATT), a move the administration had long sought. According to one U.S. participant, the administration was "amazed" that Mexico could come to such a politically difficult agreement and believed that Mexico needed firm support to survive this transition period.[71] In anticipation of the August meeting, a Mexican aide to De la Madrid recalled, "The Americans called and virtually asked us what we would like to have happen during the meetings. We are very encouraged because they have never behaved in this way before."[72]

Even the Central America issue, which had been so explosive at the Mexicali summit in January, was more subdued. By mid-1986 the Contadora effort was petering out, the U.S. Congress had approved $100 million in aid to the contras in July, and Mexico was considerably less active on Central America. On the drug issue, administration officials said they were trying to emphasize cooperation over confrontation. The administration announced a $266 million initiative, "Operation Alliance," to strengthen enforcement along the border in cooperation with Mexican authorities.

A number of participants in the August 1986 meeting indicated that there was no mention of the Chihuahua elections or any other political topic at the meeting save Central America.[73] When asked in a written question from *El Excelsior* about the recent criticisms of some U.S. officials concerning democratic violations in Mexico, President Reagan avoided answering. His comments instead reinforced that these were minority views. He stated, "[I]t's important to distinguish very carefully between the policy of the United States Government and the private views of individuals, whether they are political figures or ordinary citizens."[74] The only outspoken voices on elections and democracy during the August meeting came from the Mexican opposition, not the United States. PAN officials had organized a public protest outside the National Press Club, where President De la Madrid was speaking.

Press Focus Continues Longer

By the early fall of 1986, the official U.S. government—the State Department, U.S. Embassy, the White House, Congress—had returned to its status quo calm of not commenting on Mexican internal politics without contradiction by any minority. For a few more months, though, the U.S. press continued its focus on Mexico. Three major papers ran series on Mexico: the *New York Times* (October 1986), the *Chicago Tribune* (December 1986), and the *Wall Street Journal* (November 1986). These series were not investigatory; rather, they recapped the events over the period of high tension, focusing on drugs, democratization, political stability, and corruption issues. From this reemerged the view in Mexico that members of the administration were still coordinating a campaign against Mexico. Yet after these series ran, press attention on Mexico also quieted down. Mario Ojeda attributes this to press preoccupation with the Iran–Contra affair.[75]

Tensions Subside: Post–August 1986

After the fireworks of the summer of 1986, there was a marked decline in U.S. public statements regarding the Mexican political system, both from the minority in Congress and the executive branch. The fate of Mexico's troubled economy now became the predominant concern for the administration, with renewed drug cooperation another key concern. This shift in policy priorities was no more evident than in the atmosphere surrounding the August 1986 meeting in Washington. The desire to infuse a more congenial tone into relations was also evident in the comparatively mild reaction to the arrest and torture of another DEA agent, Victor Salazar. Salazar, in contrast to Camarena, survived, and his torture was quietly announced publicly. Attorney General Meese, one of the key figures extending apologies to the Mexicans for the hearings, reacted angrily to the news, but there was no comparison to the intensity of concern that had surrounded the Camarena case.

What explains the disappearance of public criticism? Some have speculated that the Reagan administration must have made a concerted policy shift to stem all public criticism following Mexico's debt agreement in August 1986. To do so requires evidence that the administration was deliberately orchestrating a campaign against Mexico's anti-democratic practices and then ordered an about face. The decline in public criticism, however, must first be seen in the context of the convergence of a series of policy and bureaucratic trends all in mid- to late 1986. These trends include key personnel changes, changes in U.S. policy priorities, decreasing tension on Central America policy, and a shift in congressional and executive attention to the Iran–Contra affair. As these trends converged in late 1986, they lessened both the motivation and the opportunity of the decreasing number of critics to speak out against Mexico.

Changes at the U.S. Embassy

John Gavin startled the Mexican public with a surprise announcement that he was retiring by the end of May 1986. By this point, tensions were highly strained between Washington and the U.S. Embassy.[76] Gavin was getting more flak from upper level State Department officials. "Rather than have the carte blanche he had in 1983 when I came in, there were people in late '84–'85 who were beginning to question some of the things Gavin was doing or how he was doing it. . . . He wasn't used to being questioned by the Secretary of State or the Assistant Secretary for Latin American Affairs or Henry Kissinger."[77] Mexicans had long been complaining about the ambassador's style but had no advance notice of the resignation. In truth, Gavin was told by Shultz that he could stay on for a second term. Reportedly, he had been trying to get another post in the second administration, with Senator Helms's assistance, but was not satisfied with what he was offered.[78]

Charles Pilliod, a former chairman of Goodyear Tire, was named ambassador to Mexico and assumed the job in October 1986. The personnel shift between Gavin and Pilliod made a noticeable difference in the level of public rhetoric about democracy. Pilliod clearly had a more low-key, conciliatory approach toward Mexico. Cathryn Thorup found: "In the wake of the period of intense Mexico-bashing between early 1985 and mid-1986, Ambassador Pilliod adopted a rather low profile presence, taking a more generally positive stance toward Mexico, staunchly defending the Mexican political system publicly, and emphasizing the benefits of foreign investment in Mexico."[79] Pilliod accentuated the positive in United States–Mexico relations and rarely gave interviews to U.S. reporters. In contrast to his predecessor, Pilliod did not battle the Mexican press, criticize the political system in any way, point out contradictions or anti-American statements in Mexican government pronouncements, or speak out on drug trafficking or corruption.[80]

It was interpreted in Mexico that the U.S. government had finally responded to Mexican complaints about Gavin's "in-your-face" style and was seeking a different kind of ambassador. But Elliot Abrams explains this wasn't so. He says the State Department did not deliberately seek out someone who would be more conciliatory, nor did they give policy direction to the new ambassador to do so. Pilliod actually wanted the Brazil post and took Mexico when he didn't get it. "To the extent that Gavin was a thorn in the Mexican side they [the Mexican government] probably interpreted that their complaints against Gavin were heard and that we looked for someone more conciliatory. It had nothing to do with it; he was a businessman, it had no policy meaning at all."[81]

As soon as he arrived in October, Pilliod had reportedly ordered his aides to send upbeat reports about Mexico to Washington.[82] This was his own doing or, at least, his interpretation of what relations needed in the wake of financial crisis. Mexico Country Director John St. John remembers that there was "no indication that there was a specific policy direction [to Pilliod] to reduce tension."[83] In an unusual moment of commenting on Mexican elections, the ambassador told reporters that "there is democracy" in Mexico and that the PRI would win the next year's presidential elections because it would get the most votes.[84] Pilliod's comments were praised by the *El Excelsior* paper and criticized by the PAN. The ambassador's only negative comment was on Mexico's Central American policy. The ambassador criticized Mexico in a speech to the Chamber of Commerce in Guadalajara for interpreting principles of nonintervention and self-determination selectively for countries like Nicaragua and Cuba. Reportedly, Pilliod was under instruction from Washington to pressure Mexico more on its Central American policy. With this speech, "he ... covered his butt," remarked one Washington source.[85]

Cleaning House in Washington

Back in Washington, the more ideological wing of the Republican party was being edged out of foreign policy positions by the middle of the second Reagan term. The more conservative wing of the party was further damaged by poor performance in the November 1986 midterm elections, the Iran–Contra affair, and the declining luster of the Moral Majority. By August 1986, most of the political appointees known for more vocal views on Mexico had moved on. There was no attempt to make personnel shifts in particular to change Mexico policy. Rather, Secretary Shultz was edging out the more ideological wing of the administration as he tried to take greater control of foreign policy more broadly in the second administration. Constantine Menges had been moved in late 1985 to a more ambiguous post handling global affairs and was edged out completely by May 1986. He argued that he had antagonized the State Department and certain White House officials over Central American policies and had become isolated in the administration, losing support of NSC Advisor Poindexter.[86]

For those who stayed on, there seems to be little evidence that the administration explicitly directed a policy of silence on internal political developments in Mexico, or that it needed to. Interviewee after interviewee indicated there was no explicit internal directive nor even much discussion of what U.S. policy toward democracy in Mexico should be.[87] The string of administration apologies and conciliatory letters after the Helms hearings did indicate that an acceptable line had been crossed with the Helms hearings. Customs Director Von Raab explains he did not receive any explicit orders to contain external criticism but that he stopped his negative comments for a while in late 1986 and then slowly inched his way back. He first tested the waters again commenting on Mexican drug corruption on a news show that aired after 2 A.M. in August 1986. He then tried for a half-hour interview with a local public television station in Washington DC, mentioning Mexico in a low-key but not uncritical way. "I'm building slowly back into this. . . . I'm feeling my way," he explained.[88]

Congressional Attention Shifts

From a brief high point in mid-1986, the few in Congress speaking out on Mexico policy seemed to have been quickly diverted to more pressing controversies. In the fall, Congress passed the Simpson-Rodino immigration bill, imposing sanctions on employers for hiring illegal aliens. This measure diffused for the time being the need to "do something" about the ever-increasing flow of illegal aliens across the border. Whether or not it was in response to U.S. pressure, many in the administration perceived that by mid-1986, Mexico had become considerably less active on Central America. This decreased the motivation for some of the few remaining critics in the administration to push Mexico further. Regarding Central America, Abrams argues: "It was merely annoying. It was not a big deal in the Reagan second term; they [Mexico] were out of the game."[89] Drugs continued to be a prevailing concern among Congressmen from the border states and Florida, in particular regarding Mexico.[90] More dramatically, by late 1986, Washington became engulfed in the Iran–Contra scandal, drawing the attention of the Congress and the media away from Mexico. The scandal raised the temperature of the battles over assistance to the Nicaragua contras and left little political space for any continued focus on Mexico.

Policy Redirection/Coordination Effort:
National Security Decision Directive on Mexico

Following the tensions of 1985 to August 1986, there was an internal, interagency review of U.S. policy toward Mexico conducted in 1987.[91] The primary impetus for the review came from the State and Defense Departments,[92] with the State Department taking the lead role. There was an underlying concern among participants about the need for greater interagency cooperation on Mexico policy; the State and Defense Departments were still concerned with internal stability in the wake of the economic crisis. The classified policy document that resulted from this interagency review (National Security Decision Directive-291) is still not available publicly; however, a few participants were willing to discuss the contents of the document.[93] The document provided a moment in time to review the key areas of political controversy over the administration's tenure.

The first section of the document dealt with United States–Mexico political relations. It stated that Mexico bashing and the leaking of information about Mexico was not effective and that it was more important to establish a climate of mutual trust and respect. The document also addressed the "volcano" theory: the proposition that Mexico was a tinderbox ready to blow, including through armed uprising. The document concluded with skepticism about this theory, claiming that Mexico had withstood many crises before. Interestingly, the document did discuss Mexico moving to a two-party system (PRI-PAN) but concluded that it was not likely to happen in the short term, particularly in the next two to three years. The Mexican government had long claimed that this was the intention of the United States government in supporting the PAN in the 1980s. On Central American foreign policy, the document adopted the position that the United States couldn't change Mexico, so it should just ignore it. This ended up being one of the most controversial items in the document. The NSC eventually signed off on the text, but reportedly never fully endorsed this laissez faire approach to Central America.[94] The document did include some discussion of whether the United States should take a more active approach to supporting the PAN but did not call for a new policy direction. All in all, on questions of democracy and human rights, even in a classified document, at least one participant recalled that "some questions were still straddled."[95] The document and review process came very late in the Reagan administration, but at the staff working level (U.S. Embassy–State Department Mexico Desk) it did contribute to an overall framework for relations for the remainder of the term.

Political Aid: Late and Disconnected from the Administration

The Reagan administration had launched the National Endowment for Democracy (NED) in 1983 to fulfill its new commitment to supporting democracy abroad. Modeled after European party foundations, NED was comprised of four separate institutions: one for each of the two major political parties; one for trade union development run by the AFL-CIO; and a final institution for private sector development. After a few years of rocky funding, NED and its affiliates had begun to support a broad range of political activities around the world. Within the Agency for International Development (AID), the Reagan administration had also provided a range of political assistance under the label of "Democracy Initiatives" provided in areas such as: judicial reform, electoral assistance, and police aid. Large portions of funding were directed to Central America.

During the Reagan years, there was little attention to financing political initiatives in Mexico either on the part of NED, its affiliates, or AID. There was no particular pressure to ensure that Mexico was a priority in the Republican party affiliate, the International Republican Institute for International Affairs (IRI), despite the impression that the administration was an avid supporter of the PAN. Janine Perfit, the IRI officer for Mexico, remembers she was assigned to Mexico, a low priority, because she was "the new kid on the block."[96] Her first meeting with PAN officials was not until 1987 in El Paso, with no direct Reagan administration encouragement. The meeting was cordial, but both sides were cautious in developing relations. IRI would, over the coming years, fund two principal programs: a new pro-democracy institute (*Instituto Superior de Cultura Democratica*) in Mexico City, formally nonpartisan but with PAN sympathies, and supporting PAN party participation in a series of international meetings aimed at building a corps of like-minded, center-right Latin American parties. Political assistance by NED, IRI, and the National Democratic Institute for International Affairs (NDI) did not really get underway in Mexico until the early 1990s, and even then on a limited basis. The low priority given to political aid to Mexico was driven not only by U.S. sensitivities but also by the lack of requests for assistance from Mexican groups leery of taking U.S. funds. The limited political aid from NED affiliates that did occur was not linked directly to any administration policy. Perfit recalls only one contact with the State Department's Director for Mexico to discuss IRI's 1987–1988 program but recalls she basically got the impression: "Thanks for telling me; don't come back and tell me anymore."[97]

In contrast to the virtual absence of pro-democracy aid, what was noticeable under the Reagan administration were huge amounts of economic assistance whose political dimension was supportive of the Mexican government. One U.S. analyst argues:

> In fact, with regard to Mexico, the overwhelming amount of U.S. assistance has gone from government-to-government in the form of bridge loans, debt management, assistance and similar supports. Although not defined explicitly as political aid, this kind of economic assistance has had important political results. On repeated occasions, such assistance has been used to bolster the Mexican government during times of economic or political upheaval, boosting its standing in the face of public criticism and political instability.[98]

Spotlight on Mexico's 1988 Elections

The return to relative calm in United States–Mexico relations over the question of democracy was put to the test in the 1988 Mexican presidential elections. U.S. government officials fully anticipated a PRI victory, as had been true of every previous election. Before the PRI had named a candidate, NSC staffer Kim Flower remembers Colin Powell, deputy NSC Director, asking who was going to be the next president of Mexico. "He didn't ask me who the party candidates would be and who would win. It was never assumed that the winner was going to be anything other than the PRI. The PRI would make sure they won.[99] The assumption of a PRI victory was also echoed by Vice President Bush. Prior to meeting with PRI candidate Carlos Salinas, Bush was quoted as saying he would soon meet with the "next President of Mexico."[100] Bush was criticized by PAN candidate Manuel Cloutier for his public presumptions.

The election did not follow past patterns. The left-wing candidate, Cuáuhtemoc Cárdenas, had broken off from the PRI and formed the Party of the Democratic Revolution (PRD in Spanish). He ran strongly, capturing at least the capital city and neighboring states. Just as Cárdenas was showing strong returns, a "computer failure" mysteriously occurred and election results were frozen for a week. Opposition parties claimed to have seen ballots burned and stashed away. Numerous times during the week, the press was told that the election results would be announced, only to be told later that there was another postponement. The foreign press and opposition speculated that Salinas may well have lost the election and that the PRI was moving to reengineer a victory. The official results gave Salinas a slight majority victory—the lowest margin of any Mexican presidential election (PRI candidates had typically won in the 70 percent range.) Cárdenas claimed that inside sources informed him that he actually won the election, and he refused to accept the Salinas victory. Years later, a PRI official would admit that the plug on the computers was deliberately pulled.

The U.S. Response

Inside the Reagan administration, there was some disagreement over how to respond to this election. No Mexican presidential election had ever come close to this level of controversy. U.S. government officials said that they did have knowledge of electoral fraud, but they were not sure as to the extent of it. Elliot Abrams recalled, "We start with a faulty knowledge base.... We had fractionary pieces of evidence that probably Salinas had fallen a little bit short."[101] Evidence from the CIA and the U.S. Embassy was saying that there was fraud on both sides,[102] although CIA evidence "wasn't fully believed" by the State Department because of Casey's ideological imprint on intelligence in Mexico.[103]

As for the appropriate U.S. response, no one in the State Department or the NSC advocated condemning the election or being neutral, saying the United States didn't know what happened. Abrams remarked: "One thing you can say is the truth, we don't know, here's what we suspect, that's probably unwise in any case."[104] The State Department was arguing that if the United States didn't know completely what happened, it should not say anything publicly. The State Department's Office of Mexican Affairs wrote the first draft of a U.S. government response. The NSC felt the United States should be taking a stronger position, that the United States should be "more forthcoming in our defense of democracy, and that we should express our explicit concern."[105] Phone calls and a few memos passed between the NSC and State Department over a one-to two-day period. "I wouldn't call it a debate; I would call it a discussion," characterized Elliot Abrams.[106] Ultimately, the State Department's "don't know, don't tell" position prevailed. The United States, along with Spain, became one of the first countries to congratulate the president-elect. State Department press guidance telling officials how to respond publicly to the Salinas election directed officials to offer congratulations and indicate: "The elections appear to have been an important step toward greater pluralism in Mexico's political system."[107]

Despite the official reaction, many of the U.S. officials interviewed in the three administrations believed that Cárdenas had likely won the election. Abrams says the PRI was smart not to let in foreign observers because "they knew they were going to steal the election."[108] The position of not having full information begs this question: Why wasn't the United States government prepared to know? U.S. officials interviewed confess that the United States reaction was tempered very much by "who" was involved in winning the election. The administration had been very pleased with the signals from candidate Salinas and his advisors on economic policy. From the U.S. standpoint, remarked Abrams, "Salinas just looked great."[109] U.S. officials were skeptical of Cárdenas, who was clearly more anti-American, and they were not particularly impressed by his advisors or their pro-democratic credentials. "To be particularly frank, the one we wanted to win, won," explained State Department Director for Mexico, John St. John.[110] Elliot Abrams mused further, "An interesting theoretical would be what if you had the exact same circumstances and the candidate was, pick your least favorite recent Mexican president, Echeverria. That was not what we had."[111]

The policy imperative for the United States was to support Salinas, especially since his legitimacy was being questioned internally. U.S. officials though, were not particularly worried about Mexico's political stability following the election. "The PRI had clearly stolen elections in the past and they could make them stick."[112] Interestingly, the strongest ever electoral performance of the Mexican left did not raise the specter of communist-inspired instability as it might have in the early 1980s. Most of the main adherents of this view had left the government. As well, the circumstances in Central America were changing, rendering the domino theory less threatening.

To some, the Reagan administration's turning a blind eye to the claims of electoral fraud in 1988 was particularly glaring given its professed global policy to support democracy and its more purist reaction to other cases of alleged electoral fraud (e.g., in the Philippines). But in truth, the Reagan administration had never before publicly condemned a case of electoral misconduct in Mexico at the time of the infraction. The criticisms of Mexico's internal politics had come previously from a fringe minority of political appointees and senators. The 1988 case stands out more glaringly not as a change in policy toward Mexico but as a contradiction in the administration's professed overall policy toward promoting democracy when the eyes of the world were watching. There was a notable change in 1988 in U.S.–Mexico policy. That change was a more enthusiastic rallying around the winner. Lawrence Whitehead remarked:

> The breadth of the apparent US consensus in favor of Salinas was startling to those who had grown accustomed to the polarized rhetoric of the Reagan years; it was even more striking in the light of Washington's strictures on the purity of suffrage in Chile and Nicaragua. But the record is clear. The US foreign policy establishment, as well as the US media from left to right, closed ranks as one to assist in the consolidation of the Salinas administration.[113]

Post-Electoral Shifts

Following the 1988 election, Mexican opposition leaders noted a shift in contacts with U.S. officials. The left and the new PRD party were suddenly objects of administration curiosity. Before the 1988 election, Reagan administration officials had little contact with the Mexican left. "Contacts were extremely sparse, not serious," maintained PRD member Ricardo Pascoe.[114] PAN officials felt they slipped to being just another opposition party in the Reagan administration's eyes, as their performance dropped by one million votes from the 1982 to 1988 presidential elections.[115] This decline in interest went even further with the Bush administration.

The Reagan Administration Record

For a four-year period from 1982 to August 1986, a vocal minority was able to raise the public profile of democracy in Mexico. Thereafter, the public record fades into status quo silence regarding Mexico's internal politics. There is little evidence of an explicit policy to undermine the Mexican ruling party or promote democracy. Rather, a more complicated picture arises in which public criticism was permitted to air in an environment of heightened bilateral tensions, poor internal control, and policy avoidance.

Those who openly criticized Mexico's internal politics represented a small group of political appointees and, predominantly, Republican senators and staff members. Various terms have been used by U.S. officials to characterize this group. One official divided the administration between "pragmatists" and "nonpragmatists"; another called them the "nut group" for a variety of views they held.[116] While of a similar idealogical bent, the minority was actually quite diverse in views and lacked coordination. They raised the issue of Mexico's internal politics not toward a specific end, but as their criticisms supported and explained other pressing concerns about Mexico. These concerns—prominently Central American policy, drugs, corruption, and instability—differed substantially in weight and urgency among the minority.

The Reagan administration's reaction to the minority vacillated between indifference, quiet agreement, and active refutation. The administration clearly suffered from poor bureaucratic control of its more rogue members, inappropriate press leaks, and the like, but this was true not only of Mexico policy. More specifically in this case, criticism of Mexico was able to flourish because of both the antagonistic nature of bilateral relations and, ironically, the lack of an explicit policy toward Mexican democracy. In an overall environment of antagonistic bilateral relations, relations characterized by "digs in everything including diplomatic notes"[117] and pressures for change in Mexico's foreign and drug policies, the "pragmatists" had little incentive to reign in the "nonpragmatists." In addition, there was little to call a U.S. position on Mexican democracy from which this minority deviated.

Despite the higher profile given to Mexican politics in the Reagan years, administration officials indicated there was surprisingly little internal discussion as to what the U.S. position toward democracy in Mexico should be. Official after official recounted that democracy in Mexico just wasn't discussed. "There wasn't even an attempt at consensus; we didn't talk about it," remembered Crigler.[118] Elliot Abrams confessed that the administration did not know what policy to pursue: "When you get finished with all the questions of having varied interests and of not wanting to harm your economic interests [and] immigration, you have . . . an intellectual problem. . . . I don't think we were terribly confident about what to do about Mexico."[119] The lack of an explicit administration policy gave those who disagreed, even slightly, room to maneuver. Abrams explained: "One of the reasons there wasn't that much control over Gavin was, what is the basis on which you are going to say no this is wrong?" U.S. officials remarked that neither Ambassador Gavin nor Pilliod was given explicit instructions on how to treat the subject of Mexico's internal politics. Even the classified NSD directive straddled the issue of what should be U.S. policy toward emerging Mexican democracy.[120] It was easier to continue to avoid confronting the question of internal politics in Mexico when the bilateral agenda was already overcrowded and complex. "Virtually every U.S. government agency and department has programs, major interests in Mexico ... so that when you come up with your list of most important issues between the U.S. and Mexico there are going to be twelve very compelling interests that you're looking at, [and] none of them is democracy or human rights."[121]

What served as the de facto U.S. policy on democracy in Mexico for the majority was an unspoken operational belief against saying or doing anything publicly about democratic developments in Mexico. Interviews found that the operational belief was not uniform in intensity among policy officials, but it was omnipresent. The agreement against public criticism was acknowledged by all Reagan administration interviewees, even, surprisingly, by many among the minority faction. Menges, often cited as one of the more extreme critics of Mexican democracy, claimed in an interview that he perceived the need to "quietly encourage democratic pluralism over time" in Mexico. Central America, he argued, needed more overt action and public support.[122] Most U.S. officials in the pragmatist camp said they favored political liberalization in Mexico, but did not see it coming about for many years. As a result, pragmatists could assert their support for the long-term goal without challenging in any way their internalized belief against open criticism. With liberalization so far away, there was little reason to assess whether the United States should or could change its role in supporting political change in Mexico.

There were principally two different assumptions underlying this operational belief articulated by Reagan administration officials. U.S. officials believed either that speaking out on democracy in Mexico would damage other, more critical parts of the bilateral relationship or that it was counterproductive, doing more harm than good for democratic development in Mexico. "My perception is that it was stupid and futile for the American government to overtly try to either, on the one hand, help the PAN, or, on the other hand, beat up on the PRI very vigorously for not opening up their politics. ... Either it was, on the one hand, too principled or, on the other hand, too Machiavellian for the reality that we confronted," recalled NSC staffer Philip Hughes.[123]

The strength of the operational belief in anchoring U.S. unspoken policy toward democracy in Mexico is evident in yet another way. Compare the criticisms of Mexico by the minority and meetings with the PAN, for example, with Reagan administration explicit electoral financial support and intervention in the plebiscite in Chile, public repudiation of the election of Ferdinand Marcos in the Philippines, or the military invasion of Grenada. The Mexican case pales in comparison. With the exception of Jesse Helms, no specific evidence has been found that administration officials ever directly accused the Mexicans of electoral fraud during this period,[124] asked for an accounting of allegations of fraud, or weighed in on the need for certain political reforms in Mexico.

Human rights performance—such a key topic for the administration in other countries—was rarely, if ever, mentioned in the case of Mexico. According to Elliott Abrams, the administration was less willing to criticize the human rights performance of De la Madrid because he was pursuing the kind of economic policies the administration endorsed.[125] The administration's annual human rights reports on Mexico, while mentioning problems of corruption and specific charges of others of electoral fraud, were not perceived as being particularly troublesome for or critical of Mexico.[126] Also, the administration got little outside pressure to respond to human rights conditions in Mexico from either U.S. nongovernmental organizations (NGOs) or its own right-wing supporters. Central America consumed the human rights communities as it did the administration. The push of U.S. and Mexican NGOs to get human rights on the United States–Mexico agenda would shape different dynamics under the Bush administration, but this was not so in the Reagan years.

A number of other factors affected the context and the content of the actions during the Reagan years, rendering them more potent than they appear in today's light. First, one of the principal actions taken by the administration was to initiate meetings with the right-wing opposition. Such meetings with the Mexican opposition are more readily accepted today, but in the 1980s, they represented a substantial change in the baseline of relations in a country deeply sensitive to U.S. intervention. Second, the public comments of the U.S. minority faction were given impetus by greater PAN activism at the time. The PAN itself had begun to break internal taboos in speaking with international institutions, officials, and the press and in advocating the case of Mexican democracy abroad. There was much conflict within the PAN over this strategy. It is hard to imagine that Senator DeConcini would have initiated the draft resolution on the 1986 Chihuahua elections without the urging of PAN leaders. Third, the actions of some Reagan administration officials may have seemed more systematic because of the more active U.S. press role in Mexico. Mexican government officials made frequent references to a U.S. government–orchestrated press conspiracy against them. In retrospect, there were reasons for the greater press attention on Mexico in the 1980s—the debt crisis, drugs, the Camarena murder, and more competitive electoral politics among them. Reagan administration officials did not take on the press for negative reporting about Mexico, and some officials must have fed it; indeed, this negative information perhaps substituted for more frank discussions in bilateral relations. One diplomat recalled "We certainly don't control the U.S. press. On the other hand, when there are those outspoken comments on the electoral process, it does give you a free ride to at least have people aware that there are those that criticize the election process."[127] In other words, this "free ride" allowed the Reagan administration to maintain its operational belief against open criticism of Mexico, handing over the tougher job of "telling it like it is" to the U.S. press.

The actions of this minority of officials over an eight-year period did not fundamentally alter the belief of the majority against open criticism of Mexican politics. Rather, their contribution to deteriorating relations of the period seemed to reinforce the inadvisability of open criticism. As the Reagan administration neared the end of its term, the 1988 Mexican presidential election introduced a new dynamic—the concern that less than full support for President Salinas would jeopardize his internal support and the U.S.-favored economic agenda in Mexico. It was this enhanced symbiotic relationship—where the United States staked its policy agenda on a particular Mexican presidency—that served as the foundation of the approach to democracy in Mexico taken by the Bush administration.

4.

The Bush Administration and NAFTA

The 1988 election of Carlos Salinas, so controversial in Mexico, was quickly overlooked in U.S. policy circles in favor of a warm embrace of the new reform-minded president. The November 1988 Houston, Texas, meeting of the newly-elected presidents, Bush and Salinas, set a new tone for close relations, dubbed the "Spirit of Houston," which prevailed throughout the Bush term. The issue of democracy in Mexico arose principally in the context of the debate over fast track authority for NAFTA and, to a lesser extent, over anti-drug policy. Throughout the Bush term, administration officials strictly and consistently restrained from criticizing the Mexican political system. The administration's public silence to political infractions was reinforced by the emphasis on more cordial relations embodied by the "Spirit of Houston" and by the administration's principle focus on securing NAFTA.

While retaining a low-profile status, the issue of democracy in Mexico took on a new dimension during the Bush years. The administration came to depict reform and democratization as being embodied by the economic modernizer Salinas and his policy team. This positive view and public praise of Salinas clashed over time with a congressional minority that came to the forefront during the debate over fast track authority. This positive-only characterization also contrasted with academic interpretations of Salinas as consolidating his rule through anti-democratic means.

While democracy was a minor issue in the NAFTA fast track debate, even this dim spotlight placed internal events in Mexico under greater scrutiny and expanded who in U.S. policy circles was talking publicly about democracy in Mexico and how bluntly it was done. This early

NAFTA debate did begin to widen the scope and visibility of Mexico's internal politics within U.S. policy circles, but this was not sufficient to substantially erode the more widespread constraint on public criticism under which relations had traditionally operated.

The Bush Administration Framework: The Spirit of Houston

The Bush administration clearly moved from the outset to distinguish its approach to United States–Mexico relations from the years of high tension during the mid-Reagan years. The shift in tenor was evident to all. Mexican analysts Héctor Aguilar Camín and Lorenzo Meyer summarized: "In mid-1989, U.S.–Mexico relations at the government level were notable for the lack of friction or substantial disagreements. A similar atmosphere had not prevailed since the end of the 1960s."[1]

The Spirit of Houston

These more cooperative and cordial relations came to be symbolized by the first meeting of the two newly-elected presidents in Houston in November 1988. State Department Country Director for Mexico Dick Howard called it a "whole new start."[2] President Bush characterized the Spirit of Houston as "our joint commitment to create a framework of mutual trust and understanding."[3] Georges Fauriol has argued that the Bush positivism on Mexico came in the context of its whole Latin American agenda and greater cultural affinity with Mexico via Texas.[4]

Mexican diplomat Walter Astié-Burgos, who was stationed at the Mexican Embassy in Washington, DC, wrote of this period: "The understanding of the Presidents translated into a more fluid communication and a better disposition at all levels of government with responsibility for bilateral relations."[5] This priority of the two presidents created "peer pressure" to cooperate between both governments, remembered Robert Zoellick, Bush administration Undersecretary of state.[6] With a strong secretary of state who was close to the president, cooperation was reinforced by a State Department that had "more leverage in the bureaucracy."[7] Internal policy divisions and personnel frictions were fewer under the Bush administration than under Reagan, which further contributed to a common policy line toward Mexico.

"The Texas factor" also reinforced personal links with key officials in the new administration: James Baker, Commerce Secretary Robert Mosbacher, FBI Director William Sessions, and the president were all Texans with ties to Mexico. This affinity was reinforced through Ivy League school ties and economic interests. The Texan background, according to Salinas, made the Bush administration "more sensitive to the way that Mexicans think and act, which has been reflected in the care and tact with which President Bush has managed relations with Mexico, and that is something we appreciate."[8]

U.S. Policy Dimension behind Better Relations

It was more than cultural factors and a desire for better relations that underscored the change in the tone of relations; key areas of conflict from the previous administration had dissipated. With the receding Cold War, newly appointed Secretary of State James Baker embarked in his first year on a bipartisan compromise on Central American policy (Nicaragua/El Salvador). He did not want Central America to embroil and dominate this administration as it had the last. Rather than an adversary this time, Mexico was an ally, particularly in encouraging the Salvadoran peace process. "We were very focused on Central American diplomacy; we wanted Mexico to be helpful and supportive of what we were trying to do," remembers Bernard Aronson, the administration's Assistant Secretary of State for Inter-American Affairs.[9] Salinas was making deliberate steps to take a less confrontational role with the United States in foreign policy. This included not only Central America, but also abstaining from a UN vote on human rights in Cuba, providing increased oil exports to the United States, and taking a more favorable position on the December 1989 U.S. invasion of Panama. Economic policy disagreements had also diminished. While Mexico's economic situation was still precarious, the administration saw the economic reforms they had so long advocated being openly pushed by Salinas. The administration would announce the Brady Plan in 1989, named after Treasury Secretary Nicholas Brady. The Brady Plan would move beyond payment rescheduling to actual debt reduction, and Mexico would be the first target.

The Mexican Dimension behind Positive Relations

Underneath the "Spirit of Houston" lay an unspoken dimension—the internal political situation in Mexico. Meyer and Aguilar have argued that there were several Mexico-based factors behind the shift to more positive relations in the shadow of the 1988 elections.[10] The 1988 elections had revealed deepening cleavages in Mexican politics. Salinas had the lowest electoral margin of any Mexican president and faced opposition from the left in the Cárdenas-led movement. A number of prominent academics were arguing that the Mexican political system had reached a crisis stage in 1988–1989, in which both internal and external forces compelled reform of the one-party state well beyond the regime's traditional coping mechanisms, such as co-optation and corruption.[11]

The challenge for Salinas and Mexico, summed up in an edited volume of the Center for U.S.–Mexican Studies, was now "to reform the PRI and at least some elements of the broader political system . . . without tearing it apart in the midst of unprecedented internal and external pressures."[12]

The meaning of the 1988 elections was not being prominently studied within the administration. Bernard Aronson feels, in retrospect, that the 1988 election "should have been a salient issue, but it wasn't . . . it wasn't on the table."[13] The administration was clearly sensitive about publicly reinforcing Salinas and what his weakening might mean. Early in the administration, Secretary Baker laid out a position repeated often during the four years: "The Mexican government, led by President Salinas, is taking the road of economic and political reform. It is a difficult road, and we are determined to help."[14] An internal 1990 Latin American Strategy Development Workshop at the Pentagon found United States–Mexico relations to be "extraordinarily positive." But they warned of any move toward democracy. In an unusually explicit, albeit classified statement, the document warned: "A 'democracy opening' in Mexico could test the special relationship by bringing into office a government more interested in challenging the U.S. on economic and nationalist grounds."[15] This document follows what Denise Dresser termed a common line of reasoning in U.S. policy: "Mexico's successes in economic stabilization and restructuring (along with the fears awakened by the near-triumph of a perceived leftist in 1988) dramatically reduced interest in political change in Mexico."[16]

The Early Bush Administration Years

The "Spirit of Houston" prevailed in the first year of the Bush administration, despite some early rough spots that revealed undercurrents of tension. This early record shows that Bush administration officials had already assumed a noncritical approach to Mexican internal politics well before the announcement of the free trade proposal in June 1990. The Bush approach stemmed from a broad-based belief about how the United States should deal publicly with Mexican politics, reinforced by the Spirit of Houston and the desire to support Salinas. This approach toward Mexico vastly contrasted with the administration's more open vocal criticism of undemocratic politics in countries such as Panama and Nicaragua.

Early Rough Spots: Negroponte Nomination/Webster Comments

Tension briefly interrupted the Spirit of Houston over the nomination of John Negroponte to be U.S. Ambassador to Mexico. Then the deputy National Security Advisor, Negroponte was close to Bush but had been a controversial figure in Central American policy during the Reagan years. Negroponte had been ambassador to Honduras at the time and was viewed as a key figure behind getting Honduran authorities to permit the Nicaraguan contras to train, base, and launch a war from their soil, a war actively opposed by Mexico. Critics on the left and right in Mexico condemned the nomination. They argued that Negroponte was being sent to intervene in Mexican affairs. "Anyone with half a brain should have been able to figure out that Negroponte would be a problem. He is going to be a symbol of right-wing intervention from the United States," wrote Mexican historian Manuel Garcia y Griego.[17] The Mexican government said it did not want to cause a controversy over the nomination and accepted it. Negroponte made numerous statements expressing his respect for Mexican sovereignty. "It is not my intention to bring about intervention of any sort."[18] The controversy soon died down for, in practice, Negroponte kept a low profile regarding Mexican internal events, in keeping with overall administration policy.

A second early rough spot emerged over a press interview given by CIA Director William Webster, in which he talked about increasing instability in Latin America. In contrast to the optimistic Bush line, Webster expressed particular concern about unrest in Mexico, citing labor strikes, protests, severe economic problems, and official corruption linked to drug trafficking:

> I know that the administration would like to give Salinas all the support that it can and help them through their debt problem so that it would become one of the anchors in a good, sound Latin American policy. But it's like every other place down there, it is fragile. . . . [T]he U.S. has enormous intelligence responsibilities and concerns in Mexico.[19]

Webster's comments prompted the U.S. Embassy in Mexico to issue a rebuttal: "The administration's assessment of the Mexican economic and political situation is well-documented and may be at variance with the version attributed to Mr. Webster."[20] Webster's comments were relatively unique in the administration. They are the only early U.S. government statement found that expresses concern about Salinas's Mexico, and they were quickly dismissed.

Emphasis on Low-Profile Relations and Aid

More fundamentally, this first year of the administration shows a clear attempt to steer away from any criticism of the regime. The constraint on anything that could be viewed as challenging the new administration can be seen in the more delicate way the Bush administration officials handled relationships with the Mexican opposition and in the limited support it offered for democracy-promotion activities. While the Reagan administration had encountered criticism for meeting directly with PAN officials, Bush administration officials were mindful of offending the Mexican government with any such meetings. Ambassador Negroponte explains that he met "very discreetly with the opposition." During his tenure, he had just a few breakfasts with PRD leader Cuáuhtemoc Cárdenas. Negroponte confirms that he "declined ever to comment on the political situation in Mexico," recalling that he was often asked to comment by the press, even on his last day. "I have a lot of thoughts on the Mexican political situation . . . but I didn't say anything."[21] This went similarly for private discussion. Ambassador Negroponte confirms that with the Mexican government "we didn't talk much about internal political developments in Mexico."[22]

In later years, Ambassador Negroponte recalled that there were some Mexican government complaints about how they were depicted in the State Department's annual human rights reports. Negroponte points out that this did not reflect a particular policy direction toward Mexico, since, as for all countries, the reports had become more transparent and critical.[23] Mexico was just affected by a broader trend. The reports, written by either contractors or staff to the Human Rights Bureau of the State Department, received little public attention and were not considered particularly controversial within Mexico. [24]

The lone critical voices in the early Bush years came from a minority in Congress arguing that Mexico was not doing enough to combat the illegal drug trade. Administration officials wholeheartedly backed the Salinas administration in April 1989 by certifying Mexico as cooperating with U.S. anti-drug efforts. This was done despite complaints from critics like Senators Helms (R-NC) and D'Amato (R-NY), who argued that Mexicans were not doing enough.[25]

Similar caution can be seen in the U.S. Agency for International Development (USAID) activities during the Bush years. USAID was wary of supporting any programs oriented toward political development in Mexico. The 1991–1992 USAID action plan for Mexico states that democracy-building activities in Mexico would be "counter-productive."[26] USAID's program stayed largely within its traditional strengths in development and family planning. Democracy-building activities, such as training and visitor exchange for Mexican law enforcement, if undertaken, typically supported the PRI government.

The National Endowment for Democracy (NED) and its party affiliates, the National Democratic Insitute (NDI) and the International Republican Institute (IRI), were just beginning operations in Mexico in the early 1990s. While funded by the U.S. Congress, these institutions maintain a level of political independence and nongovernmental status. NDI began its activities by supporting Mexican citizens' groups conducting electoral observations, the first being a "quick count" conducted in the Mexico state elections in 1990. IRI continued its support for the *Instituto Superior de Cultura Democratica*, which was sympathetic to the PAN. These activities were set apart from Bush administration policy and relied more on the initiative of the NED affiliates.

Salinas Takes on Early Reformer Role: 1989 and Onward

Salinas undertook a number of actions in his first two years to initiate internal reforms as well as to strengthen the PRI and his role within it. These actions helped reinforce the administration's vision of Salinas uniformly as a reformer. Salinas made dramatic promises saying he would end the one-party state, separate the party and government, and ensure transparent elections and respect for the vote. Soon after taking office, he led a campaign against corruption and, not unlike past Mexican presidents, jailed a number of prominent leaders, both enemies and friends. He arrested *La Quina*, the prominent leader of the petrochemical workers union, as well as a prominent drug trafficker, a police officer, the head of the teachers' union, and a top businessman (for stock fraud). By unseating entrenched labor leaders who had failed to deliver the PRI vote in 1988, Salinas seized the moment to appoint less independent replacements, restoring the official labor sector back into the PRI fold, "a key factor in Salinas' rapid consolidation of power."[27]

Not all of Salinas's early actions were considered reformist, even by the U.S. government. Analysts note a greater tendency by Salinas to appoint reformers to economic positions, but old-line politicians to more political posts. One of Salinas's most significant policy moves was to create a new social program aimed at addressing dire local needs. The National Solidarity Program (known as PRONASOL in Spanish) permitted local communities to petition the federal government directly for resources for small projects. Here too, Denise Dresser has argued that the reformist package had implications that were not necessarily democratic: "PRONASOL may strengthen institutions and practices—such as presidential power and unfair competition among parties—that constitute the main obstacles to political change in Mexico."[28]

A final significant event in the early Bush–Salinas years was the election of the first opposition governor in July 1989 in the state of Baja California. The U.S. government cited this historic event repeatedly over the next three years as a sign of Salinas's openness to democracy. Asked whether the Baja California election would make U.S. policy officials look differently at Mexico, Mexican Ambassador to the United States Petricioli replied: "The relationship between Mexico and the U.S. should be based on matters of really deep significance in the governments of our countries, not on who is going to be mayor in San Diego or Tijuana."[29] As 1990–1991 unfolded, however, this positive electoral step of permitting a PAN governorship would be juxtaposed against a series of reverse images. Electoral fraud was charged in a number of state and local contests. In the same month as the Baja California election, widespread fraud was alleged in local elections in Michoácan, Cárdenas's home state, and later again in December. The trend in U.S. policy would be to say nothing on the negative events and to highlight the positive ones.

State Visit: October 1989 and Debt Agreement

The low-to-no profile on democracy and elections was clear as Salinas made his first state visit to Washington in October 1989. Both presidents expressed great optimism about the United States–Mexico relationship, as talks focused on debt, trade, and narcotics. President Bush characterized Mexican drug cooperation as "fantastic."[30] During this visit, it was reported that President Salinas had largely dismissed the idea of a free trade agreement with the United States, saying the unevenness of the two economies made the idea unrealistic.[31] In President Bush's remarks, not a word was said about Mexico's internal political situation, nor was mention made of the Baja California election. Ironically, President Bush did stress building democracy, but in countries other than Mexico: "[A]s major trading partners we [the U.S. and Mexico] must explore ways to expand our commerce and, as American states, discuss how democracy can be restored to Panama and free and fair elections held in Nicaragua."[32]

The presidential visit was followed in February 1990 by the signing of a historic agreement to restructure and reduce Mexican foreign debt. Previous debt plans had merely "rolled over" existing debt. Under the Brady Plan, this agreement actually reduced Mexico's $48 billion debt and lowered Mexico's payments in real terms. It was the first and most important test of the Brady Plan. Author William Orme, Jr. called it a "conceptual breakthrough in third world debt management."[33] Nearly five hundred participating creditor banks agreed to forgive principal, reduce interest, or lend new money to Mexico. At the signing ceremony, the agreement was said to mark the "concluding chapter" of Mexico's eight years of frustrating debt negotiations. However, Salinas was to soon find that the agreement alone was not enough to bring large flows of foreign capital back to Mexico without a trade opening as well.

Political Reform Comes Front and Center: May–June 1990

Tarnishing the image of a reformist Mexico was a series of human rights and electoral disputes that came together in May–June 1990, just as President Salinas was set to announce his support for free trade negotiations. In May, prominent human rights activist Norma Corona was shot death-squad style in

Sinaloa by, as was later determined, members of the federal government's Federal Judicial Anti-Narcotics Police. Corona was investigating the torture-murder of four people by the squad. Corona's murder put the Mexican human rights situation on the front pages in a way that was an embarrassment to the Salinas administration.

Later in May, tanks rolled into Michoácan for yet another electoral dispute with the PRD. After nullifying December elections in Urúapan, the PRI had conducted a door-to-door electoral census for a new election. The result of the new census, according to the independent Mexican Council for Democracy, was that "the government had adulterated the electoral registry by striking out 18,000 legitimate voters and inserting the names of 14,500 real and fictitious persons, none of whom was eligible to vote."[34] In this new, more sophisticated effort at fraud, the PRI gained a two-to-one victory in a town that the PRD was widely believed to have won six months earlier.

Electoral disputes received an even greater international hearing when the Organization of American States (OAS) finally ruled on fraud complaints brought by the PAN party in the case of 1985 and 1986 elections in Durango and Chihuahua. In the first ever international hearing of electoral fraud in Mexico, the OAS ruled that the electoral codes of the two states violated the OAS Human Rights Convention which guarantees citizens the right to vote in genuine and periodic elections. The Mexican government refused to recognize the jurisdiction of the OAS, but the case, nonetheless, brought embarrassing international attention to the Salinas government.

A week after the OAS case broke, as President Salinas was visiting the United States, he was informed that Americas Watch was about to issue a highly critical report on Mexico's human rights situation. The report claimed that human rights abuses had been "institutionalized" in the current government and that the government lacked the "political will" to end them.[35] It blasted the government's federal anti-narcotics police as responsible for the most serious cases of torture, murder, extortion, and robbery. The *Washington Post* followed with an extensive article highlighting the gruesome conclusions of the report.[36]

Had it just been the Corona murder, Americas Watch Mexico specialist Ellen Lutz thinks the Mexican government might have been able to contain the negative publicity.[37] But the combination of the OAS ruling, the Americas Watch report, and a DEA report published on the still unresolved Camarena case—all just before the expected announcement to initiate free trade talks—prompted action. President Salinas announced the formation of a National Human Rights Commission (CNDH in Spanish), an advisory body that would conduct investigations on human rights cases and issue recommendations. While an important step forward, the commission had no independent authority to compel adherence to its recommendations, nor could it take up political or labor rights. "Creating the Commission on Human Rights served to preemptively defuse the issue by making it appear that the Mexican government had its human rights problem under control."[38] The United States supported the move and subsequently referred to it extensively as a sign of President Salinas's openness to reform. There had been no discussion about such a Commission within the Mexican government. Rather, Salinas "created the commission in forty-eight hours because he wanted to create a card for his trip to Washington," argued Mexican political analyst Sergio Aguayo.[39] Immediately upon the creation of the commission, Salinas sent a team of prominent advisors to the United States to explain the plans for the commission. Salinas gave the commission powers to promote Mexican human rights work around the world, which Aguayo noted is further evidence of the commission's external purpose. Mexican law gives such external relations powers only to the Mexican foreign ministry.

An interesting observation on this pre-NAFTA moment of anti-democratic news from Mexico is how little was said by the Bush administration, save compliments on the creation of the commission. If Salinas was sensitive to external criticism, it was more likely perceived to come from Mexico's image in the U.S. press, among potential opponents to the treaty, and from critics of Mexican anti-drug policies.

NAFTA Case Study

On June 10, 1990, President Salinas formally proposed to President Bush that they begin immediate talks to create a free trade area. Many analyses, as well as a statement by Salinas himself, indicate that Salinas changed his mind to favor North American integration after a widely publicized and disappointing investment-promotion trip to Europe. Believing that European resources would be directed largely toward Eastern Europe, he saw Mexico's reform program and growth linked to deepening trade and investment ties with the United States. Ambassador Negroponte remembers that Salinas "concluded he needed something dramatic. He wanted something to consolidate domestic [economic] reforms."[40]

From this impulse to deepen United States–Mexico economic ties, this case study will examine how the issue of democracy arose and receded in the U.S. policy debate and intermingled with internal political developments in Mexico. It will show that concern for anti-democratic practices arose only from a minority that stood outside of the political mainstream and that this critique and concern was overwhelmingly in the context of the potential trade agreement. Throughout the administration, and even within elements of the minority to a different extent, constraint against criticizing the Mexican regime dominated. Public silence to anti-democratic practices was reinforced by the administration's desire not to publicly challenge Salinas and to see him as a reformer.

Early U.S. Trade Discussions: Preliminary Lines Drawn

Chief NAFTA trade negotiator Julius Katz recalled that before any U.S. announcement of support for trade talks, U.S. officials went through a series of discussions with the Mexicans and key U.S. interests groups to test the basic outlines of any agreement. With the Mexicans, they wanted to ensure that talks would be comprehensive and not exclude any key areas, particularly the sovereignty-sensitive area of oil. They also wanted to make clear that there would be a negotiation of equals, with no concessions for Mexico being a developing country.[41]

In testing out a potential agreement with key leaders of U.S. industry and labor, Katz was assigned to approach U.S. labor leaders with the proposition. He talked with Tom Donahue, the Secretary-Treasurer of the AFL-CIO. Donahue's initial response was "we're going to fight you on this," but Katz recalled that he indicated some flexibility in that the price for labor's support would be a good trade adjustment policy for U.S. workers. Katz left thinking they might be able to leverage labor's support in some way, but within the next few months, he argued, they saw no chance for labor support. The first inkling of opposition, apart from labor, came in a June 1990 letter from the U.S. environmental organization Friends of the Earth. The letter to the International Trade Commission (ITC) detailed reservations on a trade agreement with Mexico because of its negative environmental consequences. It also touched on concerns of improving the living, working, and health conditions of Mexican workers.

Anticipating some opposition, but not the strong opposition that was to come, President Bush announced in August 1990 that he would seek congressional authority to pursue a United States–Mexico free trade agreement on a "fast track" basis. Under "fast track" procedures, the Congress agrees beforehand to bar any amendments to the implementing legislation, permitting itself only to vote yes or no within sixty days of introduction. Such procedures are considered important to assure nations, and in this case Mexico, that the Congress will not undo concessions negotiated by the two governments.

Early Democracy/Human Rights Dimension

No public statement was found by either president (Mexican or U.S.) or other high official in these initial announcements of negotiations about a potential relationship between trade negotiations and democratic development, even on the positive side of arguing the trade agreement's contribution to democracy. During the presidential campaign, Bush in fact had made this trade–democracy link. He had stressed his commitment to promoting democracy in the Americas and said that Mexico would be given a high priority, given its proximity to the United States. He had also stated that the U.S. objective in Mexico should be to strengthen democracy and free enterprise.[42] Once in the White House, this language all but disappeared.

With the subject off-limits to both governments, what began first was a "cat-and-mouse" game between a minority of liberal U.S. congressmen and Mexican leftists, which centered on the potential for including democracy and human rights concerns in the agreement. In September, Rep. Kostmayer (D-PA), who headed the House Foreign Affairs Subcommittee on Western Hemisphere Affairs, took the administration to task publicly and privately for turning a blind eye to massive vote-stealing in 1988 and other state and local elections and to police torture and other human rights abuses.[43] Kostmayer directly called for the talks to include human rights issues. In early November, Congressmen Donald Pease (D-OH) and Terry Bruce (D-IL) circulated a draft letter to their fellow members to send to President Bush, which rejected fast track authorization and called for negotiations to confront tough issues like the environment, human rights, labor rights, and anti-narcotics measures.

The Mexican government began to respond to these ruminations about links between trade and democracy. President Salinas made clear, in his State of the Union address in early November, that Mexico's democracy was "not subject to external evaluation."[44] Mexican Foreign Relations Secretary Fernando Solana announced defiantly that the agreement would only be about trade and investment, insisting that Mexico would reject the inclusion of political conditions in the agreement.[45] These statements by Solana raised the ire of Congressman Pease, who felt the Mexicans were dictating terms unilaterally. Pease issued a statement calling the Mexican government's position unacceptable.[46] Salinas also made much of parallels to Eastern Europe and the Soviet Union, signaling that Mexico would not rush into political reform risking instability. Salinas declared that Mexico would not "imitate" the path of others but would work out its political model its own way.[47]

Salinas's Political Reform: August 1990

While clearly attempting to communicate to international audiences that major political changes were not a priority, the Salinas administration did, for a host of reasons, seek to solidify its political base and to satisfy some opposition demands through a political reform package passed in August 1990. While all Mexican presidents have pursued some form of political reform, Salinas was the first to include an opposition party in the negotiations. The resulting new Federal Code of Electoral Practices (COFIPE in Spanish) had skillfully garnered the support of the PAN, but not the PRD, enabling the PRI to depict the PRD as anti-reformist.

Heavily played up by the Salinas administration, the COFIPE contained a number of important liberalizing measures. It established a new Federal Electoral Institute (IFE) to replace the much-maligned institute that crashed the computers in 1988. IFE was an important step forward both in efficiency and in expansion of non-PRI participation in its governing board. Nonetheless, the president and his party still controlled the majority, and IFE rank-and-file staff remained dominated by PRI supporters. The lack of IFE's independence was a principal reason cited by the PRD and one-third of the PAN when they voted against the reforms. Also of importance, the Salinas reforms prohibited two parties from nominating the same presidential candidate, preventing any PRD–PAN alliance that could challenge the ruling party. The "governability" clause continued to guarantee the PRI a 50 percent majority in the Chamber of Deputies outright as long as they got 35 percent of the national vote in a complicated formula. Academic critics saw these reform moves in a different light. As Peter Smith described it: "Recent reforms of the electoral system may contribute to 'liberalization' of the authoritarian regime but they do not necessarily indicate a commitment to 'democratization.'"[48]

Fall 1990 "PR" Tour

Following on the summer reforms and President Bush's announcement that he would seek fast track negotiating authority, the Salinas administration initiated a more public campaign in the United States to "allay suspicion about its political practices and to polish its reformer image."[49] Less oriented toward the Bush administration, where support was solid, the Mexican government was reportedly concerned about U.S. public opinion and the upcoming U.S. congressional elections, where Democrats were thought likely to make gains. Democrats were viewed as less supportive of a trade agreement overall and more likely to press Mexico on touchy issues such as internal politics. The Mexican government sent a team of officials, sympathetic academics, and business representatives to Harvard University in October to speak on Mexico's political aims and economic progress. Extensive and unprecedented efforts were made to reach out to Mexican and Mexican American constituencies in the United States and to lobby U.S. Congressmen directly.

Mexico State Elections: November 1990

As the Mexican government was trying to advance its reformist image in the United States, elections were held in early November 1990 in the State of Mexico. The PRI claimed to have won 116 out of 121 municipalities by "unbelievable margins,"[51] in a state that even the government had admitted went to the PRD in 1988 by a 2 to 1 margin. M. Delal Baer, head of the Mexico Program at the U.S. Center for Strategic and International Studies, wrote:

> Recent local elections in the state of Mexico, viewed by analysts as a bellwether of President Salinas's commitment to democratization, were rife with irregularities. The president's snail's pace on reform is beginning to look uncomfortably like intransigence.[50]

The Mexico state elections had another impact, according to Denise Dresser:

> Partly as a result of irregularities in the mid-November elections in Mexico state, an important segment of the foreign press began to intensify its criticism of the Mexican political process. For the first time since the 1988 election, some of the criticism was directed toward Salinas personally. This marked a significant contrast to the generally supportive attitude of the foreign press during the first two years of his tenure, when reporters tended to make negative judgments of the PRI on the one hand, and positive evaluations of Salinas on the other.[52]

Examples of U.S. press criticism can be seen in a *Time* profile of Salinas that called him a "man obsessed with his public image" who was dragging Mexico back to "an era of paternalistic rule by an all-powerful *caudillo*."[53] The *New York Times* published an editorial following the Mexico state elections pointing to their irregularities and stressing the need for more political reform.[54]

The timing of the Mexico state elections was not fortuitous for Presidents Salinas's and Bush's efforts to solidify support for fast track. Less than a week after these contentious elections, Bush and Salinas were to meet in Monterrey for a much-heralded summit. The summit was to showcase the future of free trade in the home base of Mexico's private sector. The trip was also to launch a six-nation tour by Bush to promote the Enterprise for the Americas Initiative (EAI). The EAI was the capstone of the new Bush administration approach to Latin America. It was a three-pronged initiative to promote trade, investment, and debt reduction through a hemisphere-wide free trade zone, a new multilateral investment fund, and a program of (official) debt reduction. Neither administration wanted the summit to be tainted.

As the summit approached, a number of U.S. academics typically considered sympathetic to the Mexican government wrote that they believed the elections would cast a pall over the summit and that President Bush might need to press Salinas to move forward with political reforms.[55] But rather than exert pressure for democratization, however, the Bush administration took extraordinary steps to assure Mexico that the United States would not do so.

Monterrey Summit Makes It Explicit: Trade Agreement without Political Reform

Despite the concerns expressed, the summit went off without a hitch. The Mexican delegation reported, "This meeting was the most cordial of the six that we have had. President Bush didn't ask for anything. He didn't touch upon anything that would be considered 'thorny.'"[56] The disclosed issues of the meeting were trade, drug trafficking, violence on the border, the Gulf crisis, and the conflict in El Salvador. Ironically, the only human rights issue touched upon was the treatment of illegal Mexican immigrants in the United States, which the two presidents jointly condemned. Aronson recalls very informal discussions with Cordoba and Solana over the issue of electoral observers, although nothing was pushed publicly and it would be four years before the Mexicans would accept them.[57]

White House spokesman Marlin Fitzwater went further to mollify the Mexicans by publicly announcing at the summit that political reform "is not on our agenda." He stated that it was a subject to be discussed only at a private level between the presidents.[58] Aronson just days before had struck a similar chord. Political reform in the talks was out. "It's already been decided: commerce and investment, nothing more."[59] Ambassador Negroponte confirmed as well: "For us to impose political conditions would be counterproductive, a red flag ... that might even jeopardize the free-trade agreement."[60]

In the context of the image-driven Monterrey summit, the Bush administration went further than mere silence on political issues. They made clear not only that political reform was not to be a part of the trade agenda, but also that the United States had no concerns at all about the nature of political reform in Mexico. When questioned by a reporter about the viability of Mexico pursuing economic reform without substantial political reform, Commerce Secretary Robert Mosbacher replied that it wasn't a problem because "Mexico enjoys more stability now than at other times."[61] Statements made by the administration expressed only support for the program that Salinas chose to pursue, with no urging or support to go further or concern about negative trends. Focused on the image of the trade agreement, these statements gave the overall impression of indifference by the administration to undemocratic trends in

Mexico. When pressed at a press briefing on President Bush's visit to Monterrey, Assistant Secretary of State Bernard Aronson expressed no concern over current political events, only full confidence in the Salinas administration. "President Salinas has stated as his own goals both economic and political modernization in Mexico, and we support those efforts."[62] Aronson repeated the emphasis on positive political events, noting that Mexico had its first opposition governor and that the PRI intended to carry out political reforms. He struggled to avoid any comment on the maligned 1990 Mexico state elections, saying only that the United States saw "press reports" of charges of irregularities, but had no ability to make an independent judgment. When pressed whether the embassy had even filed a report on the elections, Aronson replied, "We haven't received a report on that particular subject."[63]

As if the Bush administration had not sent enough signals, President Bush himself weighed in to give assurances that the United States had no pro-democracy agenda with Mexico. In an interview for the Spanish language newspaper *Univision*, Bush evaded a question about democracy in Mexico, making clear that the United States was not seeking "to impose any model" on Mexico. The president went further in downplaying events in Mexico by saying that it was difficult to judge the Mexican government when, until recently, the dead voted in Texas.[64]

In reviewing the public record, this clear and repeated denial of what was not to be in the free trade negotiations is striking. There were no other issues treated with such a blunt denial: not drugs, not immigration, not the environment, not even oil, which was the most sensitive political issue for the Mexicans.[65] It could be that the administration was either responding to a direct Mexican request to make it clear that democracy was off the table or was operating again on implicit assumptions against publicly criticizing or calling for change in Mexican internal politics. Aronson feels U.S. officials were largely operating implicitly, trying to support Salinas who was taking a political risk by opening up the economy."[66]

More than just responding to Salinas, administration officials maintained that the issue of whether to include any political dimension to the trade talks was a nonstarter from the very beginning of the administration. There was some noise made by trade agreement critics that the administration should pursue a more politically-oriented economic community like the European version, which did set political conditions for entrance. But within the Bush administration it was never debated or considered. "I don't think it was well thought out," argued Aronson, "but rather it was more of a 'classic argument' that political conditions are not part of a free trade agreement."[67] A chief aide to Senator Hollings (D-SC), one of the principal proponents of incorporating a democracy dimension to the talks, maintains that the administration was "totally dismissive" of their concerns of democracy in Mexico.[68]

Pease–Bruce Letter on Fast Track Conditions: December 1990

The clear "hands-off" position of the Bush administration on political issues was creating a division with some more liberal Democratic members. In mid-December, Congressmen Pease and Bruce sent a letter to the administration urging the consideration of a range of nontrade factors in the agreement. The letter urged Bush to incorporate a social charter into the agreement to "address fundamental labor, health, environmental and political polity differences." It also stressed the need for sweeping changes to the Mexican political system and greater democratization.[69] The letter stressed that its supporters were not trying to derail the trade agreement but rather to get closer congressional scrutiny. The letter was signed by thirty-five members of the House, importantly by the majority (thirteen) of the members of the Ways and Means Committee who had legislative jurisdiction over fast track legislation. Opponents were gathering in the Senate as well. Senator Hollings (D-SC) introduced a resolution to deny fast track authority that had thirty-seven cosponsors.

Mexican Government Signals Slowing of Political Reform

With the Bush administration position solid and the issue of Mexico's internal politics emerging among only a few critics of fast track legislation, the Mexican government sent a number of signals that suggested the slowing of political reforms near the end of 1990. President Salinas made a number of press statements announcing that any further political liberalization would come only after economic goals had been reached.[70] In a December 1990 address, Foreign Minister Solana defended Mexico's right to continue to bar international observers from polling places and said that an attempt by the OAS to rule on the fairness of Mexican elections "would constitute an unacceptable act of intervention."[71]

The Bush administration voiced no concern about the economic reform first strategy nor inquired just what Salinas meant by publicly putting the brakes on political reform. Asked in a later interview about the Salinas strategy, Aronson replied: "Because he [Salinas] was doing political things at the same time, we didn't question his economics first strategy. If they had been like the Chinese it wouldn't have been acceptable."[72]

Fast Track Opposition Builds: January–February 1991

As a vote on fast track authority loomed in the spring of 1991, opposition began to spread from Congress to the NGO community. Up until this point, opposition had been vested principally in a minority group of congressmen and senators and the major labor unions. Cathryn Thorup cites a Capitol Hill meeting on January 15, 1991, as the genesis for lobbying against fast track approval:

> It was not until early 1991, however, when a meeting was held on Capitol Hill to lay out some of the concerns of labor, environmental, and agriculture groups that members of Congress and a variety of domestic activists entered into a series of discussions that would raise the political profile of the free trade discussion.[73]

The forum was organized by a number of U.S. and Mexican groups, including the International Labor Rights Education and Research Fund, the National Wildlife Federation, and United States–Mexico *Dialogos*. Among the workshops sponsored were ones specifically on human rights, social charters, and health and safety, some of which touched on issues of democracy and labor rights. These organizations saw a trade agreement deepening social disparities between the countries, worsening environmental pollution, and reinforcing poor labor conditions in Mexico. The democratization theme was appropriated in a different way: "Democratization of the negotiations" was a term applied by NGOs to label fast track authority as undemocratic as it barred changes to the agreement. In February, the talks were officially broadened to include Canada, which brought a number of Canadian organizations into the developing cross-border opposition.

The minor role played by democracy in the opposition to fast track legislation was echoed in two Senate Finance Committee hearings on the United States-Mexico free trade agreement in February. The hearing focused on the effect of free trade on jobs and on congressional prerogatives to amend the treaty. At these hearings, hardly anything was said about the interrelationships of trade and democracy or about political conditions, save an ambiguous statement by Senator Heinz (R-PA). Heinz posed a classic dilemma of U.S. policy: "It is equally as important that Mexico become politically more pluralistic and stable if those are not mutually inconsistent."[74]

Even in the NGO community, democratization and human rights did not play a prominent role. In the fast track period, the NGO coalition was just in its early, immature stage and was focused on convincing Congress not to give up the right to amend the treaty, not on the merits of the treaty itself. One activist described it as "pandemonium," focused only on the congressional vote.[75]

A second factor limiting the expression of NGO concerns about democratization in Mexico was that these NGOs found themselves constrained by fears that calling for political conditions implied criticism of Mexico and they would be perceived as Mexico-bashing. Scott Paul, an activist with the Citizen's Trade Campaign, recalls that there was internal pressure from the Latino community not to speak out against Mexico.[76] Beliefs against public criticism of Mexico were also present in the NGO community and would create greater division later on during the debate over NAFTA approval.

Congressional Opposition Intensifies: March–May 1991

As the legislative timeline required, the Bush administration formally requested an extension of fast track authority for GATT and the United States–Mexico–Canada talks on March 1, 1991. This started the congressional clock ticking—Congress now had sixty days to deny fast track authority or it would be automatically granted. This time frame intensified the congressional and executive focus on the vote and raised, just somewhat, the prominence of the democracy issue within it. During this period, both opponents and supporters developed tentative positions that would be played more fully in the debate over the treaty itself over how free trade would affect democratization in Mexico and Mexican politics.

A key defining point came in a March 7 letter to President Bush from the two chairmen of the committees with jurisdiction over fast track legislation, Dan Rostenkowski (D-IL), Chairman of the House Ways and Means Committee, and Lloyd Bentsen (D-TX), Chairman of the Senate Finance Committee. Their support for the agreement was not in doubt, but the letter, plus a similar one from Majority Leader Gephardt, served as a warning to the administration that trouble was brewing within Democratic Party ranks. The letter advised Bush that fast track legislation was in danger unless the administration took steps quickly to address opposition concerns on the environment, health and safety, and workers' rights.

The letter indicated to the administration the key issues that had to be addressed to persuade the growing contingent of doubters. Democracy, political conditions, or a social charter were not explicitly mentioned. Rather, the letter reflected only the narrower issue of how the Mexican political system limited labor rights. The administration took the Rostenkowski-Bentsen and Gephardt letters seriously, recalled Julius Katz, the administration's chief trade negotiator. "We knew they were not blowing smoke. . . . [W]e saw the letter as an opportunity."[77] The administration promised to respond publicly to congressional concerns by May 1.

In the meantime, the battle lines were being drawn more sharply between the administration and congressional opponents of fast track legislation. The Democratic National Committee came out against it. While this was merely symbolic, it was indicative of how party lines were being drawn. High-ranking Democrats, namely the number two and three Democrats in the House, Majority Leader Dick Gephardt (D-MO) and Chief Deputy Whip David Bonior (D-MI), were lining up in opposition. Republicans were largely supportive of the president's position, staying relatively silent on the issue of democracy.

While, again, references to democracy and human rights were not dominant among those opposing fast track legislation, liberal Democrats and independents did raise these issues in hearings and in the press in more explicit terms than in the past. Independent House member Bernie Saunders (Ind-VT) called Mexico a "human rights emergency" and pointed to specific events: the fraudulent 1990 Mexico state elections, the rulings of the OAS against Mexico, and Salinas's 1988 election.[78] Other members also directly criticized Mexico's human rights record and long record of electoral fraud.

For opponents, labor rights, as a subset of political rights, was the most direct way the Mexican political system affected the trade agreement. Rather than free trade raising living and working conditions in Mexico through greater prosperity, they argued that authoritarian and anti-democratic practices had and would continue to prevent economic gains in Mexico from accruing to Mexican workers. These gains, they argued, had been going to just a small elite group supportive of the government. Often cited was the Mexican government's effort to control wage rates, restrict collective bargaining, and permit health, safety, and child labor abuses. Opponents pointed out how wage rates in Mexico continued to decline, even as productivity increased. If labor conditions and, in particular, wages did not improve, opponents argued that U.S. workers would be unfairly disadvantaged. U.S. firms would have distorted incentives to relocate to Mexico.

President Salinas went on a seven-city speaking tour in the United States, fretting publicly that the fast track vote could be lost and trying to target specific congressional constituencies. Salinas tried to assure U.S. audiences that Mexico was seeking better wages and didn't want Mexico's cheap labor to be their principal contribution to NAFTA. With fast track legislation in jeopardy, Salinas broke with a policy decision made in June not to bring the issue of labor into the debate.[79] In his tour through the United States he spoke only of human rights concerns on the U.S. side, specifically the poor treatment of Mexican immigrants in the United States. Press speculation was that he was doing so to rebut U.S. criticism of Mexico's human rights record.

Over time, some supporters of fast track legislation began to put forward the alternative view that free trade would encourage democratization in Mexico, although this was more common later in the debate over NAFTA approval. In an unusually public move, twenty-three academics at the initiative of Sidney Weintraub of the University of Texas and M. Delal Baer published a letter urging congressional support for fast track legislation. In the April 1991 letter they argued that the free trade agreement "would give a push to political democracy that cannot be achieved through external exhortations or flagrant U.S. interference in Mexican affairs."[80]

Administration officials, however, rarely used a democracy rationale for the treaty. In testimony before the Senate Foreign Relations Committee, for example, Bernard Aronson stressed that consolidating democracy and advancing human rights was one of the five basic objectives of the administration in Latin America. He did not, however, indicate that he felt the trade agreement with Mexico would advance this goal. Rather, Aronson concentrated on the job advantages for the United States, the positive relations with Mexico over antinarcotics operations, and the negative effect that fast track legislation disapproval would have on growth and market opening all over the region.[81]

Administration Responds to Environmental and Labor Concerns

A turning point in support of fast track legislation came in the Bush administration's response in May to the nontrade concerns raised in the Bentsen-Rostenkowski and Gephardt letters. The administration announced an action plan in the three principal areas of concern: environment, workers' rights/health and safety, and labor adjustment. Dubbed the "side letter," the contents included a promise to work with Congress to assist U.S. workers and industries negatively affected by the agreement, to appoint environmental representatives to the trade and advisory boards, and to develop a border environmental plan.

The workers' rights provisions—a side-door entrance to broader democracy and human rights concerns—promised the least of all. The side letter was either complimentary or defensive of Mexico regarding worker issues. "Protections afforded by Mexican labor law and practice are stronger than generally known—Mexico's laws provide comprehensive rights and standards for workers in all sectors."[82] The side letter mentioned how a greater percentage of the Mexican labor force was unionized than in the United States, without mentioning that the vast majority belonged to the state-sponsored union and had little choice but to join, given difficulties in organizing alternative unions. The only labor problems alluded to in the letter were "enforcement problems" attributed largely to lack of resources. The Bush administration agreed in the letter to undertake joint actions with the Mexican Labor Ministry through a to-be-negotiated Memorandum of Understanding (MOU) outside the agreement. Unlike the environmental commitments, the workers' rights provisions did not promise any new oversight of compliance or enforcement, did not promise participation of workers or workers' rights experts in the talks, and did not promise to improve any standards or workers' conditions in Mexico. The workers' rights provisions in the side letter clearly did not challenge the administration's approach to Mexico's political system: they contained no substantial criticism of the regime and did not pressure the Mexicans toward any actions not provided for in joint cooperation agreements.

It was the trade adjustment assistance and environmental provisions, that swung a number of members and NGOs over to the pro–fast track legislation side. La Raza and the National Resources Defense Council (NRDC) immediately offered their support. Majority Leader Gephardt announced he was satisfied with the new commitments and developed a resolution confirming them, which was later passed by the House along with the fast track legislation. From the outset, the Bush administration's strategy had been to try to divide the opposition, and in the end it succeeded. Cathryn Thorup wrote:

> Efforts to mitigate the impact of the anti-fast track effort focused on carrot and stick attempts to split the coalition. The Bush administration believed that environmentalists—many of whom, after all, were not opposed to an FTA [free trade agreement] per se—could be weaned away from the coalition if they felt their concerns had been adequately addressed.[83]

Chief NAFTA negotiator Julius Katz agreed that the environmental provisions of the side letter was more concrete than the one for labor and workers' rights. They did not expect to get labor support with the side letter. "Labor was only a memorandum of understanding. . . . [T]he environment was really agreements." Katz added that workers' rights were fraught with enforcement problems.[84]

Democracy and human rights concerns were eventually confined to the obscure corner of workers' rights and obscured even further because the minority who raised such concerns did not realistically expect to have them addressed in a trade agreement. In the words of one congressional aide: "Bush's plan gave many members the protection they needed. They didn't want to be seen as anti-trade, but they wanted to look strong on labor and the environment. This made it easier."[85]

Congress Votes to Extend Fast Track Authority

With support firmed up with the side letter, the actual vote in Congress in May 1991 was anti-climactic. Fast track legislation won by a vote of 231 to 192 in the House, 59 to 36 in the Senate. Democracy and human rights concerns were raised on the floor of the House and Senate, but these concerns were two of many brought up by opponents and were never prominent. The most fundamental stab was made by Sen. Moynihan (D-NY), who consistently opposed fast track legislation, stating: "We are for the first time being asked to consider a free-trade agreement with a country that is not free."[86] Moynihan stressed that Mexico had no independent judiciary and lacked full respect for civil and political rights. Further, he added: "On workers' rights we need more from the administration than a compilation of how good Mexico's laws are."[87] The few who openly spoke on democracy and human rights concerns were largely liberal Democrats. Rep. Duncan Hunter (R-CA), a conservative congressman from the San Diego area, was one of only a handful of conservative Republicans who said anything on democracy: "The real issue is political freedom. Mexico needs political freedom, and if they have political freedom they will have prosperity. We cannot give political freedom to Mexico."[88]

Trade Negotiations Begin

With fast track approval secured, the administration moved quickly in June 1991 to open negotiations toward a free trade agreement. Labor issues were kept on the back burner. Ambassador Negroponte wrote in a confidential memo: "The FTA process can also be helpful in dealing with environmental, labor and other 'flank' issues but within carefully defined limits." He stressed the need to be careful in not promising too much in the way of flank issues and to stress what Mexico had already achieved.[89] One commentator described the democracy dimension to the newly initiated talks: "It's the invisible ghost at the bargaining table. Everybody knows it's there, but it will not be touched."[90]

Mexican Midterm Elections: Summer 1991

Just as the negotiations were getting underway, Mexico faced midterm elections for its entire Chamber of Deputies, half of its Senate, six governorships, and a number of state assemblies. This was the first nationwide vote of the Salinas era, and it was seen as a referendum on his leadership. But in contrast to earlier regional elections, Salinas was now enjoying a groundswell of popular support. His growing support was fed by his economic success in reducing inflation and the fiscal deficit and by his Solidarity program which was helping build direct political links to local communities.

The combination of Salinas's popularity, the lackluster performance of the Cárdenas-led PRD, and, persistent electoral fraud, according to opposition forces, helped the PRI achieve significant gains in the 1991 elections. The most hotly contested local elections were the governorship races of San Luis Potosí and Guanajuato where PAN support was strong. Citizen monitoring groups recorded significant levels of fraud. The PAN claimed all-out victory in

Guanajuato. Salvador Nava, the joint PAN–PRD candidate in San Luis Potosí denounced his loss as "the biggest and most elaborate fraud ever perpetrated with the help of computer technology."[91] The *Wall Street Journal*, typically supportive of Salinas, came out with an editorial criticizing the fraud in both elections, as did a number of major U.S. papers.

Salinas responded in an unusual way. While not calling for new elections or an investigation, he forced the resignation of both PRI governors-elect. He replaced one, in San Luis Potosí, with another PRI official and the other, in Guanajuato, with a PAN party member, although not with the PAN candidate who would have won, Vicente Fox, a nationally popular candidate who would run for president in 2000. Reporter Tim Golden believes Salinas was hoping to reduce damage to his international image with the move:

> Objectively there was not enough strength in the opposition in San Luis Potosí and Guanajuato to force the PRI to give in. The new element was the concern over the foreign press. The government got rid of Aguirre [PRI-governor-elect] the day *The Wall Street Journal* editorial came out, but before that they called several foreign correspondents to brief them on what was about to happen. The event seemed more directed to the foreign audience than the local one.[92]

Despite the high profile coverage of these elections, no official U.S. reaction was found in public statements at the time. Nor was any direct response from Congress noted, save a mention about early reports of irregularities by Congressman John LaFalce (D-NY).[93] There was a reference made by U.S. Trade Representative Carla Hills insisting that the United States would not take such events into account: "[T]he political events in Mexico will not be part of the trade negotiations."[94] At a later date, the administration's annual Country Reports on Human Rights Practices did take note of the elections. It cited credible evidence from nonpartisan observers that "distorted the outcome" of the races.[95] It also turned it around to note the positive response of the Mexican government nominating interim governors pending new elections, although it was incorrect in stating that there would be new elections.

NAFTA Negotiation Period: 1991–1992

There is little doubt that Salinas was concerned about his and Mexico's image in the United States during the negotiation period. This concern was more focused on NAFTA critics than the administration. In January 1991, Salinas embarked on an unprecedented expenditure of government funds on public relations and media firms, aimed at garnering support for the trade agreement and improving Mexico's image in the United States. In the end, this spending totaled more than $6 million.[96]

As in the lead-up to the NAFTA negotiations, the actual negotiation period contained no public criticism or expressions of concern about Mexican internal political developments from the Bush administration. There were reports that during the negotiating period Bush administration trade negotiators had encouraged the Mexicans to use a more conciliatory, diplomatic tone on political questions for congressional (not administration) consumption.[97] Head negotiator Katz did not remember any specific instances of this. He did recall the Mexican government occasionally "expressing their irritation" at what the U.S. Congress was saying about them, saying "it was unhelpful." The U.S. reply, Katz remembered, was, "You have your politics, we have ours."[98]

During the talks, a private channel of communication emerged between President Salinas and his chief aide José Cordoba and Robert Zoellick in the State Department, who would communicate to Secretary of State Baker and National Security Advisor Brent Scrowcroft. This provided the Bush administration with advance notice of major political and reform moves by the Salinas government as well as serving as a way for the Mexicans to raise unresolved or troublesome issues in the negotiations. This was not used to apply any overt pressure on the Mexicans to make political changes. Zoellick would have conversations with Cordoba about election-monitoring from time to time, following conversations about economics, but he stressed that this was more conversational from the standpoint of emphasizing the advantages to the Mexicans. Regarding elections for example, the advice was "ultimately they'll never believe you unless you bring in third-party observers."[99]

During the negotiation period, it was only from congressional critics and the NGO community that the specter of democracy was heard. This came particularly in the October 1991 hearings of the House Foreign Affairs Committee. Subcommittee Chairman Rep. Robert Torricelli (D-NJ) raised the specter of the link between Mexican internal performance and the free trade agreement. He argued that: "Every human rights denunciation and legitimate complaint of fraud by those concerned about democratic elections is a nail in the coffin of a free trade agreement."[100] Holly Burkhalter, Americas Watch Washington Director, criticized the Bush administration and Congress in her testimony at the hearings. She also criticized the Bush administration's lack of concern for human rights abuses, especially if they got in the way of anti-drug activities. She cited Bush administration annoyance at internal Mexican reforms to curb human rights abuses that slowed anti-drug investigations.[101]

Over time, NGO opposition to the trade agreement was taking on greater and broader organizational dimensions. In particular, there were joint anti-

NAFTA campaigns by trade unions and by human rights, environmental, and religious organizations across the three countries. These groups struggled over what role democracy and human rights were to play in their crusade. They were divided, in particular, because advocating democracy meant openly criticizing Mexico's current politics, and many in the movement did not want to be seen as anti-Mexico. Senator Ernest Hollings (D-SC) spoke publicly about reforming Mexico first before a trade agreement.[102] He tried to push an alternative to NAFTA that was more on the European model, which required initial democratic conditions, but according to his aide, this "never went anywhere."[103]

Throughout the negotiation period, the administration held steadfast to its bright image of a reformist Mexico and the separation of democracy and human rights concerns from the trade agreement. Secretary of State Baker went so far as to call Mexico "a model nation."[104] The administration had hoped that talks would be completed early in 1992, in plenty of time to obtain congressional approval and present NAFTA as a major achievement of Bush's first term. For many reasons, the negotiations lagged and were not completed until August 1992. This left the question of congressional approval to the winner of the November 1992 presidential election and thus propelled the trade agreement to major prominence in the presidential campaign.

U.S. Presidential Election Campaign: NAFTA and Mexican Politics

Bush had made NAFTA and its promise of more U.S. jobs and exports a focal point of his re-election campaign. Independent candidate Perot and Republican challenger Buchanan came on strong in criticizing both the Mexican regime and the agreement as a job drain on the United States. The liberal democratic voices who had spoken out on internal conditions in Mexico earlier now found the issue taken over and sensationalized by the right during the presidential campaign. Perot and Buchanan critiqued Mexico repeatedly. Perot labeled Mexico a corrupt, destitute, one-party state. In describing Mexican labor practices he went so far as to say: "If and when there's a strike, they send in the state police, shoot twenty or thirty workers, clear the place out, get rid of the union, cut the wages, put everybody back to work."[105]

As U.S. presidential politics over Mexico heated up during the summer of 1992, Mexico was experiencing its own *verano caliente*. The PAN opposition party had finally won the Chihuahua governorship in 1992 that it claimed the PRI had stolen from it in 1985. The PRD lost the governorship of Michoacán, the state of its greatest strength. Protests ensued to overturn the Michoacán elections. Before taking office, the PRI-elected governor of Michoacán resigned, saying he was not able to govern effectively. Salinas replaced him with another party member. In a rare coupling of Mexican domestic politics and NAFTA negotiations, U.S. trade negotiators in Mexico City were visited by a delegation of PRD supporters and pro-democracy groups following street protests. The groups petitioned the negotiators to reflect on the recent electoral fraud, vote manipulation, and demands of the Mexican people for liberty.[106] There was no U.S. government response.

Candidate Clinton and NAFTA

Democratic candidate Clinton had supported NAFTA "in principle" early in the campaign, but had been vague about his views until October. Nor had Clinton said much about internal political conditions in Mexico during the campaign. His team was deeply divided over how to position Clinton politically on NAFTA. Clinton, overall, supported free trade, but he did not want to directly antagonize labor and feared the loss of votes to Perot, particularly in the Midwest. One month before the election, in a speech in Raleigh, North Carolina, Clinton finally staked out his position: He would support the treaty, only with the incorporation of separate side agreements on labor and the environment. It was unclear at the time just what the content of any labor side agreement would be. Anti-NAFTA groups and trade unions were split between those who were optimistic about such side agreements and those who were not. Clinton's position on NAFTA would later place him in a delicate position after his victory in November. The newly-elected administration had to ensure congressional passage of an agreement that it had vaguely committed to "correct" with side agreements.

From Bush to Clinton

The Bush administration followed an uncompromising stance of no public comment on negative political events in Mexico, rooted in a belief on the inadvisability of public criticism of Mexico. This belief was reinforced by the administration's own emphasis on more cordial relations and, in particular, that criticism would be seen as showing less than full support for the Salinas presidency and the free trade initiative. According to administration officials, the low-profile approach also included low-visibility contact with members of the Mexican opposition and low-profile democracy assistance, if at all. Explaining that this was an approach that didn't need to be widely debated, State Department Undersecretary Robert Zoellick explained that it was "more assumed that we shouldn't speak out. Why would you want to do this?" [107]

One frequent assumption held was that public criticism would damage other aspects of the bilateral relationship. "The cost you pay for being openly, publicly critical is you risk harming interests in other areas," reminded Ambassador

Negroponte.[108] This damage would occur needlessly, many officials felt, since overt pressure or statements were unlikely to have a positive impact on Mexico. "The best way to encourage change in Mexico is by having initiatives appear home-grown," remarked Zoellick.[109] There was little concern expressed in interviews that public criticism would have an impact on Mexican stability;[110] rather, it was viewed more narrowly as potentially reducing Salinas's margin of policy maneuverability.

The Bush administration, however, went further than the absence of criticism or acts that might offend the Mexican government. It painted a uniformly positive political image of Mexico, setting up both contrast and confrontation with the image portrayed by NAFTA critics, the Mexican opposition, and some academics. The repeated public praise for positive events such as select PAN victories, without reference to negative trends, such as claims of electoral fraud, torture, or corruption was particularly striking during the Bush years, especially given the more prominent reports from the American press.

By sticking so uniformly to a positive-only approach, the Bush administration may also have constrained how it evaluated and judged politics in Mexico during the period. Salinas was viewed as an unequivocal political and economic reformer without a single blemish. In retrospect, a number of Bush administration officials felt that this total embrace of Salinas went too far. Bernard Aronson explains that there was never a debate or discussions about alternative views of Salinas within the Bush administration or even of negative trends in human rights or elections, about which some academics were writing. "People didn't look beneath the surface as much as they should have."[111] "Maybe he never intended to fully open up," commented the State Department's Mexico Country Director.[112] Subsequent investigations revealed widespread corruption linked to drug trafficking within the Salinas administration, touching the president's brother Raul and very possibly Salinas himself. Aronson notes that during his tenure, however, not only was this not examined, but also he recalls no internal memos and communications incriminating the president's brother.[113]

The unblemished view of Salinas was neither examined nor reconciled with other accounts because it reinforced so well the assumed pattern of silence and fit so importantly within the overall "Spirit of Houston" framework. This public silence well preceded NAFTA and was, again, assumed rather than openly debated within the administration. Positivism on Salinas provided the veneer of consistency with stated U.S. pro-democracy goals and offered a tidy response to NAFTA critics. It was clearly reinforced by realist-rational actor calculations at the same time that public criticism might jeopardize or make more difficult the passage of NAFTA, drug policy, and the continuance of macroeconomic reforms in Mexico along free market lines. While administration actions can be understood as coming from both realist calculations and assumed beliefs about the inadvisability of public criticism of Mexico, there was also criticism at the time that the administration was a damper on democratization in Mexico. As Gentleman and Zubek wrote in their comparison of the Mexican and Polish transitions, contrasting Poland where the United States openly pushed for democratic change:

> We also conclude, in contrast, that the momentum for political democracy in Mexico was undercut by Mexican elite perception that the United States would not insist upon the democratic condition as a prerequisite for integration and was, in fact, prepared to sacrifice progress in this political area for the sake of protecting the initiative for economic integration.[114]

Would the incoming Democratic president, who had committed to "fix" NAFTA through side agreements, recast U.S. policy toward democracy in Mexico as well? NAFTA, which had dominated United States–Mexico relations for the Bush administration, was now left in the hands of Bill Clinton and his policy team.

5.

The Clinton Administration
Secures NAFTA

With NAFTA negotiated but not approved by the U.S. Congress, it was now up to the incoming Clinton administration to make the vision of free trade in North America a reality. The new president had already established some ground rules. He would not open up the completed negotiations but would arrive at separate labor and environmental side agreements. In the campaign, Clinton had emphasized democracy and human rights, criticizing broadly the human rights policies of the Bush administration. Would he now depart from the dominant policy line of his predecessors regarding democracy and human rights in Mexico? Would the first Democratic administration in twelve years take a new direction in United States–Mexico relations?

This chapter follows the first year of the Clinton administration from its initial policy trends through to the approval of NAFTA in November 1993. Securing NAFTA would come to dominate the first year of the administration to the consternation of top advisors who pushed for a domestic agenda. The review demonstrates surprising continuity in this first year between the Clinton and Bush administration approaches to democracy in Mexico. One can see the persistence of restraint on public criticism of Mexico within the executive branch, irrespective of party.

The democracy issue continued to play a minor role in the debate over NAFTA approval, although its visibility broadened. In keeping with the stepped-up drama of the debate, both supporters and opponents were now making sweeping claims about Mexican politics and the political impact of free trade to support their position on the treaty. Still only a minority of NAFTA opponents spoke critically of Mexican internal politics. The most extreme comments from Perot and Buchanan came to over-shadow and discredit other NAFTA opponents. While raising the public pro-file of internal politics in Mexico, the NAFTA debate did little to alter the way democracy in Mexico was treated in U.S. policy circles or to shape any more explicit policy toward Mexican democracy.

The Clinton Administration: Initial Policy Approach

With the victory of Bill Clinton in the November 1992 election and a Democratic majority in the Congress, there was some speculation in the United States and Mexico that the new administration and Congress might press Sali-nas harder to liberalize politically. Candidate Clinton had criticized the Bush administration's policy toward China and Haiti for ignoring human rights abuses. Clinton had also taken a strong stand against dictatorial regimes in Latin America. These positions, plus stronger Democratic Party traditions on human rights, translated to open speculation among Mexican intellectuals and the political opposition that these same principles might be applied to Mexico. This speculation was not, however, based on specific statements made by the Clinton team about Mexico. Leftist commentator Adolfo Aguilar predicted, for example, "a foreseeable revision of the complacent attitude of the government of the United States with respect to the abuses of political power, human rights, electoral fraud, and lack of democracy in Mexico."[1] Jorge Castañeda expressed a similar view:

> The newly arrived Democrats in Washington will probably not dispatch squadrons of observers led by Jimmy Carter to monitor elections and censure human rights violations in Mexico, but they will not maintain the Republicans' systematic indifference to such matters.[2]

Initial Policy Follows Bush Administration Lines

Despite the speculation, it is difficult to detect any appreciable shift in the administration's attitude toward speaking out or more openly supporting democratic change in Mexico during this first year. A State Department desk officer for Mexico explained the continuity between the two administrations as: "amazing, no significant changes in the way things are done."[3] Clinton administration officials interviewed did not indicate any internal consideration given to broadening NAFTA to political concerns or, as critics had argued, using the opening to NAFTA to advocate greater political reform. Richard Feinberg, the administration's new Director for Latin American Affairs on the National Security Council, indicated that the administration supported political reform and more competitive party politics in Mexico, but their approach was "we don't get involved in the details, don't make headlines."[4]

The new administration was walking a tight line: it was accepting the trade agreement negotiated by the Bush administration while trying to win over some of NAFTA's opponents through side agreements. This did not leave much room, nor was it an opportune moment for policy experimentation on political questions. The Clinton administration adopted wholesale the Bush administration's arguments in favor of NAFTA; it did not really try to bring in a different political perspective. As Sidney Weintraub observed: "Have the people in the Clinton administration thought this through? I don't think they have. They are taking it [Salinas and the Mexican government policies] as an article of faith."[5] A Clinton administration State Department document, reminiscent of the Bush administration, read:

> Under President Salinas, political reforms have opened the political process and have led to significant opposition gains at the national, state and municipal levels. While the ruling *Partido Revolucionario Institucional (PRI)* still dominates, President Salinas' reforms have raised public confidence and reduced complaints of significant election irregularities.... President Salinas also has attacked longstanding problems of government corruption and worked to improve respect for human rights.[6]

This upbeat spin on Salinas was not entirely expected as Salinas had scarcely concealed his support for the re-election of George Bush. Clinton followed in the footsteps of his predecessors by reserving his first meeting with a foreign head of state for Mexico. While lacking the effusive friendliness of the Bush–Salinas meeting, the first meeting between President-elect Clinton and Salinas showed little difference in approach. The meeting did not succeed in clarifying the timing with which the new administration would pursue the negotiation of side agreements, or what these side agreements would actually contain.

NAFTA under Clinton

NAFTA Opposition Heats Up: Democracy Debated

As President Clinton took office in January 1993, a more systematic organization of NAFTA opposition groups was taking shape. As these labor, environmental, and human rights groups began to organize, they debated internally: What is our message? How can we most effectively win congressional votes against the agreement? In internal discussions, the issue of whether to raise fundamental questions about Mexican democracy was actively discussed. But NAFTA opponents were not of one mind.

Among NAFTA opponents, there was a consensus about the Mexican political system: its fundamentally undemocratic nature and its abuse of human and labor rights. Yet the opposition held dissimilar views about whether democracy and human rights issues should be raised as a rationale against the agreement, let alone the more concrete question of whether NAFTA opposition groups should push for specific political conditions. There were many factors at play— some tactical, others more deeply rooted in strong beliefs against publicly criticizing Mexico. First and foremost, there was concern about confusing the message for voting against the agreement. Opponents to the treaty had largely agreed on U.S. job loss as the principal rationale. Democracy and human rights were too intangible in the face of rationales with direct impact on the United States. Second, many groups themselves did not want to criticize Mexican internal politics, and this was reinforced by the position of Latino groups. An internalized belief against speaking out against Mexican internal politics can be seen to run much wider in the United States than just U.S. government officials and was reinforced by Mexicans themselves. As one activist recalls: "There was a lot of pressure within the Latino community not to speak out about Mexico. . . . [T]he Mexican nongovernmental organization community was split on whether they wanted us to speak out or not."[7] There was fear that the leftist community would be perceived as "Mexico-bashing," a term that had been applied to the ugly rantings of the far right, such as the likes of Jesse Helms and Pat Buchanan. U.S. citizen groups were also receiving mixed messages from their NGO counterparts in Mexico. Although the latter agreed with their U.S. counterparts, some Mexican activists urged their U.S. colleagues not to say anything publicly. Third, NAFTA's chief opponent, the AFL-CIO, was facing a credibility problem in linking worker and human rights to NAFTA. Prior to NAFTA, the AFL-CIO's international wing had been known to directly support the Mexican government-aligned trade union, the CTM (Confederation of Mexican Workers) as well as repressive, state-dominated unions in Central America. To now claim to be championing the rights of workers to organize independently seemed opportunistic at best. As one Democratic Senate aide described it, because of the AFL-CIO's past links to repressive trade unions they had "zero credibility."[8] A final factor was the weight of the administration's positive portrayals of Salinas-led reforms. "They characterized it [NAFTA] as a referendum on reform in Mexico; you're against reform in Mexico if you're against NAFTA."[9]

With internal divisions within the anti-NAFTA movement, only a small group of congressional members and NGO leaders took it upon themselves to include references to Mexico's political system in their arguments against the agreement. Chief Deputy Whip David Bonior (D-MI) became the lead organizer in the House against the NAFTA agreement, and one who frequently mentioned Mexico's internal politics. Bonior regularly invited Mexican activists and human rights leaders to meet with congressional members and staff to discuss the Mexican political situation. Many Mexican activists feared reprisals back home if they were to formally testify at congressional hearings, but felt comfortable with more informal meetings held in congressional offices. For Bonior, his opposition to Mexico's political system and human rights record followed logically from his activism on Central America.[10] Bonior's efforts to broaden and link NAFTA opposition to Mexico's internal political situation, however, were not widely embraced by opponents.

The net effect was that NAFTA supporters perceived democracy and human rights concerns as an afterthought of opponents. Worse, democracy and human rights perspectives were dismissed by NAFTA supporters as coming from extremists or oddballs like Perot. Chief negotiator Katz labeled the democracy and human rights arguments as "just baggage they carried along with other arguments."[11]

Mexican Intellectuals Try to Inject Political Conditions in U.S. Debate

An interesting new dynamic arose in early 1993, triggered not by a minority voice in the U.S. Congress or NGO community but by a few Mexican intellectuals who were seeking to have congressional consideration of NAFTA include political conditions. Given historical Mexican sensitivities, this was an unusual move. It was not, however, so different from what opposition figures from other countries might ask of U.S. officials. Jorge Castañeda and Adolfo Aguilar Zinser visited the State Department and Democratic congressmen, specifically seeking support for the conditioning of the NAFTA agreement on international observation of the upcoming 1994 Mexican presidential elections.

Castañeda explained that he "received different sets of negative responses, but no positive ones."[12] The Clinton administration, he reported, was totally opposed to political conditions and would not consider it. They told him he was being interventionist. In Congress, Castañeda recalled his conversations with Senators Ted Kennedy (D-MA) and Christopher Dodd (D-CT). He maintained that most senators held simplistic views of Mexican politics, with Senator Dodd arguing that the Mexican left was communist and was merely trying to kill the agreement.

Castañeda's and Aguilar's conversations with U.S. leaders were not typical of the Mexican opposition during the NAFTA period. The PAN had not ventured back into activism in U.S. policy circles since its decidedly mixed experience in the mid-1980s. Ricardo Pascoe, a chief aide to the leader of the PRD, Cuáuhtemoc Cárdenas, explains that for its own reasons the PRD tried to distance itself from the U.S. debate over NAFTA. Many of the PRD's obvious allies in the United States (e.g., unions, environmental groups) were engaging in "Mexico-bashing arguments," he pointed out, accusing the Mexicans of trying to take jobs away from the United States. Many in the PRD did agree with some of the things NAFTA opponents were saying about Mexico on human rights and electoral fraud, but they didn't want the U.S. Congress intervening in Mexico's internal politics. Pascoe explains that "because of the way the U.S. uses those criticisms against you, to try and extract concessions.... [Y]ou can't become allies of these people criticizing Mexico."[13] The PRD was not entirely hands-off, though. PRD allies in the United States were actively expressing disagreement with NAFTA, and some had informal relationships with NAFTA congressional opponents.[14] Ironically, it was the Mexican government—not the opposition—who most tried to influence the U.S. debate through sustained lobbying and Salinas's public appearances in the United States.

NAFTA Prospects, Side Agreements Reached: Spring–Summer 1993

By the spring of 1993, prospects for NAFTA ratification appeared dim. Leon Panetta, Director of the Office of Management and Budget (OMB), inopportunely mentioned to the *Washington Post* in late April that he felt NAFTA was "dead" for now. This prompted denials from the White House and assurances from House Speaker Tom Foley (D-WA) and Majority Leader George Mitchell (D-ME) that the agreement would indeed pass once the side agreements were finalized.

When the side agreements were completed in August 1993, divisions within the NAFTA opposition came to the forefront. The environmental agreement immediately garnered support from a number of important groups, dividing the environmental movement right down the middle. The labor side agreement did not win many converts. The side agreements created independent panels for labor and the environment that can hear disputes involving enforcement of existing laws and, in certain circumstances, impose trade sanctions. Not all labor laws were subject to this review. The Mexican government made clear that rights such as freedom of association, collective bargaining, and the right to strike would not be covered. Enforcement of minimum wage laws, health and safety, and child labor laws would be subject to the dispute resolution mechanism. Another key provision protected U.S. industries from sudden NAFTA-related import surges.

The unions criticized the labor side agreement for leaving too much out and for having no teeth. Majority Leader Gephardt made it clear that he was voting against the agreement and that labor rights was one of his key concerns. The administration had apparently written off trying to please Bonior and

Gephardt, and instead targeted more centrist Democrats. The administration "wrote labor people off very soon. That's why the labor side agreement is so weak; it's a joke," recalls a Democratic aide.[15] Gephardt and others pointed out that the Mexican government had shown its willingness to make concessions on environmental issues during the negotiations, such as shutting down a controversial oil refinery in Mexico City, but not on labor issues.

Democracy Argument as Vote Draws Near

As the NAFTA vote drew near, the democracy card was played by both sides in more sweeping terms than ever before. A minority of critical voices, mainly liberal Democrats, were pointing to Mexico's political system in their statements against the agreement. NAFTA's supporters, meanwhile, had turned this argument on its head. They argued that Mexico was more democratic than not and that NAFTA would bring further democracy. These pro-democracy claims for NAFTA appear to have been articles of faith, based on the notion that free markets eventually break down authoritarian political systems. In truth, little analysis was done to indicate how this might actually work in Mexico or why this article of faith did not apply to all countries, such as Singapore and South Korea, which had succeeded in developing free markets without democracy.

On the occasion of signing the side agreements, President Clinton invited the former living presidents to the White House lawn for a "photo-op" display of bipartisan support. Sweeping democracy rationales for the agreement were invoked. President Clinton linked NAFTA to an overall U.S. policy to support democracy: "For decades, we have preached and preached and preached greater democracy, greater respect for human rights, and more open markets to Latin America. NAFTA finally offers them the opportunity to reap the benefits of this."[16] Former President Carter, while arguing that Mexico "still has a long way to go to have a truly honest, democratic election," made the claim that "the single most important factor that will bring democracy and honest elections to our next-door neighbor is to have NAFTA approved and implemented."[17] There were few distinctions among the arguments, no questioning that perhaps it was not a certainty either way.

During the fast track debate, Senator Moynihan had spoken out forcefully against a free trade agreement with a country that was not free (democratic), but he was strangely silent during the NAFTA debate. He was now Chairman of the Senate Finance Committee with a Democratic administration and had a responsibility to shepherd the NAFTA legislation through the Senate.

Even though Congress was not proposing any specific political language for NAFTA, President Salinas was reportedly still worried that this might happen. The PRI feared, according to Mexican Ambassador Jorge Montaño, that if

NAFTA was delayed much longer it would be close to the 1994 Mexican presidential elections and more likely that NAFTA opponents in Congress would try and link the two.[18] They had been observing the efforts of Mexican intellectuals like Castañeda to do just this, not realizing the limited effect such efforts were having on U.S. officials.

A crowning moment for NAFTA supporters came in the televised debate between Vice President Gore and Ross Perot just before the final November vote on the trade agreement. Perot was clearly outgunned. Gore laid out a somewhat more open admission of the status quo in Mexico than had been heard from a U.S. official during the NAFTA debate. Gore invoked the classic argument used in the China case, that the United States would lose its ability to influence political changes without a specific economic lever. Gore stated:

> Mexico is not yet a full democracy. They do not yet have full protection for human rights. But they've been making tremendous progress, and the progress has been associated with this new relationship with the United States. The question is whether or not we will have the ability to influence what they and their Government decide.[19]

Critics argued that the moment to use the economic lever was before treaty approval. They contended such an argument loses forcefulness if there is little intention of pushing a political agenda with this better economic relationship as in the case of Mexico.

NAFTA Vote: November 1993

The congressional floor debate over NAFTA followed similar lines to the positions taken in the months leading up to the vote. The Clinton team pulled out all the stops to win. Although 60 percent of House Democrats voted against the pact, Republican votes were enough to give the administration a 234 to 200 victory in the House and an easier victory in the Senate. When it came down to the wire, democracy and human rights played a subordinate role in the arguments of both supporters and opponents. Even some liberal Democrats who had raised the democracy issue during the lead-up to NAFTA, such as Representative Torricelli, ended up supporting the agreement in the end.

Marcy Kaptur (D-OH) argued on the House floor that the absence of democracy and human rights from the agreement was a "tragic omission" and reprimanded the administration for not using the agreement as leverage to push the Mexicans further on the road to democracy.[20] Days after the vote, Mary McGrory wrote a column castigating the administration for moving away from its initial human rights commitment and for characterizing Mexico's record as "not as bad as China."[21] But these were rare mentions of the democracy dimension, which was clearly overwhelmed by more compelling and tangible economic interests that swayed votes in the U.S. Congress. In contrast to Gore's assertion that the United States would have more leverage with Mexico under NAFTA, President Salinas reminded North Americans after the vote that "the only thing we negotiated was free trade."[22]

NAFTA's Aftermath

Shortly after the vote, Vice President Gore made a trip to Mexico City. Days before his arrival, the Mexican opposition had charged the PRI with committing widespread fraud in elections in the Yucatán. Also, just before the trip, Salinas had handpicked Luis Donaldo Colosio as the PRI presidential candidate for 1994. In an embarrassing faux pas, press secretary Dee Dee Myers congratulated Colosio and not the opposition candidates, calling him the new president of Mexico.

During his trip, Gore evaded press questions on whether he thought Mexico was a true democracy, on the Yucatán elections, and on the Colosio nomination. Instead, he called for a general commitment to democratic political culture and announced a Western hemispheric summit in Miami to gather together the community of democracies, including Mexico. U.S. aides traveling with Gore indicated that the vice president intended to convey a message with his repeated reference to democratic values, but he would not raise the democracy issue directly with Salinas.[23]

NAFTA Introduces a New Dynamic

While questions about Mexican democracy ultimately did not decide votes, the NAFTA debate itself provided the impetus for a much wider airing of views on Mexico's internal politics than had occurred previously. From 1990 to the end of 1993, some form of public dialogue addressing contrasting views of the Mexican political system is discernible. This dialogue, highly stilted, reached a wider audience on a more sustained basis than ever before. The quality of the debate over the nature of Mexico's political system suffered from the extreme polarization and simplification of arguments on both sides. This was true of the whole NAFTA debate, not just of democracy.

Only a minority of NAFTA opponents raised questions regarding Mexico's political system. This time it was principally liberal Democrats with a few conservative Republicans. What was not completely expected was evidence that the minority, while holding a different political view of Salinas and Mexico, also largely subscribed to, or was torn by the longstanding belief against public criticism of Mexico. The raising of democracy by the minority also revealed that some other pressing issue, in this case the vote on NAFTA, was needed for the minority to overcome existing norms against speaking publicly about Mexico's internal politics.

Because Mexico's internal political system had been subjected to so little public scrutiny to this point, the polarized debate never challenged either administration to confront their own beliefs or unequivocal view of the Salinas regime. The "NAFTA-as-a democratizing-instrument" argument was sweeping and unequivocal. It was not that NAFTA might not have such effects; it was the certainty with which this was depicted. Such sweeping claims reflected their own brand of opportunism. As Georges Fauriol noted: "They knew Mexico was undemocratic. They knew it would take years before democracy would come through freer markets. It was a meaningless argument."[24]

While the NAFTA debate provided a new spotlight on Mexico's internal politics, it also substituted for a lack of more sustained critical analysis of Mexico and an explicit policy toward emerging Mexican democracy. As NAFTA became the dominant issue in United States–Mexico relations, both the Clinton and Bush administrations viewed the democracy issue as one of many vehicles for selling NAFTA, not as a focus of U.S. policy itself. The public messages sent by the U.S. government during this period were clear: unequivocal statements that the United States would not consider any political dimension to NAFTA, no public statements of criticism or concern regarding Mexican internal politics or complaints of electoral fraud from 1989 to 1993, and only supportive statements regarding the pace or direction of political reform under Salinas.

Regardless of the poor quality of the debate, the NAFTA negotiations infused a new dynamic in U.S. political relations with Mexico. Mexican human rights activist Marie Claire Acosta argues that NAFTA opened a door with more members of Congress for direct interest in Mexico's political system, a door that was opened further with the Zapatista rebellion in Chiapas in 1994.[25] Whether simplified and rhetorical, the very existence of NAFTA compels the U.S. government to respond more to political events in Mexico. "The whole issue of trade will never be the same again because trade has invaded the area of worker rights, consumer rights and human rights."[26] While the long-standing operational belief in the U.S. policy establishment had escaped relatively unscathed from the NAFTA period, it would be increasingly difficult to maintain this with the same tenacity in the future. As Denise Dresser wrote: "In the past, the costs of overlooking Mexico's authoritarian regime were almost insignificant, but North American integration has heightened these costs. Mexico is no longer an exotic anomaly but part of a North American community."[27]

6.

The Clinton Administration and the 1994 Mexican Presidential Elections

The Bush and Clinton administrations' carefully groomed image of Mexico as a modernizing society, to be further democratized by NAFTA, was put to the test almost immediately. Mexico's image of political stability was rocked by the news of an armed uprising in Chiapas in January 1994, and later that same year, by two high-profile political assassinations. Mexico was not fitting neatly into the characterizations laid out by NAFTA supporters or opponents.

The specter of instability cast a shadow over the upcoming August 1994 Mexican presidential elections. President Salinas had hoped to preside over peaceful elections and to hand his reform program over to a successor whose electoral legitimacy was unchallenged. There was speculation that he also wanted to advance his reputation as a candidate to head the new World Trade Organization (WTO). U.S. officials had important motivations for ensuring that the cloud of electoral fraud that surrounded Salinas's election in 1988 would not be repeated in 1994. The NAFTA agreement was just getting underway and the administration was proposing to extend it throughout the hemisphere, building a network of free trade democracies. If Mexico were to exhibit starkly undemocratic behaviors it would undermine the credibility of the upcoming Summit of the Americas and NAFTA as well.

It was in this unusual political context that the Clinton administration ultimately supported international observation of the August presidential elections through providing funds for a high-profile U.S. visitor delegation and for a Mexican citizen alliance observing the elections. This important evolution in the U.S. relationship with Mexico over democracy to more overt political assistance, was largely accomplished within the parameters of traditional policy.

The case study in this chapter will track how the Clinton administration and Mexican government came slowly and fitfully to support international electoral observation in the 1994 Mexican elections. It will show that the prevailing belief against open criticism of the Mexican political system continued to operate simultaneously with this policy shift and was not dramatically challenged by this incremental change. The change came about in this case not from an outcast minority, but by the interplay of key individuals both within and outside the administration. The political context leading up to the elections began to shift with the dramatic rebel offensive in Chiapas.

Chiapas: The Specter of Instability Rises

On January 1, 1994, the day NAFTA came into force, armed rebels seized several key towns and took control of roadways in the southern state of Chiapas. One hundred forty-five people were left dead in brief fighting between the Zapatista National Liberation Army (EZLN in Spanish) and the Mexican army. The rebels said their military offensive aimed to address human rights, discrimination, and land tenure rights for the Mayan Indian population. They claimed that they were declaring war against the "illegitimate" government of Carlos Salinas de Gortari and seeking political reforms for the entire country.[1]

The Mexican government first attempted to put the rebellion down militarily, but then shifted to a strategy of negotiations. Press headlines accused the military of committing human rights abuses against the local, primarily indigenous population. Charges of rape and murder were prominent, including the claim of the summary execution of seven to nine suspected rebels in Ocosingo, Chiapas. Manuel Camacho Solis, a respected party official, was appointed Commissioner for Peace and Reconciliation to work out a peace agreement with the Zapatistas. Other government representatives were assigned to seek political agreements with the key opposition parties. While peace negotiations with the Zapatistas dragged on, the government was able to reach a significant political agreement with the political parties. On January 27, the Mexican government and major opposition parties agreed to a series of political reforms, including the creation of independent electoral authorities and greater media access for opposition parties.

U.S. officials say they were caught completely off guard by the uprising. The first senior Washington official to hear the news was Bob Felder, the State Department's Country Director for Mexico, who got a call from the State Department's Operations Center on New Year's Day: "At first, I thought it was a joke."[2]

Richard Feinberg, Senior Director for Inter-American Affairs at the NSC, also recalled that it "caught us by surprise."[3] A September 1991 classified CIA report that had been distributed to all senior State Department and NSC officials had not predicted any such uprising. The fifteen-page report, "Mexico's Troubled South: Being Left Behind," stated that "high-level corruption, reportedly including the Governor of Chiapas" was "undermining local authorities and contributing to sporadic violence."[4] The document predicted that political conditions would "lead to increased political discontent," but it fell short of predicting an armed uprising or identifying the existence of armed groups.[5] Ted Wilkinson, a political officer at the U.S. Embassy at the time, recalled that there was no hard intelligence on the presence of armed groups. He said that one attaché's report cited armed groups in Chiapas, but "I didn't consider it then."[6]

Assistant Secretary of State for Inter-American Affairs Alexander Watson stated that the U.S. government raised human rights concerns "at the very highest levels from the outset of this crisis."[7] This public statement marks a rare moment in which U.S. officials indicated publicly that they spoke to the Mexican government about internal developments within Mexico. While important, this shift is an incremental one for administration officials did not actually criticize the regime or express concern for the Mexican government's handling of the crisis or the roots of festering inequities in Chiapas. Rather, while noting references to human rights events, U.S. officials predominantly made positive and encouraging statements about the regime's handling of the crisis and the Mexican political system overall. Some of the franker statements arose from the first congressional hearings on a political topic in Mexico since the discredited Helms hearings in 1986.

Congressional Hearings on Chiapas

The title of the hearings on February 2 made clear that they would not avoid the topic of democracy: "Mexico: The Uprising in Chiapas and Democratization in Mexico." Representative Robert Torricelli (D-NJ), who chaired the Western Hemisphere Affairs Subcommittee, opened the hearings stating he knew he was breaking a taboo: "There are those who will wonder about the right of the United States to be asking questions about political reform in Mexico."[8] He drew justification from the new trade relationship:

[W]hen the North American Free Trade Agreement was agreed upon, clearly we entered into a different relationship. We have not simply that right, but more importantly, the responsibility for the interests of our investors and indeed of our larger national concerns to inquire about the political stability of our new partner.[9]

This was still a minority view within Congress, taken up now by a few Democrats. Even among liberal Democrats there was disagreement about being openly critical of Mexico. Representative Joe Kennedy (D-MA), considered quite liberal in speaking out on human rights and democracy in Central America, was more circumspect about Mexico, according to his aide.[10] Kennedy, asked to testify at the hearings following a visit to Chiapas, felt he did not want to publicly criticize the Mexican government or its political system.[11] The Mexican government's response to the hearings was heated. Assistant Secretary of Foreign Affairs Andrés Rosenthal declared: "It must be made very clear that the enactment of the free trade agreement does not give anyone outside Mexico the right to erect himself as a judge of affairs that only we Mexicans should resolve."[12]

Administration witnesses generally characterized Mexico as undergoing dramatic political change and supported the Mexican government's handling of the Chiapas crisis. Assistant Secretary of State Alex Watson put a positive spin on Chiapas: "We are also witnessing dramatic transformations in the Mexican political system. . . . Chiapas, rather than representing a reversal in the process of economic and political transformation in Mexico, has proven to be a further energizing factor contributing to a deepening of the reform process."[13] In a sign of more openness, Assistant Secretary of State for Human Rights and Humanitarian Affairs John Shattuck cited reports of human rights abuses and, quite unusually, stated that it appeared that the Mexican army was responsible for summary executions in Ocosingo. At the same time, he praised the reform process and Mexico's efforts to investigate human rights abuses: "This [Mexican government activity] is precisely the kind of human rights activity and effort to get on top of human rights abuses that countries all over the world ought to be engaged in. Mexico has many human rights problems, to be sure. All of us do."[14]

Shattuck and Watson emphasized that they talked privately to the Mexicans about democratic reform, although the substance could not be revealed publicly. "We press the Mexican government on democratization issues all the time when we talk to them," remarked Watson.[15] For the first time in the public record, a U.S. official stressed that Mexico was not an exception to the overall U.S. policy toward promoting democracy:

I want to emphasize the seriousness with which President Clinton and all elements within the administration take the issue of an evenhanded approach toward issues of human rights and democratization. It is a pillar of the President's foreign policy precisely because all nations of the world are looked at in a very consistent and fair way. In the case of Mexico, there has been no lack of serious treatment of the human rights abuses and the problems of democratization.[16]

Clinton administration characterization of its policy and Mexican government performance was contrasted in the hearings with the testimony of human rights representatives and a few congressional members. Juan Mendez, Executive Director of Americas Watch, for example, stated:

> We believe that the United States, the Clinton administration, has not been forceful or forthcoming about human rights violations in the context of this conflict, as should have been expected from the seriousness of the violations. We don't doubt that there have been important approaches of a quiet diplomacy kind, but we believe the seriousness of violations that we have heard today warranted a frank and honest and public expression of concern.[17]

In the hearings, the administration was questioned about a controversy that surfaced in the U.S. press over the use of U.S. military equipment against the rebels and their peasant supporters. U.S. press reports had revealed the use of U.S. aerial drug eradication helicopters by the Mexican army in Chiapas. After a written request for clarification from the Committee, the State Department later acknowledged that sixteen U.S. planes were deployed in Chiapas, but that senior U.S. Embassy officials (note: not Mexican officials) assured Washington that the planes were used in "a logistical, non-combat support role."[18] The Mexican government then quietly withdrew the U.S. helicopters from Chiapas. A similar question arose over Mexican government requests for additional military supplies and hardware, including helicopters and weapons during the time of the military conflict. The State Department acknowledged that Mexico had purchased military rations from U.S. stocks and had made inquiries about the price of helicopters and other military equipment. But administration officials indicated that, under current law, most of these items were not subject to export controls.[19] These controversies over the use of U.S. military equipment revealed how difficult the policies were to maintain. Those helicopters were clearly not provided to support counterinsurgency operations, yet the United States felt hemmed into its response by not wanting to criticize either the Mexican government or the operations themselves.

Response to Chiapas in Context

The Clinton administration's response to the Chiapas conflict had elements of a more open policy toward internal political events in Mexico, yet it still largely reflected the traditional U.S. approach of avoiding any direct criticism of the Mexican political regime. Jorge Castañeda commented:

It's remarkable, in a sense, that someone, a president of the United States, who spoke about Mexico almost every day for a couple of months last year during the NAFTA debate, has managed not to say a word about Mexico, not even pronounce the word Mexico in public over the past month, given that the Chiapas uprising is arguably the most important political event in Mexico in 25 years.[20]

The administration also struggled to avoid giving too many details of the positive acts it maintained the Mexican government had taken. It spoke largely in broad brushstrokes. As part of the congressional hearings, Representative Torricelli had requested specific details of human rights investigations conducted by the Mexican government. The State Department later provided a five-paragraph response that did not detail progress on any specific investigation; rather, it referred to general categories of ongoing investigations. As U.S. human rights groups maintained, the truth was that little progress had been made.[21]

The unprecedented news of an armed insurgency active on Mexican soil put an undeniable strain on the traditional positive-only pattern of approaching political developments in Mexico. The public record does reveal an incremental change in how the U.S. administration publicly dealt with the conflict, but it did not imply a whole reshifting of U.S. thinking on how it should approach political development in Mexico. Denise Dresser commented: "Clinton's response to Chiapas suggests that the administration has not yet articulated a strategy for assisting Mexico to strengthen its democratic institutions. Nor has it decided how much it wants a democratic Mexico and how much it is prepared to invest in that outcome."[22] The State Department political officer for Mexico also confirmed that the changes in Chiapas did little to prompt a U.S. rethinking: "Chiapas didn't impact directly on U.S. views for democratization."[23]

Case Study:
The 1994 Mexican Presidential Elections

Even before the Chiapas crisis, there was concern within the administration that electoral fraud in the Mexican presidential elections could pose serious problems for U.S. policy. Although the administration had publicly praised Mexican democracy during NAFTA consideration, there was widespread "fear of 1988" within the administration, remarked Ann MacDonald at the U.S. Agency for International Development (USAID).[24] Electoral fraud on the scale of 1988 offered the prospect of damaging a range of U.S. interests and initiatives. To ensure passage of NAFTA, the administration had staked its reputation not only that Mexico was democratizing, but also that NAFTA would accelerate reform. A new administration initiative, the Summit of the Americas, was scheduled for the fall and was to showcase a plan to extend free trade and democracy throughout the hemisphere. Nondemocratic states were to be explicitly excluded from the summit. The administration made clear that Cuba and Haiti would not be invited.[25] But how awkward would it be to showcase Mexico if its leader was perceived to have won through deliberate vote-rigging? Fraudulent elections had the potential of marring the implementation of NAFTA, evoking criticism of Mexican participation in the Summit of the Americas, and raising questions about Mexico's lead role in a hemisphere-wide free trade initiative of democracies, summed up NSC official Richard Feinberg.[26]

In late 1993 and early 1994, there was quiet speculation about the prospect of international observation of the elections. Mexico had traditionally opposed such observation as tantamount to foreign intervention. At a United States–Mexico workshop in January, U.S. congressmen had questioned two Mexican senators about their reluctance to admit international observers for the August elections.[27] Representative Torricelli also commented during the February hearings:

> I think it is legitimate for us to discuss the terms and conditions under which elections are being held. The Mexicans are very resistant to having international observers at their elections, but perhaps there can be some halfway point of having nongovernmental officials looking after the elections process.[28]

International electoral observation was just one potential policy option, but one that had become standard fare in the U.S. pro-democracy menu. Whether the United States would openly push Mexico to change its policy, however, was another matter. Uncertainty over which direction U.S. policy should take was evident in an initial meeting with U.S.-based NGOs at the State Department late in 1993.

State Department Meeting: December 1993

In early December, State Department and USAID officials invited U.S. NGOs to their offices to talk about their potential activities around the 1994 Mexican elections. U.S.-based NGOs had taken a particular lead in conducting international observation throughout Latin America. Among the participants were representatives from the Carter Center, the National Endowment for Democracy (NED), Freedom House, the National Democratic Institute for International Affairs (NDI), and the Washington Office on Latin America (WOLA). The meeting was led by Norma Parker, Deputy Administrator for USAID's Latin America and Caribbean Bureau; Arturo Valenzuela, Deputy Assistant

Secretary for Mexico designate (confirmed in January 1994); and Joanna Mendelson, USAID special advisor in the Democracy Bureau. Each of the NGO representatives was asked to explain in turn what activities they were considering around the upcoming elections. Michael Shifter talked about NED's work to date supporting Mexican citizen observation of local elections. Other organizations then spoke. NGO representatives later said they weren't quite clear what State and USAID officials were after. "There was an interest, but they were very ambivalent," recalls Shifter. "They were not really sure how hard to push."[29]

From the government perspective, some participating U.S. officials felt they were starting by making an effort to touch base with the NGO community. Norma Parker recalled that under the previous Deputy Assistant Secretary for Mexico, Donna Riley, there had been talk of trying to put together a coalition of NGOs in Mexico, but nothing came of it. She admitted that less than eight months to the election, they didn't have any clear direction: "Even in December 1993, we weren't talking about observation."[30]

By January 1994, discussions over the question of electoral observation were beginning between the respective governments and U.S. NGO officials, all out of the public eye. U.S. officials were talking to the Mexican government about ensuring that the legitimacy of the 1994 elections was not questioned and about specific electoral procedures. Santiago Oñate, then head of international affairs for the PRI and later president of the party, was asked by U.S. officials to consider accepting OAS electoral observers. He turned down the proposal. The United Nations (UN) was also considered unacceptable because for so many years the Mexican government had opposed UN "intervention" in other countries. NDI President Ken Wollack and Santiago Canton, Director for Latin America, met on March 13 with Luis Donaldo Colosio, the charismatic PRI candidate for the presidency, pressing him to accept national and international observers. Although Colosio told them NDI was welcome, NDI officials responded that they did not operate where there weren't conditions for domestic observation.[31] The Mexican government had still not formally decided on what terms it would allow its own countrymen to observe the elections. Ten days later, amidst these tentative discussions, came another dramatic jolt to Mexico's international image of stability.

Political Assassination of Colosio

PRI presidential candidate Colosio was gunned down while campaigning in Tijuana. The assassination sent shockwaves through Mexico and the international markets. Mexico, proud of its decades of political stability but shaken by armed revolt in January, now faced an unprecedented political assassination. The next day, President Salinas, concerned about a run on the Mexican peso, closed the banks, currency exchange houses, and the stock market.

President Clinton issued a strong vote of confidence, declaring that the Mexican government was in "sound shape" and that he did not believe that Colosio's death was a sign of instability that would disrupt the growing trade and investment between the two nations.[32] U.S. Ambassador Jim Jones even went so far as to make a pronouncement that the killing seemed to be an act of random violence, although he cautioned that the Embassy did not know what motivated it.[33] Just hours after the shooting, Treasury Secretary Lloyd Bentsen revived an existing standby agreement and set up a $6 billion credit line to help Mexico withstand any financial market jitters. The Mexican stock market fell one hundred points at first, but then recovered with only a small downturn after news of the U.S. readiness to step in. Ernesto Zedillo, Colosio's campaign manager, a technocrat and former education minister who had never held elective office, was later named the PRI candidate.

Electoral Rumblings: April/May 1994

By April, there was still no clear indication of whether the Clinton administration would back any explicit support or activities surrounding the election or, conversely, whether Mexico itself would permit international observation. Privately, U.S. officials were telling U.S. NGOs that they were having informal discussions with the Mexicans about electoral conditions and observation.[34] Publicly, the administration continued to express confidence in the fair outcome of the elections and in the Mexican political system. There was a series of public statements by the U.S. ambassador, Assistant Secretary of State Watson,[35] and the president himself during this period, well before any Mexican commitment on observation, all expressing such confidence. "I believe that Mexico will hold full, free, and fair elections," declared President Clinton.[36] Ambassador Jones also announced that the U.S. government was prepared to work with a president from the opposition.[37]

The Clinton administration's glowing characterization of the prospective election was tarnished by a press report on April 27 that the Mexican government had imported from the United States millions of dollars worth of riot equipment, including water cannons, remote-controlled television systems, barricade removers, and guns with optional features to dye targets so they could be identified later.[38] When asked about these sales, Watson replied that he had no information: "You'll just have to ask the Mexican government why they bought this equipment and for what purpose.... Maybe it's nothing special, maybe it is, but you'd have to ask them. I don't think anyone is anticipating anything like Chiapas elsewhere."[39] U.S. congressmen would later use this report to suggest that the Mexicans were not planning the clean and fair election that the State Department was ready to certify.[40]

The spotlight on the upcoming elections continued with a second hearing on Mexican political reform chaired by Representative Torricelli on April 20. He asserted: "The United States cannot silently accept fraudulent elections in Mexico this August. It is our responsibility as a major trading partner and as the leader of the free world to insist that Mexico's next president be elected in an open and honest vote."[41] More outspoken calls for free and fair elections could be heard from a small group of House members, mostly liberal Democrats, echoed principally at this second House hearing in April. The administration was pursing a quieter, more contained approach, as evidenced by Secretary Warren Christopher's trip to Mexico.

Secretary of State's Trip to Mexico: May 1994

This rare trip to Mexico was under the auspices of the United States-Mexico Binational Commission and was Christopher's first trip to Mexico as secretary of state. There was a full agenda including: trade/NAFTA, border issues, and drug cooperation. But sandwiched into the official discussions was a remarkable thirty seconds at a lunch with Foreign Minister Manuel Tello.[42] Christopher prefaced his remarks by saying that the administration was aware of the sensitivities of the Mexican government and people to affronts to their national sovereignty. He stressed, however, that it was important to ensure the legitimacy of the election. He then went on to mention international observation as a way of supporting the legitimacy of the election. Left unclear was what the United States was specifically looking for Mexico to do. It was an unusual moment wherein the U.S. secretary of state raised a topic touching on Mexican democracy with a Mexican cabinet official. According to press reports, President Clinton also raised the issue of electoral observation with the Mexican ambassador to the United States on May 5.[43] Back in the public eye, however, Secretary Christopher adopted the same refrain as other U.S. officials, saying that he expected the elections to be free and fair.[44]

State Department aides disclosed to the press some of the main lines of United States-Mexico discussions on democracy and electoral observation on the condition that the informants not be identified. They stressed that any kind of challenge to the legitimacy of the election would be a tremendous problem for the United States-Mexico relationship. Their assessment of the political reforms was slightly less than the totally laudatory public position: "There is a feeling that the general lines of the electoral reforms they have laid out are in the right direction. There's less confidence that these things are working out in the way they should."[45] These officials told the press that they were deliberately understated in public but more direct in private. "The Mexicans read these statements very carefully and are hypersensitive to any sign that we are interfering in their internal affairs. So we didn't want to come on too strong in public."[46]

Shortly after the secretary's visit, the Mexican government decided to formally legalize foreign "visitors" to the elections. Mexican Foreign Minister Tello and other officials reportedly opposed international observation, while Salinas favored it. Colosio, prior to his death, had also said he favored it.[47] Some in Mexico linked the decision to U.S. pressure.[48] Mexican NGO groups had first used the term "visitor" in the summer of 1992. These groups were trying to get around Mexican government opposition to foreign electoral observations by inviting foreigners not to observe the elections, but to "observe the observations" done by Mexican citizens.[49] It was always an informal term, but now the Mexican government had co-opted it for its own purposes. While a welcome development, "electoral visitors" was clearly less than what the U.S. government had been seeking and added to the uncertainty of just what the Mexican government would permit on election day. A number of U.S. congressmen and senators continued to push for full electoral observation.

Torricelli–Bonior Resolution on the Mexican Elections

In preparation for the April hearings on Mexican political reform in the House of Representatives, Torricelli's staff mused about the possibility of writing a congressional resolution to complement the hearings. Jane Thiery, Congressman Torricelli's aide, remembered the thinking: "Well, we're going to have hearings. Should we do a resolution? All right, if we did a resolution, what would it be like?"[50] Such resolutions are a dime a dozen and rarely draw much attention from members of Congress since they have no force of law. But from a rather commonplace origin arose the first congressionally-passed resolution in modern times commenting on Mexico's political system.

The draft was worked on by Torricelli's staff, the staff of Chief Majority Whip David Bonior (D-MI) (the principal co-sponsor along with Torricelli), staff of Majority Leader Gephardt, and the House Parliamentarian. The relatively small group was drawn from three members all openly critical of NAFTA. When the resolution was introduced on May 17, Representative Bonior announced: "The United States has a new relationship with Mexico—our futures are intertwined. We have both the responsibility and the opportunity to ensure that there are fair and free elections in Mexico on August 21st."[51] The resolution called for the Salinas government to go further than inviting foreign visitors by permitting full-scale international observation. The opening clauses of the resolution mentioned specific instances of electoral fraud and undemocratic practices, citing in particular charges of fraud in the Yucatán and Morelos within the previous year. "The people of Mexico today are struggling to overcome decades of rigged elections and entrenched political corruption," remarked Bonior.[52]

The press conference was sparsely attended and received very little media attention in the United States. Only about fourteen members of Congress, mostly liberal Democrats opposing NAFTA, signed on as co-sponsors of the resolution. "It wasn't a big coalition";[53] these were still minority views within the Congress. The attention in Mexico, however, was intense. The Mexican embassy, government, and Congress all issued harsh statements condemning the resolution and the right of anyone in the U.S. Congress to comment on Mexican elections. The Mexican press was also filled with condemnations. A statement issued by all the major parties in the Mexican Chamber of Deputies read: "We reiterate that Mexican electoral procedures should be based on our principles and laws, and we will not allow our national sovereignty to be violated under any argument whatsoever."[54]

While no companion resolution moved in the U.S. Senate, twelve senators signed a letter asking Secretary of State Christopher to convey to the Mexicans the need for internationally recognized observers. They described U.S. interests this way: "Allegations of flawed elections, even if baseless, could cause political strife that would affect the success of NAFTA, exacerbate immigration problems in U.S. border states, and spark controversy in both countries."[55]

U.S. Government Support Coalesces: Mid-May 1994

Although administration officials had been having informal discussions with the Mexicans and the Mexicans were now to invite visitors, it was still not decided whether the U.S. government itself would be supporting any pro-democracy activities directly or sending observers. An important event that would help give direction to U.S. efforts was a decision by the principal Mexican pro-democracy groups to unite under a large umbrella organization that they christened *Alianza Cívica,* the Civic Alliance. A number of the organizations making up the alliance had been supported by NED affiliates, and NDI was instrumental in convincing some of the major Mexican organizations to unite, as there were just too many to fund.[56]

Norma Parker of USAID remembered that the U.S. decision was made after a Civic Alliance presentation and was "more spur of the moment. It was made one day to the next."[57] The Mexican government had just decided to let the United Nations in, but it was not permitted to conduct electoral observation. The Mexican government would instead train domestic observers, largely with Mexican government funding. Joanna Mendelson of USAID's Democracy Unit explained that "the UN was the fig leaf" they needed; now the United States would not be standing out or stepping too hard on any diplomatic toes by supporting electoral activities.[58] USAID and the State Department reached a decision on two key activities: to provide funds to the Civic Alliance through NDI and to fund an official observer/witness delegation through NDI and the International Republican Institute for International Affairs (IRI). These two activities totaled about $1.2 million.

While the UN provided one layer of cover, financing electoral activities through third parties created another. Nothing was to have the official U.S. stamp. The U.S. government would provide a grant to NDI, which would support the Civic Alliance's domestic observation. The State Department would fund NDI and IRI to run an eighty-person "witness" delegation, many of whom would be from outside the United States. Despite the cultivation of fig leaves, USAID and State officials were still concerned about Mexico's reaction because it would be the first time that the U.S. government had taken such public steps around a Mexican election. Interesting, Parker recalls that they did not get the negative reaction from the Mexican government that they expected.[59]

All told, U.S. officials emphasized that the resulting policy outcome came about less from a planned policy on Mexican democracy than from a slow evolution of official views and response to external groups. USAID's Mendelson and Parker emphasized that NDI ultimately brought a proposal to them to finance the Civic Alliance; they did not solicit one or broadly plan a U.S. approach to the elections.[60] Parker recalls: "Nor was there much consideration of other alternatives or activities. We never considered anything beyond electoral observation."[61]

The lateness of the decision by the Mexican government on what it would allow, and the similar late start of U.S. government activities, clearly constrained the quality and thoroughness of what could be observed. Janine Perfit of IRI recalled that she first argued that IRI should not participate; the delegation would only be dropping by Mexico a few days before the election and would not be conducting crucial pre-election observations, which were particularly important in the Mexican case. However curtailed, Perfit conceded that there was "pressure from the administration, even a Democratic one," to participate plus key Republican interest from Representative David Drier (R-CA) and others who clearly wanted IRI there.[62] Mexico's decision, and the U.S. response, ultimately came together with less than three months to go to the elections.

Controversy over Bias in the Civic Alliance

Although funds were to be provided via NDI to the Civic Alliance, USAID and State officials were not entirely comfortable with the decision. Some feared that the alliance might not be objective in reporting electoral fraud, as a number of prominent leaders had displayed sympathies for the opposition parties. Others contended that the Mexican situation was no different than that of other countries. Those motivated to monitor against fraud were not going to be party regulars. This did not mean they could not be objective. NDI official Santiago Canton recalls that USAID had "a lot of concerns and nervousness with Civic Alliance. We had concerns ourselves . . . but you just had to wait for election day."[63]

The bias controversy was brought into the public light on June 3 through an article by analyst M. Delal Baer. Baer, with the Center for Strategic and International Studies, wrote that the alliance was heavily slanted toward the PRD, and this bias impugned their ability to be objective. "It will be hard for alliance leaders to discipline themselves and the passions of thousands of members," she wrote.[64] She called for a reconsideration of funding for the alliance. The Civic Alliance was outraged by the accusations, and some Mexicans raised questions of Baer's own bias toward the PRI.[65] The NED board reviewed the claims and, ultimately, went ahead with funding. This U.S. strategy to support electoral observation was, ironically, coalescing just about the time the Mexican race was heating up.

Mexican Presidential Race Appears to Tighten

By mid-May, the PRD's candidate, Cuáuhtemoc Cárdenas, despite his strong showing in the 1988 elections, appeared to be lagging in public opinion polls. But the first-ever Mexican presidential television debate on May 12 ignited the hopes for PAN candidate Diego Fernández de Cevallos. Fernández appeared feisty and combative, taking on PRI candidate Zedillo, who appeared stiff and insincere.[66] Speculation was rife that Fernández might now become a consensus, anti-PRI candidate, drawing a wide range of disaffected voters, perhaps even leading to Mexico's first coalition government. In Mexico City, a group of intellectuals calling themselves the San Angel Group met to consider the possibilities of a coalition government or negotiated transition, as well as to discuss the country's electoral conditions. The group consisted of writers, economists, and academics and included people identified with each of the major parties.

In Washington, however, there was not much consideration of the possibility of a coalition government.[67] Some U.S. officials viewed the speculation as wishful thinking by Mexican left-wing intellectuals, promoted by Jorge Castañeda and others sympathetic to his views. Reportedly, only one U.S. official, Cathryn Thorup, a USAID official detailed to work under Richard Feinberg at the NSC, raised the question of a coalition government internally. The NSC wanted an internal policy paper on the subject, but the State

Department rejected the request, fearing that if it got out, it would offend the Mexican government.

As often happens in Washington, even minor speculation was twisted out of proportion. House Speaker Newt Gingrich and nineteen other House Republicans wrote a letter to President Clinton expressing their concern that a high U.S. official had told the Mexican ambassador to the United States that it was time to consider a PRI–PRD coalition. In words reminiscent of the 1980s, the letter read:

> We are very concerned that the election results could lead to a coalition of far-left elements coming to power as a result of precipitous violence and instability. . . . It may set the stage for a handful of PRD supporters in the U.S. Congress and in your administration to react to the turmoil and argue for the application of political and economic pressure to foster a PRD coalition.[68]

The Mexican newspaper *La Jornada* later identified the Republicans' source as Constantine Menges, the Reagan aide considered alarmist on Mexico in the 1980s. The Mexican ambassador categorically denied having said what was attributed to him in the letter or of knowing Menges.[69] There is little evidence that the Clinton administration was ever seriously planning for other potential political scenarios, including a coalition or non-PRI Mexican government. U.S. officials, in fact, had little sympathy for the PRD; if there was any expected upset winner, the United States thought it would be the PAN.[70] Ricardo Pascoe, a former PRD congressman and a close aide to Cárdenas, maintained: "I never got any sense they [the Clinton administration] were thinking of alternatives to PRI in the 1994 elections . . . they are completely committed to the PRI."[71]

Torricelli Resolution Advances/Trip to Mexico

In keeping with its positive approach to the upcoming elections, the Clinton administration did not want any unwelcome comments on the Mexican political system coming from the Congress. As the Bonior-Torricelli resolution was advancing to a public hearing in June, it became an increasing thorn in the administration's side, contradicting its positive portrayal of electoral conditions in Mexico. Ambassador Jones personally lobbied on the Hill against the resolution.

When Representative Torricelli suggested that he would like to go to Mexico in June to investigate pre-electoral conditions and the situation in Chiapas, the State Department tried to discourage him, telling him "this was not the appropriate time."[72] Torricelli, known to grab headlines, had the potential to unravel the administration's delicate portrayal of the elections and international observation. A delegation did depart in mid-June, and the Embassy was clearly concerned about the delegation's trip, particularly to Chiapas and its meetings with Zapatistas. In the end, the more prominent incidents came from protests by the Mexican left angered at Torricelli's anti-Cuba legislation.

Once back in Washington, Torricelli worked with his co-sponsor Representative Bonior to advance the resolution. With administration protestations and Mexican public criticism, Torricelli and Bonior revised the resolution with the help of House Foreign Affairs Committee Chairman Lee Hamilton's staff. The administration stopped short of calling for the defeat of the resolution; they knew a revision was in the works. As Torricelli explained the revisions: "[R]emoved several clauses from the original resolution that may have been viewed as an effort to simply criticize Mexico for its past. I have also eliminated a provision from the body of the resolution that calls for full-scale international observation of the election."[73] The revised version expressed no overt criticism but rather the support of the U.S. Congress for the efforts of the Mexican government, parties, and civic groups to ensure free and fair elections and urged full implementation of the January 1994 political reforms. This watered-down version passed the full House of Representatives by voice vote on June 3. While praising the new text and Representative Hamilton, in particular, for "a constructive effort," the Mexican government made clear its disapproval even of the revised version. Its formal comment stated: "Mexico cannot accept this type of proposal intended to qualify and determine the Mexican electoral process."[74]

What was more interesting than the ultimate passage of the now benign, nonbinding resolution was that the State Department could not have judged the criticism to be as damaging as it was portrayed and was not trying very hard to have it removed. Torricelli aide Jane Thiery recalls: "We didn't feel heavy pressure. If we would have felt heavy pressure, we would have dropped it. It wasn't worth it. How many votes was it going to get Torricelli? Three?"[75]

Conditions Right before the Election

As the elections approached, the political chances of the ruling party candidate, Ernesto Zedillo, were looking better and better. Diego Férnandez's star seemed to be fading. Political polls were now predicting an easier victory for the PRI. Since polls are notoriously suspect in Mexico, there was still some speculation that the election could be close, but the general atmosphere was more upbeat for the PRI than it was in May around the time of the debates.

By this time, U.S. official statements were all but certifying the election would be free and fair before it happened. The Mexican government had spent millions on a massive overhaul of the electoral rolls and computer system and called in U.S. accounting and auditing firms to review the system. These were important efforts. At the same time, no public mention was made of any of the reservations about pre-electoral conditions raised by the Mexican opposition parties, civic groups, or the U.S. media. These reservations included: opposition access to the media; media bias, particularly in television; and misuse of public resources. Ambassador Jones told a group of U.S. correspondents: "We don't see any evidence of a pattern of systematic irregularities or abusing of the system. There may be operational glitches, but [there is] no systematic pattern of irregularities."[76] In a letter to Senator Ben Nighthorse Campbell (R-CO), the State Department admitted that "we would have preferred a system involving foreign observers," but argued that a consensus favoring such observers was not possible before the August elections.[77]

In keeping with the positive depiction of the upcoming election, there was no public comment by the U.S. administration when the highly respected Jorge Carpizo resigned as head of the electoral commission in June. Carpizo claimed that party forces were resisting reform and undermining the commission's independence. Administration officials had earlier praised Carpizo and had lauded his appointment as evidence of the independence of the new electoral commission and a key indication that the elections would be free and fair.[78] There was also no comment as well when, two days later, President Salinas convinced Carpizo to stay on.

The U.S. government was not only expressing the utmost confidence in the cleanliness of the upcoming elections, but also claiming little need for a planned U.S. response if the elections were not all that was predicted. Responding to questions about what President Clinton would do if the elections were not honest, Ambassador Jones stated and later repeated:

> As a practical matter there is nothing the U.S. government needs to do because private investors in the United States will be so put off by not having political freedoms follow economic freedoms that investment will dry up and the economic hopes of Mexico will go with it. That is far stronger than anything the government can do.[79]

The ambassador did not explain the basis on which he believed that American business would react so uniformly to political events in Mexico when they had not done so before: not to political murders, not to Chiapas, not to the 1988 presidential elections. If fraud would ensure the continuance of economic policies supported by U.S. investors, why would American businesses react harshly? The private sector operated in countries far more repressive than Mexico. Even so, was the possible reaction of the U.S. investment community a substitute for a U.S. government policy response?

The U.S. government's upbeat pronouncements on the election contrasted somewhat with those of the U.S. media, which continued to raise questions of overall electoral fairness. A *New York Times* editorial on the eve of the election observed:

> Some doubt remains whether the election will prove clean enough to assure internal stability and continued smooth relations with the United States.... [E]lection supervision at the local level remains the subject of manipulation, and foreign observers have been limited to an indirect role. Meanwhile, television and newspapers have given Mr. Zedillo greater and more favorable coverage than his rivals.[80]

The caveats of a few in the U.S. media aside, as election day approached few from the United States observed major preoccupations regarding potential violence or fraud and a PRI victory.

Election Day: August 21, 1994

With all the many preparations, a number of observers found election day anticlimactic. There was no massive computer breakdown, no major incidents of violence, no hotly contested match between the reigning PRI and the opposition. The day passed peacefully, with an impressive 78 percent of the population going to the polls. The quick counts and exit polls all pointed to PRI candidate Zedillo winning with a comfortable margin. In addition to the eighty-plus delegation organized by IRI and NDI and the private U.S. groups and academics observing, the U.S. embassy deployed its own personnel across the country and had them accredited as observers. Together with State and USAID personnel from Washington, the U.S. government contingent was around fifty to sixty in total. It seemed like the embassy "sent everybody, even the cleaning staff, out to observe."[81]

This is not to say the day passed without controversy or concerns. Numerous organizations and the opposition parities documented a range of electoral irregularities and fraud. PAN candidate Férnandez called the elections "profoundly unjust and unfair"; Cuáuhtemoc Cárdenas called them a "colossal fraud."[82] One of the bigger problems was the lack of sufficient ballots for those Mexicans voting outside their hometown in special voting places set up around the country. Tens of thousands of voters were turned away. The comfortable margin for the PRI came as a surprise to many in the NGO community. For many in the Civic Alliance, the media bias, the illegal use of government funds to support the PRI, and the strong-arm tactics of the PRI, including providing food to voters, all pointed to an unfair election to start with, even if, technically, the balloting was relatively clean. The Civic Alliance had "one hell of a discussion" over how to report its conclusions.[83] Alliance members ultimately concluded in their report that the electoral process was "deeply flawed.... This election cannot be disqualified in one fell swoop, but equally unacceptable is the triumphalism that holds this election up as a model of transparency and cleanliness."[84] In a report on the elections, Jared Kotler of the Washington Office on Latin America wrote: "If there is a consensus among knowledgeable observers, it is that the elections were relatively free, but not fair."[85]

The U.S. government reaction was more favorable and less unequivocal than that of the Mexican opposition or the NGOs. "These elections have been the most open and transparent in modern Mexican history.... As such, they represent a triumph for the Mexican people," announced the White House.[86] Ambassador Jones's statement read: "These elections are a milestone in Mexico's progress in political reform and democratization and complement the dramatic economic reforms undertaken over the last decade. Reports from international visitors were generally consistent: irregularities were not significant in the outcome of the elections."[87] This embrace of the uncritical view can also be seen in how the U.S. post-election statement draws selectively from the NDI-IRI observers' report and fails to acknowledge the statements and views of "other" Mexicans, namely the opposition parties and the civil organizations that U.S. funds supported. This is not to say that all opposition claims had validity and required comment, but rather that the United States lost some of its image of neutrality by not acknowledging different viewpoints. Some U.S. government officials did have concerns regarding the elections. USAID's Joanna Mendelson felt that there were "a lot of problems" on election day. She and other USAID members watched as riot police were brought out in Oaxaca because electoral officials didn't know how to handle the heavy demand for ballots.[88]

The official NDI-IRI delegation did have a generally favorable impression. The preliminary statement of the delegation, issued on August 23, concludes: "This election represents a significant step forward for the Mexican democratic process."[89] The delegation documented a number of problems in the electoral process, including violence, use of state resources to advance the PRI, disparity of resources between parties, and media bias. Even with these problems, the delegation concluded that "it ... received no evidence to suggest that they would have affected the outcome of the presidential contest."[90]

Had there been substantial electoral fraud the United States would have been in a difficult political position. Could it have claimed that there just wasn't enough evidence to tell, as it had in 1988? The United States had gone out on a limb in its positive depiction of a changed Mexican electoral system. So unequivocal were U.S. public statements about pre-electoral conditions in

Mexico that it would have made U.S. criticism on election day much more difficult. In his analysis of the elections, Kotler wrote: "This uncritical posture may have made sense from the standpoint of avoiding controversy, but it also gave the impression that Washington was indifferent to problems."[91] How prepared was the United States for a range of different outcomes? There had been no policy papers outlining potentially different electoral scenarios; this was judged too politically sensitive. Richard Feinberg indicated that the NSC had a "couple of different press releases ready to go from the White House" depending on the outcome of the 1994 elections.[92] Feinberg stressed that he felt there would be a "fair amount of continuity no matter who wins. . . . I don't think policy planning went much beyond being neutral."[93]

NED Comes to Intersect with U.S. Policy

An interesting side note in the evolution of U.S. policy in the 1994 elections case is the new, more integrated roles played by the NED and its affiliates, NDI and IRI. Up until this time, under the Reagan and Bush administrations, NED, NDI, and IRI officials indicated that they barely visited the U.S. Embassy or had contact with the State Department regarding Mexico. Under the Clinton administration, two factors changed. First, Mexican civic society had evolved to the point where there were bona fide proposals from capable organizations that NED and NDI staff could present to their boards. For years, Mexican organizations shied away from soliciting funds from the United States. Second, NED and NDI in particular were playing more activist roles in advocating U.S. support for electoral observation in Mexico and meeting with administration officials. NED and its affiliates were pushing the envelope a bit, but their policies did not reflect dramatic policy differences with the administration, as over China policy, for example. "What NED was doing in Mexico was not counter to U.S. policy; rather, it was taking a piece of U.S. policy that the United States was unclear about and going with it."[94]

Post-Election Impact

After the election, the question remained whether this new focus of activity would represent a more permanent shift in the U.S. approach to evolving Mexican democracy or whether democracy would again recede from the bilateral agenda. USAID had funded a significant one-time event and was left asking what its role should now be. One observer noted, "I don't think the election experience gave USAID a clearer sense of what to do afterwards. I do think they were affirmed in what they did.[95] Ann MacDonald, acting USAID director for Latin America and the Caribbean, said that there was a general request from the U.S. ambassador to continue to show support for Mexican democracy, but that this was not highly specific.[96] USAID was having a severe budget crunch, and giving money to Mexico meant taking it away from somewhere else. Through NDI, USAID continued to support the Civic Alliance to observe local and state elections. The ambassador had been particularly interested in moving forward with a judicial reform program. MacDonald explained: "Lots of quiet overtures have been made to the Zedillo administration.... They seemed interested [in judicial reform], but then nothing happens."[97] With little Mexican government interest, the judicial reform idea withered. USAID/Washington told Art Danart, the USAID director at the Mexico City Embassy, that he could take $1 million out of his population programs and put it into democratization programs if he chose. This was an initiative he could have taken himself, but rejected. USAID's fiscal year 1995 budget for democratization programs was $235,000, with programs and recipients roughly similar to previous years.[98] Danart felt that USAID's population work was very important in Mexico and that "a little more democratization money won't matter."[99]

The 1994 presidential election provided an unusual moment in time—a single event when Mexican internal performance had the potential to disrupt and undermine the U.S. agenda with Mexico. Clarity of U.S. interests and some convergence with Mexican interests were important factors in ultimately inducing policy change toward international electoral "visitors." The U.S. NGO community played a catalytic role in the shift, but key political appointees in the Clinton administration were central as well.[100] "We pushed the agenda a little bit, and the U.S. government was receptive," explains NDI's Canton.[101] More than any other case to date, the coalition bringing about this policy shift represented more of a majority position. The rank and file at the State Department was brought along by NGO activists and key political appointees. Congressional leaders interested in pushing for electoral observation and a spotlight on Mexico were in a minority. The interpretation of the Bonior-Torricelli resolution as inflammatory ultimately moved congressional efforts to the sidelines, with little impact on administration policy. Notable in this case were the administration's shift to openly finance electoral observation and to publicly acknowledge the discussion of political and human rights issues between the two countries, even if the substance of that communication was not revealed publicly.

While a shift is evident, one should not overstate U.S. policy evolution. The event itself does not appear to have had a lasting impact on U.S. basic assumptions and policy toward Mexican democracy. The policy shifts that occurred around the 1994 elections were constrained and shaped by the simultaneous coexistence of a belief against open criticism of the Mexican regime. Rather than provide a basis for challenging this belief, administration officials found a way to bifurcate U.S. policy: pursuing two mini-policies simultaneously, but perceiving them as one. The amounts provided around the election pale in comparison to amounts spent on much smaller countries like Nicaragua and on democratic transitions in Eastern Europe. After the elections, U.S. policy was still caught in the tension between selling and defending the current Mexican government and the distance needed for a credible democratization policy.

While the United States was relatively successful in achieving its goals for the Mexican elections, this success was considered almost anti-climactic and did not result in any newfound determination or agreement to expand the U.S. role. Interviewees often portrayed the event as a one-time deal not likely to be repeated. David Beall, deputy chief of mission at the Mexican Embassy at the time felt "in the long run, it's a minor issue."[102]

In Congress, with the spotlight on the elections removed, there was little motivation for further attention on democracy in Mexico. Torricelli's subcommittee soon became absorbed in higher profile controversies: securing the release of U.S. and Guatemalan files on the murder of Jennifer Harbury's rebel husband, tightening the Cuban embargo, and the expropriation of property in Nicaragua. Despite the success of the international observation, there doesn't seem to have been much interest in revisiting or analyzing the 1994 election experience. The IRI-NDI delegation never turned in its final report, and no one at USAID pressed for it. The opportunity to build on this experience to advance the U.S. relationship with Mexico over democracy passed quietly.

Another Crisis Engulfs Relations

The results of the 1994 elections were passed over—and then more accurately, overwhelmed—by subsequent events. Less than a month after the election, Mexico was rocked by another high-profile political murder. José Francisco Ruiz Massieu, the general secretary of the PRI, was shot in downtown Mexico City just six weeks before the new government was to take office. Then just shortly after the much-promoted Summit of the Americas in December 1994, Mexico and the United States were engulfed in yet another devastating Mexican financial crisis. The emerging peso crisis prompted a new moment in time when differing perspectives on Mexico's political system reemerged for debate in the United States.

7.

The Clinton Administration and the Peso Crisis

The successful August 1994 elections laid the foundation for a smooth transition to power by Mexican President Ernesto Zedillo on December 1. Zedillo was making welcome references to democratic reform. In his inaugural speech, he promised greater political and legal reform and called for a "healthy distance" between the government and the PRI. There remained a certain uneasiness, however, about Mexico's political situation, as the Chiapas conflict and investigations into two high-profile murders in 1994 dragged on without credible resolution. Internal conflicts within the PRI, contained for the election, would soon reemerge from factions wedded to authoritarian ways. As Haggard and Kaufman have explained: "The electoral pressures of the 1994 campaign forced internal compromises, however. Technocratic factions, now headed by Zedillo, needed the old guard to continue in power; the old guard, as had been the case for many years, had little future outside of the framework of the PRI."[1]

Even this initial calm exterior was over all too quickly. President Zedillo had hardly set up his office when, one week later, protests erupted at the swearing-in ceremony for the PRI-elect governor of Chiapas. With increased tension in the southern region, the Zapatistas and government troops stepped up military maneuvers. Two weeks later, a financial crisis broke. The Zedillo administration devalued the peso by 15 percent, triggering a freefall downward as far as half the peso's value. The U.S. government was ultimately called on and compelled to help stabilize the exchange rate and restore order to North American financial markets.

To stem the crisis, the Clinton administration proposed a package of over $40 billion in loan guarantees. In negotiations with Congress over these guarantees and in congressional debates over the peso crisis and the role of NAFTA, the issue of Mexico's internal politics entered into the debate. Like NAFTA, the political dimension was a minor subplot in the overall drama. But unlike NAFTA, Mexico's political state now laid behind a host of congressional concerns, forcing cracks in the stone wall of the belief against public criticism that had held strongly for so many years.

This chapter will examine how the issue of democracy in Mexico interplayed in the larger matrix of U.S. policymaking during the brief period that encompassed the Mexican peso crisis. It will demonstrate that the Clinton administration tried to fend off political conditions on the emerging legislation, arguing directly in public forums and in private conversations with Congress over the need to prevent public criticism of Mexico. It was again a minority in Congress that rallied around the issue of democracy as part of their opposition to the peso rescue plan, linking their most immediate concerns in United States-Mexico relations to the undemocratic nature of the Mexican system. The political views of a minority of conservative Republican and liberal Democratic critics were so diverse that they would continue to constrain the development of any wider consensus on how the United States should treat political questions regarding Mexico. Restraining criticism of Mexican internal politics by the executive branch would have another manifestation during the peso crisis. It kept the administration from publicly acknowledging a political dimension to the crisis, specifically in assigning any responsibility to Mexico's political leaders for fiscal mismanagement or politicized decision making around the elections. This depiction of the peso crisis as a financial one only further fueled a disconnection with how some in Congress and in academia were portraying and understanding the crisis.

For the first time, however, there is evidence of a greater willingness by the executive branch, specifically the Treasury Department, to stretch the prevailing belief against public criticism to allow mild political conditions on the rescue bill. This relaxation of prevailing taboos for a greater political imperative never came to pass, as the congressional legislation was jettisoned in favor of more reliable executive action. Without a pressing political rationale, executive branch policy returned after the crisis to the time-honored pattern of avoiding public criticism and accentuating positive political developments in Mexico.

Case Study: The Mexican Peso Crisis

Calm before the Storm

On December 16, 1994, the State Department convened a closed meeting on Mexico with over fifty specialists. It was a diverse group, including intelligence analysts, professors, Wall Street financiers, and U.S. government officials from a wide range of agencies. The meeting marked the end of a six-month interagency review of United States-Mexico relations initiated by the new State Department Mexican Country Director, Bob Felder. While Mexico was not given a completely clean bill of health, none of the participants sounded any alarm bells. As Edward Smith, the Mexico Desk Officer for Economic Affairs at the time recalled: "The paper I wrote did not predict a crisis. . . . The analysts from Wall Street were quite concerned about their money, but they weren't pulling it out."[2]

The Peso Floats

Four days after that calm meeting at the State Department, the Mexican government announced that it was "lifting the upper limit of the band on the rate that the peso can be traded with the dollar."[3] This was finance-speak for devaluation. Mexican Finance Minister Jaime Serra Puche identified renewed Zapatista military actions as the reason for the action, saying the government was only trying to increase flexibility in light of resurgent Zapatista activity. This single-event argument fooled no one. The Mexicans were devaluing what had long been perceived as an overvalued currency for a host of political, economic, and financial management reasons. President-elect Zedillo had urged Salinas to devalue before he left office but he refused. Manuel Pastor has argued that the timing of the crisis was related to an "unfortunate convergence of political pressures and economic mismanagement, the specific causal variable was an overvalued exchanged rate that had long required correction."[4] Nora Lustig linked the devaluation principally to Mexican government fiscal and monetary policies adopted that year.[5]

The original 15 percent fall in the peso's value was only the beginning. In the days that followed, the peso would drop to 50 percent of its former value, igniting a crisis in financial markets that would tie the Clinton administration more closely to Mexico's fate regardless of whether either side wanted it that way. The origins of the peso crisis were both economic and political, and academic analyses were linking the political dimension to Mexico's authoritarian style of government and internal decision-making. Manuel Pastor has argued that the "highly exclusionary arrangements" of the Mexican system enabled policymakers to push through sweeping economic reforms but also lay behind policy miscalculations, the peso crisis being a prominent one. He concluded that "insulation and insistence on consensus among technocrats stifled any constructive dialogue within the government over the need for a shift in the exchange rate."[6] Denise Dresser stressed that the disarray brought on by devaluation was the result of centralized decisions made by technocrats insulated within an undemocratic political system.[7] This link between the political system and economic miscalculation, while discussed in academic accounts, was absent in the U.S. government's public interpretation of the crisis.

The U.S. Response

When the devaluation news hit on December 20, most of Washington was in its Christmas holiday lull. The new Treasury Secretary, Robert Rubin, was not yet in place. Larry Summers, Undersecretary of the Treasury for International Affairs, worked the phones during these early days trying to offset a possible panic rush of bank withdrawals.[8] Congress was out of session, and the House of Representatives was in a state of suspended animation with the prospect of a Republican majority after a generation of Democratic control of the House. In December, no one had been officially sworn into their new positions and there were no established lines of communication and contact with the new House leadership and their staffs. Jaime Serra Puche had been to New York to talk with Wall Street investors to reassure them of Mexico's stability and sound direction and to keep them invested. He had not been convincing.

Within the executive branch, there was talk about the need for an aid package to Mexico by late December. President Clinton stated publicly in a December 30 press interview that discussions were on going with the Mexican government about what the United States could do to help. The president drew on a political argument, maintaining that assistance was needed to support and re-ward reform: "I would have to say that if you look where Mexico is today, compared to where they were several years ago, they have made a serious commitment to economic reform, to social reform, to cultural reform and to political reform. I would like to see that commitment rewarded."[9]

But it wasn't until early January, with the new Congress and the president back in town, that the air of crisis hit the Beltway. The administration went public with its first proposal. They announced an $18 billion international package, with the United States putting up one-half of the amount. This would extend an earlier unused $6 billion credit line in the U.S. Treasury provided as emergency funds to stabilize the economy in the wake of the Colosio assassination. It soon became clear, however, that this amount of credit was not enough. On January 12, 1995, the president proposed a $40 billion loan guarantee package. With a package this big and politically sensitive, the administration now wanted congressional approval. Initially they would shoulder most of the burden alone. They felt most of the world would see Mexico as a U.S. problem.[10] It would not be long, however, before the administration would successfully "internationalize" the crisis, pulling in the European allies and the IMF, arguing that Mexico's financial instability would reverberate in international markets.

The congressional leadership initially responded positively to the administration's plan. House Speaker Newt Gingrich (R-GA), Majority Leader Dick Armey (R-TX), Senate Majority Leader Bob Dole (R-KA), House Minority Leader Richard Gephardt (D-MO), and Senate Minority Leader Tom Daschle (D-SD) issued a joint statement with the White House on January 12 endorsing the administration's rescue plan for Mexico. The joint statement read: "We agreed that the United States has an important economic and strategic interest in a stable and prosperous Mexico. Ultimately, the solution to Mexico's economic problems must come from the people of Mexico, but we are pursuing ways to increase financial confidence and to encourage further reform in Mexico."[11]

The next day, January 13, the administration held a briefing for over one hundred congressional leaders with representatives from the Federal Reserve (FED), Treasury, and State Department. Administration officials advised Congress that they needed to act quickly to avert a crisis of confidence. They warned that Mexico was close to default. In exchange for the guarantees, the Clinton administration proposed that the Mexicans agree to pay a fee to the United States and meet certain economic conditions that would better ensure Mexico's ability to repay.

Congressional Shots Fired in Opposition: Democracy Conditions Raised

Even before a congressional working group to draft the legislation got off the ground, voices were raised in opposition to the plan, many calling for stringent economic and political conditions. Conditions on the guarantee legislation could have a lot more bite than anything Congress had considered before, and the administration knew it. The Torricelli-Bonior resolution six months prior was a non-binding resolution that expressed the sentiment of Congress. This was big money that mattered. It was not some small amount for anti-drug efforts that Mexico could do without if it didn't want to meet the conditions.

Minority Whip Bonior was the strongest and most prominent voice arguing that explicit conditions for democratic reform be tied to the legislation. On January 17, Bonior stated, "The Mexican system is riddled with deep structural, economic and political problems that must not be left unchecked."[12] He suggested five conditions:

insist that Mexico tie Mexican wages to productivity; give Mexican workers the right to organize independently, the right to bargain collectively and the right to strike; insist that Mexico buy more American products; demand a continuation of democratic reforms and resolve the crisis with rebels in its Chiapas state peacefully; and passage of President Clinton's job training program for Americans who lose their jobs caused by the devaluation of the peso.[13]

A week later Bonior spoke on the House floor: "NAFTA was a missed opportunity to make real reform. I don't think we can afford to miss that opportunity again."[14] A number of liberal Democrats openly expressed their strong
reservations to the package, repeating a statement popular among Republican
and Democratic opponents: "We must not be sending money to Mexico just to
prop up a nation with the fastest-growing number of billionaires in the
world."[15] Rep. Barney Frank (D-MA) stated he would oppose the package if it
did not contain conditions to improve worker standards. Marcy Kaptur (D-
OH), Sherrod Brown (D-OH), and Dan Hamburg (D-OH) were among the
more liberal Democratic voices calling, with different emphases, for labor, environmental, and human rights/democratization conditions.

Republican conservatives, also critical of Mexico's internal politics, largely
focused on different issues: immigration, drugs, corruption, and Mexican
policy toward Cuba. The incoming House Republican freshmen added new
voices to the perceived congressional renegades criticizing Mexico. Four freshmen joined by former presidential candidate Pat Buchanan and Republican
Deputy Whip Duncan Hunter (R-CA) called a press conference to announce
their opposition to any "bailout" of Mexico. The freshmen let it be known that
among their concerns was Mexico's political system, and in particular corruption. Pat Buchanan was as explicit as he had been on the campaign trail:
"Democracy, true democracy, has to be brought to Mexico.... Why don't we
get Mexico to make reforms in its whole political process before we do this?[16]
Representative David Funderbunk (R-NC) continued in a similar vein:

> Countries like Mexico, Haiti, and Angola are not poor because we have too much,
> they are poor because their governments engage in destructive statist economies,
> central planning, and repress individual economic freedom.... Each time we
> saved the Mexican currency, the government they refused to reform itself. It is
> still rife with corruption.[17]

The freshman Republicans were not calling for conditions requiring political or any other reforms. They wanted an outright rejection of the financial
package. Mexico's undemocratic and corrupt political system, as they labeled
it, was one of a host of reasons. The 1994 Republican victory ushered in a large,
ideological freshman class who had staked their election on the leadership's
"Contract for America." Committed to proving they could turn things around
in the Congress within one hundred days, a financial crisis in Mexico did not
square with their domestic priorities. Freshman Representative Steve Stockman
(R-TX) circulated a letter to Gingrich signed by several freshmen, complaining
that the bailout interfered with the Contract and that the leadership should
change direction.

The Clinton administration was raising the stakes on the other side, claiming dire national security consequences of not acting quickly. It claimed that a 35 percent devaluation of the peso would induce a similar percentage increase in illegal immigration from Mexico to the United States. If the Mexican financial crisis deepened, 430,000 more Mexicans would cross the border into Texas, California, and the Southwest, claimed administration officials.[18]

While the opposition was just gathering steam, a congressional team quietly went to work crafting legislative language for the package with the administration. This congressional working group proceeded on a separate, more moderate track than the public critiques being heard from a minority of members on the left and right of each party. The peso crisis quickly came to be acted out on the U.S. political stage with three distinct tenors: the Republican leadership–White House nexus of public unity, the congressional-administration negotiating team of plodding moderation, and the vitriolic public debate amongst the rank-and-file congressional membership. Often going in different directions, these complicated machinations ultimately collided, unable to arrive at a majority in support of the legislation.

Congressional Negotiations Begin: Political Conditions Enter

The administration-congressional negotiating team took form quickly and began work right away on Saturday, January 14. Treasury Department officials Larry Summers and Jeff Shafer were the chief negotiators for the administration. The State Department typically sent Assistant Secretary of State for Latin American Affairs, Alex Watson, but State as a whole reportedly played a more minor role on the team. Jim Leach (R-IA), a respected moderate who was now Chairman of the House Banking Committee, led the House Republican team and became the de facto chief negotiator for both houses.

Since the legislation needed to be voted on within weeks, if not days, the plan was to develop the same legislative language for the House and Senate with the administration's agreement, in order to avoid either a House-Senate conference, last-minute negotiations with the administration, or an administration veto. While this sort of three-way drafting was not unheard of, it was unusual, reflecting the high priority the administration put on the legislation. As one seasoned aide reflected, "It was the first time I saw a drafting session with administration officials, senators and congressmen at the table."[19]

Political language started creeping into the draft bill that first weekend. One of the earliest drafts of the congressional legislation contained a sweeping sense of Congress provision, calling for more focus on promoting democracy via economic policy in reaction to its absence in NAFTA. The draft read: "It is the sense of Congress that future trade agreements should comprehensively address economic integration, including the relationship between trade and the environment, trade and worker rights, and the need for a stable, open, and democratic system."[20]

As in the past, democracy had come to be raised by Congress largely as it intersected and supported other policy objectives. This can be seen in the distinct policy priorities of the different negotiators. Dissatisfied with NAFTA and the labor side agreements, the Democratic team focused predominantly on labor, political, and environmental issues in the negotiations. Barney Frank (D-MA) was put specifically on the negotiating team to help win the support of pro-labor, anti-NAFTA Democrats. Frank made clear that Democrats wanted language that sought increases in Mexican wages in line with productivity. He argued that the nondemocratic Mexican government had kept a hold on these wages through its government-controlled trade union.[21] Republicans had different issues with Mexico that they wanted addressed in the legislation. Jesse Helms (R-NC) and others wanted to tighten the screws on Mexico's support for Cuba and crack down on drug trafficking and immigration. Helms's top priorities were drugs and Cuba policy, both of which he believed stemmed from the "synergism of the one-party state and its anti-American foreign policy."[22] There was reportedly a bit of a pull and tug within the administration with line agencies, like the DEA, arguing for "getting something for our money" and the State Department warning against conditions. The Treasury Department clearly had the upper hand in the administration team and kept at bay other agencies' desires for conditions.

Administration officials were explicit that they would accept no political conditions to the bill, only economic conditions specifically tied to Mexico's ability to repay the loan. They asserted repeatedly to congressional negotiators that Mexico should not be publicly criticized, principally, they argued, because such criticism would be counterproductive. Larry Summers told congressional leaders at a January 16 meeting that the administration would accept no political conditions because overt criticism always backfires. He emphasized to the members that the Mexican government could do more if it was not seen as acting at the demand of the United States.[23] Jeff Shafer says he argued as well with congressional officials, telling them: "We support where you're going, but don't tie our hands."[24]

Differing Administration/Congressional Stands on Conditions Emerge

Within days, differences between the administration's no political conditions stand, embedded in a belief against the inadvisability of public criticism and leaders in Congress who saw the need to bend on this given axiom, emerged. A few, like Jesse Helms and his staff, maintained that the United States should and could openly criticize Mexico.[25] In hearings before the House Banking Committee, Secretary Christopher gave the State Department's critique of political conditions: "If we encumber this package, which is so vital to the health of Mexico, with conditions that are unrelated to the matter at hand, those very conditions could undermine our intended goal of trying to encourage further reform in Mexico."[26]

The administration's no political conditions stance on an unprecedented multibillion dollar loan package conveyed to some members of Congress that the administration was more interested in satisfying the Mexicans than the Congress. An aide to Jesse Helms described the first weekend meetings to his boss: "The Administration is treating the legislation as something to be mutually agreed on between the U.S. and Mexico: they are treating this as if Mexico should have a veto on what the Congress thinks is appropriate conditionality."[27] In some cases the administration said they raised privately particular political issues/conditions with the Mexicans, but many of the congressional participants felt the administration did not even bother to ask the Mexicans whether specific conditions might be acceptable.

A more interesting variant emerged from the leader of the congressional negotiations who argued it was time to bend and engage in a little mild criticism. In a January 17 letter, Congressman Jim Leach (R-IA) let Secretary Rubin know he was skeptical about political conditions on the legislation but felt that realism should reign, using China as a model:

> Mexican officials have emphasized that they cannot consider a measure that implies surrendering sovereignty; and, paradoxically, they suggest the less said on an issue the more flexibility they have to be forthcoming. I have personal doubts that "political" language is appropriate for this bill, but from a congressional perspective it seems highly unlikely a majority vote can be garnered unless a specific commitment can be obtained on issues of concern to many on Capitol Hill. In this regard, I stressed to the Mexican Finance Minister the China MFN [Most Favored Nation] analog. The issue of MFN was economic, but nevertheless Congress insisted on certain political conditionality, and in deference to Chinese sovereignty concerns, couched such conditionality in terms of Presidential determinations. This MFN model, as much as the Israeli loan guarantee model, is the precedent for the current draft legislation.[28]

Even though the China MFN model entailed little constraint on administration policy beyond the annual certifications, the administration would not entertain anything close to this type of language for Mexico. Doing so would have broken the unspoken ban on public criticism of Mexico's internal politics and ventured into a more political relationship that had long been avoided.

Emerging Democracy Conditions

As negotiations continued, the political conditions considered by the negotiating team were strongest with regard to immigration, illicit drug flows, and labor rights. With regard to democratization and political reform, the conditions were not as dramatic or as binding as reported in some press accounts. The *Washington Post*, for example, had reported: "Chief among the issues being discussed here [Mexico City] and in Washington are curbs on illegal immigration, private participation in the government oil monopoly, an opening of banking services to foreign competition, revisions of wage scales and drastic revision of the political system, which has been dominated for 65 years by Zedillo's PRI."[29]

Despite the portrayal in the press, reviews of numerous versions of the draft congressional legislation reveal that at no stage was legislation requiring sweeping democratic reforms actually considered. Political conditions relating explicitly to democracy and human rights clearly took a backseat to higher profile "hometown" political issues of immigration, drugs, wages, and Mexican foreign relations with Cuba, although each of these issues had a political/democracy dimension.

Rep. Bonior and his staff were considered the most vocal proponents of pro-democracy stipulations. Bonior aide Matt Benson confirmed, "We did not offer language. It was considered and dismissed within our office." Benson explains that they reasoned that they would not get strong enough language to make them agree to the overall legislation and they didn't want to get backed into a corner supporting a watered-down bill. Benson maintained that Gephardt's position was more akin to the administration's of not wanting to overtly criticize Mexico.[30]

Gephardt aide Mike Wessel did place legislative language on Chiapas in the draft. This provision stated the desire that "there should be a peaceful settlement of the situation in the Mexican State of Chiapas."[31] The language had little opposition among the congressional working group or even the administration and could hardly be construed as criticism. "There was a bipartisan feeling we should say something about Chiapas," recalled one Republican aide.[32] Bonior's office, however, considered this "throw-away language"[33] in terms of any meaningful political conditions.

What did become a focal point of congressional Democratic concern with the Mexican political system were labor rights and free labor market conditions. Frank had proposed language in the early drafts that would require more explicit guarantees that Mexican wages would be tied to productivity and that the Mexican government would be required to live up more explicitly to the labor rights enumerated in the NAFTA side agreement: the right to collective bargaining, freedom of association for workers, and implementation of a wage monitoring system by the government. The NAFTA side agreement had only listed labor rights as general principles in an annex. On pushing these labor matters, Frank knew he had the support of the Democratic leadership, but the "Republican leadership was tepid."[33]

The labor rights language was clearly deferred to House minority Democrats to prepare, with Barney Frank as the point person. The general legislative approach taken was to ask the administration to make a series of determinations on labor conditions before granting the loan guarantees. Among these conditions, the January 24 draft text required that:

> The Government of Mexico has committed:
>
> (A) to allow wage growth to reflect productivity gains; and, (B) to recognize the importance of free labor markets through the enforcement of—
>   (i)   the industrial relations laws of Mexico, and
>   (ii) a fair and equitable collective bargaining system.[35]

Wider Congressional Criticism Mounts/Democracy Raised

As the congressional and administration negotiators plodded along behind closed doors, the rank and file members were going public with their grave doubts about the entire rescue package. Senator Barbara Boxer (D-CA) maintained that the pending legislation provided an opportunity to reassess U.S. participation in NAFTA. A group of fifteen anti-NAFTA representatives said they would try to force U.S. withdrawal from the agreement.[36] Prominent NAFTA opponents like Ralph Nader and Ross Perot came out against the aid. Meanwhile, the Republican leadership watched as support for the package eroded on both the Republican and Democratic sides. On January 18, Dole signaled a backing away from his initial commitment: "He [Clinton] needs to work within his party. We're not going to carry the whole load here and get hung out to dry."[37]

As part of its case for the legislation, the administration argued that the financial package would help promote democratic reform in an already democratizing Mexico. Testifying to Congress on January 25, Secretary of State Christopher said:

> The triumph of democracy and open markets in our hemisphere is certainly reflected in Mexico's experience over the last few years. Let us not forget that the Mexico of today is not the Mexico of the early Eighties. . . . Its current liquidity crisis, however, must be solved immediately. If it is not, we will have little hope of helping Mexico to continue meeting the long-term challenge of modernizing its economy, strengthening its democracy, and addressing the environmental, labor and immigration issues that affect both our nations.[38]

The administration also made its positivist political case in a fact sheet sent to members of Congress: "Mexico does face some political unrest in Chiapas. But Mexican society as a whole is stable, as evidenced by the successful conduct of elections this year, and the pro-NAFTA consensus as Mexico passed through the assassinations with no social unrest."[39]

This view of an ever-democratizing Mexico was challenged by congressional critics of the plan as well as academics who argued that the lack of sufficient political change was part of the roots of the crisis. Ernest Hollings (D-SC), an outspoken critic of NAFTA, stated in Senate hearings, "Unfortunately, Mexico's economic opening was not matched by a political opening. Instead it remained what Mario Vargas Llosa called 'the perfect dictatorship.'"[40] Mexican analyst Dresser stated: "One lesson from 1994—Mexico's year of living dangerously— is clear: economic modernization cannot flourish without political modernization."[41] The administration's positive-only depiction was a more difficult sell during the peso crisis, as officials were trying to argue that they were both supremely confident of Mexico's current political stability and financial management and, at the same time, were warning of dire consequences of rampant instability and widespread flight from Mexico if there was no package.

Opposition to Conditions in Mexico

As disagreement between the administration and Congress played out publicly, Mexican leaders reacted angrily to press reports that the rescue package might come with strong political conditions. They argued that political conditions on loan guarantees were tantamount to intervention in their internal affairs. On January 26, the lower house of the Mexican Congress voted 381 to 58 to require Zedillo to submit the loan guarantee agreement to the Congress for ratification. The Zedillo government did not divulge the details of its discussions, saying Mexico would await the results and decide whether or not to accept the terms of Washington's package, but adding that "we are not negotiating anything."[42] That statement did not completely square with reality. As one Mexican official described it later to the U.S. press, Foreign Minister José Angel Gurria "virtually set up shop" at Foggy Bottom, negotiating conditions on the loan guarantees.[43]

Negotiations Press On: Political Language Watered Down

With brewing opposition within the rank-and-file and slow, fitful negotiations with the administration-congressional team, the original schedule for bringing the legislation to a vote in mid-January could not be met. Over the next two weeks, the House and Senate working groups continued to meet off and on with drafts changing by the day and hour. It was "a negotiating frenzy, sometimes two to three versions [of the legislation] a day."[44] Leach's office found the White House very frustrating to deal with. Sometimes the "White House wouldn't respond, you never knew."[45]

As the negotiations plodded along, the labor rights language was getting watered down, but it was still prominent. The version proposed on January 30 called for the government of Mexico to "recognize the importance of free labor markets," rather than demonstrate its commitment.[46] This legislation would have required the FED to report on a number of economic items tangentially affecting the political system, including the impact of Mexican macroeconomic policy on real wages and living standards and the industrial relations policy of Mexico.[47] The January 30 text still expressed the sense of Congress that there should be a peaceful settlement in Chiapas and indirectly took a shot at the Mexican political system by declaring, "history has shown that societies that do not have a large and viable middle class have difficulty sustaining stable institutions of democratic governance."[48]

Despite the frenzied negotiating environment, lead administration negotiator Jeff Shafer felt that "we were converging" on common legislation.[49] In the final days of January, the key outstanding issue was on the labor provisions, but Shafer felt this was manageable. He believed he could have persuaded Rep. Frank to modify the language on wages and that they could have worked out some mild language, couched in presidential determinations and the like, that had little real bite. He saw differences between the Treasury Department and State: "State was more concerned than I was with sovereignty." Treasury's clear administrative lead on the financial package created the dynamic that "State would let Bob Rubin make the deal."[50] This provided an unusual opening in which existing prohibitions on public criticism to Mexico might have been breached.

Congressional Legislation Abandoned for ESF: January 29–30, 1996

But as the negotiating team limped toward resolution, congressional opposition from the rank and file continued to mount. Public opinion polls were showing that large majorities of Americans were against the Mexican rescue bill, and members feared they would pay a political price for supporting the package. On January 30, Speaker Gingrich held what one participant labeled a "cathartic" meeting in his office that included two border states' governors and key Senate and House leaders and staffs from both parties.[51] The emotional meeting made clear there was "no support for doing anything."[52] Gingrich called White House Chief of Staff Panetta and told him that Congress was objecting to the financial package and its chances for passage were slim and worsening.[53]

The White House was sandbagged from both sides. The day before, Sunday January 29, Mexico's Ambassador to the United States, Jorge Montaño, had walked into the offices of Deputy Director of the NSC, Sandy Berger. "I'm told we don't have enough foreign reserves to make it past Tuesday," Montaño relayed to Berger. "Either we have a clear sign [of U.S. support], or we have to declare a moratorium."[54]

Now the administration felt it had to act quickly. The peso was sinking to its lowest level in history, 6.35 to the dollar. "Plan B," the discretionary use of the economic stabilization fund (ESF), had been discussed with the Group of Seven industrialized nations. The president could issue an executive order drawing on the ESF funds that would not require a congressional vote. The ESF was a little-used fund within the U.S. Treasury to stabilize the dollar in financial markets. Gingrich had told White House Chief of Staff Panetta that if the president acted alone the Congress would breathe "a huge sigh of relief."[55] On January 31, the president formally announced he would provide loan guarantees directly to Mexico by using his presidential authority to draw on ESF funds. They would no longer need congressional action. As part of the package, the administration announced complementary international support from the IMF and European donors that weeks before officials had maintained wouldn't be forthcoming.

While publicly exuding confidence and arguing all along that the only concern for Mexican stability was not getting the peso agreement, administration officials were privately concerned that some political event could rock the peso and undermine the fragile agreement they had put together. Just days before the signing, Treasury officials recall receiving a report late at night over the wires of new Zapatista movements. Their hearts sank. Could another political calamity shake the peso? They quickly called the Embassy in Mexico to get more information, but the Embassy knew nothing about it.[56] In a number of interviews, U.S. officials mentioned they did not think their own government was completely on top of the political situation and relied instead on U.S. and foreign press reports. It did not turn out to be much of an event, but for a moment everything seemed to crumble before their eyes. The event underscored how vulnerable Treasury officials felt to political events in Mexico that they said publicly were so unrelated to economic policy. Jeffrey Shafer noted that they were "nervous" that some political event in Mexico could affect the negotiations. Even once the financial package was signed and in operation, "We knew that the success of the program depended on political events in Mexico to which we had less control."[57] Nonetheless, U.S. officials at the time did not indicate in interviews that they considered projecting a more guarded depiction of Mexico. As with the NAFTA debate, the general sentiment was that the positivist image would help, in the short term, to shore up support for the U.S. action. U.S.

officials had to hold their breath that their public version would not be contradicted by actual events. Luckily, the loan guarantees were provided without political incident.

Post–Peso Crisis Congressional Activity on Mexico and Democracy: February–December 1995

Relieved of having to cast a difficult political vote, the new Congress did not let up on its public criticism of the administration's rescue package and, for a few, of Mexican internal politics. In fact, the situation opened up new avenues for congressional criticism. A Republican aide explained that once there was no prospect of a vote, freshman Republicans had freer reign and "continued agitating through the spring against the plan and for some Republican action."[58]

In the months that followed, congressional efforts of principally right-wing Republicans and liberal Democrats were focused, using different strategies, on seeking extensive documentation on what the administration knew about the peso crisis and on gaining greater accountability and reporting on NAFTA and other disputed areas of United States-Mexico relations. Without the prospect of a legislative vehicle like the rescue package, political issues and criticism had a low profile but were still present. Jesse Helms got a requirement in the Mexican Debt Disclosure Act that the administration make available information on the involvement of senior Mexican officials in drug trafficking since 1991, the beginning of NAFTA.

The content of the post-crisis debate was as highly polarized and simplified as during the crisis. While the administration portrayed Mexico in glowing terms without any reference to political concerns, critics depicted Mexico as inherently corrupt and largely unreformable. Only a few congressional voices mirrored the administration's depiction of Mexico, reflecting some diminished credibility of the all-positive portrayal in the face of dramatic financial crisis. In hearings two days after the signing of the rescue agreement, Senator Alfonse D'Amato's (R-NY) political argument was as black as the administration's was white: "[T]he political system is beyond reform. I think we're operating under a myth, that the political system is one which is capable of reforming itself."[59] Rep. Tom Lantos (D-CA) went further and criticized congressional members as well:

> I'm also tired of listening to Republican colleagues who voted for NAFTA talk about Mexico's corrupt government. What did they think Mexico's government was before NAFTA when they voted for it? . . . We ignored the fundamental economic, social, and political inequities that make Mexico a potential volcano.[60]

Sherrod Brown (D-OH), a relatively junior liberal member who had been one of the voices calling for more democratic accountability for Mexico, stated at that same hearing:

> NAFTA was one opportunity. We blew that chance. This is our second opportunity to deal with some of the problems that the Mexican government has—some of the tragic things the Mexican government has done to its people in terms of keeping wages down, in terms of democratic totalitarian abuses, in terms of environmental laws, in terms of worker safety laws, in terms of wages, all of those kinds of things...And I just would like to put in my views that I would hope that we would entertain some of those issues before we got again in this situation a third time.[61]

In late October 1995, Marcy Kaptur, along with Byron Dorgan (D-ND), longstanding critics of NAFTA and the peso rescue package, introduced the NAFTA Accountability Act with five Democratic and Republican colleagues. The act required certain conditions be met for the continuance of NAFTA. In particular, the bill contained a provision requiring an assessment of NAFTA vis-à-vis Mexican democratization. The legislation did not move forward.

Post–Peso Crisis: Administration Expresses Unqualified Support for Mexico

As congressional opponents continued their sweeping political criticism, the administration painted the opposite picture of unqualified optimism and silence regarding anti-democratic political and human rights events in Mexico. At congressional hearings, State Department Undersecretary Peter Tarnoff argued: "On the important issue of Mexican political reform, Mexico is continuing its profound political and economic transformation. President Zedillo has been adamant about the need to make Mexico a full democracy."[62] Tarnoff pointed specifically to two events in Mexico that were repeatedly referred to in subsequent administration statements throughout 1995: the February 12 elections in the Mexican state of Jalisco, in which the PAN won the governorship, and the presidential elections of August 1994. Connie Mack (R-FL) and Chris Dodd (D-CT) were two senators whose statements backed up the administration argument, both mentioning the Jalisco elections. Dodd emphasized how "remarkable" was Mexico's change in the past six to eight years.[63] Senator Mack, in taking on Senator D'Amato, remarked:

> There was a recent election, Senator D'Amato, in defense of Mexico, and in their attempts to bring perhaps not Jeffersonian democracy but democratic reforms, the Pon [PAN] party, as I understand it, won big elections in Mexico

recently. I think we should be very careful before we just suggest that we cannot help them unless they become a Jeffersonian democratic experiment overnight.[64]

What wasn't mentioned in these or any other public forums were troubling anti-democratic trends during the same year. While administration statements mentioned positive February 1995 state elections in Jalisco as a sign of progress, the June elections in the state of Tabasco were unmentioned outside of the annual human rights reports. In the Tabasco governorship race, the left-wing PRD charged massive fraud against their candidate, Andrés López Obrador. There were extensive protests following the election. These protests were marked by the dramatic surfacing of vast amounts of PRI documents providing evidence of electoral misconduct in Tabasco. In a drama befitting the current Mexican political scene, a stranger had driven up to a PRD protest rally on June 5 in Mexico City and unloaded fourteen boxes of PRI documents that he wanted Obrador to look at. These boxes contained thousands of PRI party spending receipts, including payments to labor leaders, journalists, citizens, a Roman Catholic priest, and even opposition figures. In all, the documents indicated that the PRI had spent nearly $65 million, or sixty-five times the legal campaign financing limit, much of which was believed to have been public funds. This level of expenditure was nearly two-thirds of what the PRI had publicly reported it had spent for all national and state elections.

Political commentators openly questioned if the PRI had spent this to win the small state of Tabasco, home of just 2 percent of the country's population, just how much did they lie about the expenditures on other elections? In particular, the Tabasco scandal prompted the Mexican opposition to question the veracity of the PRI's reported expenditures for the "clean" 1994 presidential election. Mexican political scientist Lorenzo Meyer commented:

> It was the kind of massive documentation that had never before been available to those who are not part of the inner circle, of the Mexican *cosa nostra*. Never before had anybody outside the PRI had access to documents that allow a reconstruction of the key element of the ruling party's electoral mechanics: its payments to people to attend rallies, its ties with an unending number of [political] actors.[65]

The PRI old guard rallied behind its gubernatorial candidate Roberto Madrazo, arguing that the opposition had faked the documents. The affair has become subsequently mired in dramatic twists and turns without resolution, dubbed "Tabascogate." Wayne Cornelius, an American academic specializing in Mexico, pointed out that Zedillo and other reformist elements of the PRI were trying to edge Madrazo out but had been unsuccessful. He noted a clear anti-democratic trend in key rural states like Chiapas, Guerrero, and Tabasco, where local PRI functionaries could resist democratic political reforms or democratization emanating from the center.[66]

June 1995 marked another event that contrasted sharply with the administration's efforts to project a positive political image of Mexico. At that time, state police armed with automatic weapons opened fire on a truck filled with unarmed peasants, claiming they were linked to guerilla groups. The "Aguas Blancas massacre," as it became known, resulted in seventeen dead and more than twenty wounded, including several children, and made headlines for months in Mexico. The governor of Guerrero was later forced to resign over his role in the massacre. It came to light that state officials had doctored evidence to make it appear that the peasants had provoked the police. Again there does not appear to have been any statement by the U.S. government on either the Aguas Blancas or Tabasco events, save mention in the State Department's annual human rights report after the fact.[67] A U.S. official, asking to remain anonymous, also confirmed this silence. Such a statement would have been a break from current policy, crossing the line to directly acknowledge the involvement of Mexican government officials in wrongdoing.

These "non-events," from a U.S. policy perspective, are intended only to demonstrate the way in which the United States was portraying Mexican democracy publicly during 1995. In an interview, State Department Country Director for Mexico Dennis Hayes characterized the Tabasco events as "more of a case of overspending than the overt fraud of Yucatán [a 1996 election that also never received public U.S. comment]."[68] This lack of acknowledgment of contrary terms can be further seen in Peter Tarnoff's selective statement to the Congress that mentions no cases of controversial elections: "Elections in Jalisco in which the PAN won a resounding victory were conducted without incident and the results were accepted by all parties. The Jalisco vote was a clear sign that Mexico is evolving into a genuinely competitive, multi-party democracy."[69]

The highly polarized nature of the U.S. debate between the administration and congressional critics contrasted with a more complicated and mixed picture being presented by Mexico analysts on both sides of the border. These analysts were writing that Mexico was experiencing both positive political advances and anti-reform regression. Denise Dresser wrote:

> In the face of the modernizing directives announced by Zedillo once in office, many traditional governors and local *caciques* (power brokers) have closed ranks and opposed the central government's plans. Mexico seems to be witnessing the

growing "feudalization" of the PRI, whereby hard-line power brokers govern their states the way they see fit, often resorting to violence, fraud, and repression.[70]

Haggard and Kaufman have analyzed the relationships between economic reform and the political actions of dominant party systems. In comparing Mexico to Taiwan, they explain why political change has been more difficult in Mexico:

> Mexico differs from Taiwan in the greater uncertainty surrounding its recovery. Unsure of parties, ruling elites in Mexico proved less willing than those in Taiwan to relinquish institutional controls that were the basis both of economic adjustment and their parties' continued political dominance.[71]

October 1995 State Visit: Early Repayment of Loan

In preparation for an October 1995 state visit to Washington, President Zedillo paved the way for a smooth trip. Zedillo brought with him a substantial early repayment of $700 million on its $12 billion loan guarantees from the United States. The administration lauded the move, maintaining that the bailout helped Mexico fight off major economic disruptions and prevent large-scale immigration to the United States. President Clinton, linking the debt repayment to the larger policy agenda, said, "A strong, democratic Mexico will be an even more effective partner in the struggle against drugs and crime and pollution."[72] The Mexican government went further and repaid the entire U.S. loan by January 1997, while still owing the IMF and European allies that had been brought into the bailout by President Clinton and Secretary Rubin.

Although congressional opponents could no longer claim that the American taxpayer would be stuck with the bill, the repayment did not quell the uneasiness about Mexico's political system that lingered amongst a minority of congressional members. U.S. newspaper headlines periodically reported news from Mexico that conveyed a less stable, more uncertain environment. For instance, in November 1995, a commission to investigate Raul Salinas, the former president's brother, was set up in Mexico. The investigation was later to take wild, even bizarre, turns, ultimately leading to the jailing of the president's brother on murder charges.

In November 1995, Jeffrey Shafer, the chief peso crisis negotiator, was called to testify in support of his own candidacy for Undersecretary of the Treasury for International Affairs. Senator Moynihan (D-NY) sent word that he was going to ask Shafer about democracy in Mexico. The rambling dialogue revealed how far apart the two were in being able to discuss the topic. The disconnection is particularly telling, one of the handful of moments during this period of the Clinton presidency when administration and congressional critics engaged in any sort of public back-and-forth over democracy in Mexico. In the discourse Moynihan characterized Mexico as a totalitarian state with fraudulent elections and human rights abuses, arguing that the Treasury Department did not seem to care: "It[Mexico] is clearly in a state of crisis of some kind. Treasury does not seem to know or care, as if it is none of its business."[73]

Edging Out of the Peso Crisis

The peso crisis demonstrated the strain of the prevailing belief against public criticism in the face of the practical demands of delivering legislation with congressional approval. With the demands of "must-have" legislation, U.S. Treasury officials were poised to allow very mild political criticism to enter the legislation. So was the chief congressional negotiator, James Leach, a moderate member. Despite this privately expressed flexibility, the administration continued to assert that Mexico could not be publicly criticized as it continued to depict Mexico through only positive political events. Its positivist image of Mexico in deep crisis, so at odds with what congressional critics were saying and reading in the newspapers, reduced administration credibility. Interviews revealed that many administration officials recognized a political dimension to the peso crisis that they would not acknowledge publicly as it would imply political criticism of Mexico. Treasury officials knew Salinas held off devaluation for political reasons before the 1994 elections and knew that he pursued certain fiscal policies for political results.

While the Clinton administration demonstrated noticeable changes in its treatment of democracy in Mexico, they stayed largely within the Bush administration framework of avoiding comment on negative events and stressing positive ones. The most notable shift over time came, however, not from administration actions and attitudes, but in the political and policy framework with which democracy had come to intersect other key U.S. policy concerns. The peso crisis offers a dramatic example of how democracy and political issues have come to intersect over time with a host of U.S. concerns: drugs, corruption, labor rights, trade, foreign policy, economic management. One can see a great contrast in the larger political dimension of the 1982 debt crisis and the peso crisis of 1994–1995. The dichotomy between a more static U.S. policy pattern and a more dynamic policy environment that compels change leads appropriately to reflections on the fifteen-year evolution and future of U.S. relations with Mexico over democracy as it enters a dramatic era with the first opposition candidate victory in the July 2000 Mexican presidential elections.

8.

Conclusion

The years 1980–1995 marked an important transition to a post–Cold War world, a world more increasingly democratic, where international intervention to encourage democracy was more widely practiced and accepted. It was also an important transition period within Mexico. During these same years, Mexico underwent sweeping economic and important, but less pronounced political changes. The most critical change would come in July 2000 when Mexico elected its first opposition party president, effectively ending 71 years of PRI rule. In the midst of this dynamic external environment, U.S. relations with Mexico over the question of democracy were comparatively static. Only in the late 1990s did they begin to show more noticeable change.

In contrast to more upfront policies to promote democracy in other nations, U.S. officials avoided an explicit policy on emerging Mexican democracy. Instead, U.S. officials were found to share a common belief that it was unwise to publicly criticize or confront anti-democratic practices in Mexico. It was this belief that played a dominant role in shaping a pattern of relations characterized by public silence on anti-democratic abuses and praise for positive change. This pattern was characterized by limited political assistance in only narrow, select areas. This chapter summarizes the findings of this study, probing more extensively why U.S. officials felt they should remain silent regarding anti-democratic practices in Mexico. It explores what this pattern of relations has meant to U.S. internal and external policymaking and where change seems headed in the future.

The Pattern of U.S. Relations with Mexico over Democracy

With the exception of the period surrounding the 1994 Mexican presidential elections, U.S. government support for emerging democracy in Mexico was of limited visibility and few concrete actions. The United States never publicly articulated a policy or strategy toward democratic development in Mexico; supporting democracy in Mexico remained a relatively low priority. As a recent State Department Country Director for Mexico summed up: "The U.S. mostly didn't think one way or the other about Mexico's internal politics; there were other issues, problems that took precedent."[1] Political assistance from USAID diversified over time but continued to operate at a low profile level. A thorough review of the public record confirmed that the U.S. government rarely took a controversial public stand by criticizing Mexican anti-democratic or human rights practices.[2] Overall, what was found was not an active policy process to react to and, potentially, support democratic development in Mexico nor even an active process to arrive at a consensus on how political change in Mexico might further or impede U.S. interests. As one U.S. diplomat explained: "There was no consensus, we didn't talk about it at all."[3]

U.S. officials contend that they did not exempt Mexico from overall U.S. pro-democracy goals. Rather, many characterized U.S. policy toward Mexican democracy as one concentrated on praise and encouragement for positive developments only. One Clinton administration official termed it "rewarding them for their commitments."[4] The public record is striking in the repetition of accolades for single events as signs of political change, such as the winning of a governorship by the PAN in 1989 or the clean 1994 presidential elections, without references to other indicators that this change might be uneven. More objective depictions of Mexican political realities might have been important signals to Mexico's emerging pro-democracy movement.

Mexico has made important political advances since 1980, particularly in electoral politics. Yet beneath this positive political change lay serious and long-festering political problems. These include the explosion of crime and drug-related corruption, decomposition and violence within the ruling PRI party, rural insurgency and the growth of paramilitary forces, persistent human rights abuses by government forces, and highly weak judicial and law enforcement systems. These problems deeply affect the ability of the PRI government to continue and expand the reform process. Despite positive political changes, the nonpartisan Freedom House, for example, continued to rate PRI-run Mexico to 1999 as "partly free," a rating of 3–4 in terms of political and civil liberties (with 1 being free).[5] This is a similar rating to those given in the early 1980s. It is only with Vicente Fox's election will these ratings now change. The desire to confront these long-standing political problems lay behind the stunning opposition victory in July 2000.

The U.S. emphasis on the positive only intensified over time as the Bush and Clinton administrations strove to portray Mexico in an ever-modernizing light. This led, by default, to highly biased depictions of Mexican political realities. The United States appeared indifferent to disturbing and sometimes growing anti-democratic trends and to the less glowing perspectives of Mexican opposition and human rights groups. The United States would only mention when the ruling party met its democratic commitments, not when it did not, calling into question U.S. objectivity and the value of praise in the first place. Opposition parties and citizens' groups continued to view the United States as deeply wedded to the PRI through most of the period. So embedded were the assumptions about how the United States should treat internal politics in Mexico and so infrequent were internal debates that U.S. officials rarely had to face the contradictions inherent in a positive-only approach.

U.S. policy became characterized by two opposite poles: an executive branch that utilized a strategy of public praise and silence regarding abuses and a small, diverse minority who would critically focus on abuses largely as it intersected and justified another pressing concern with Mexico, be it drugs, trade, or debt management. This fed highly polarized and oversimplified U.S. debates over politics in Mexico. The minority evolved from a collection of far-right political appointees and conservative Senators in the 1980s to a wider, even more disparate group of liberal Democrats and conservative Republicans in Congress from the NAFTA period onward. The minority were clearly strange bedfellows. They were at political extremes in each of their parties, acting not in any organized way, but as lone wolves,[6] motivated by different concerns about Mexican politics. Only during the 1994 elections was policy evolution orchestrated more by a majority coalition, but in this case, it was accomplished only by continuing to avoid public criticism of the Mexican regime and operating at a low-profile level.

Many factors constrained the size, impact, and staying power of the minority. Few joined the ranks of the minority for fear of association with the more outlandish Mexico critics, like Helms, Buchanan, and Perot, whose views were more extreme. The minority was often discredited as opportunistic since they seemed to raise the issue of democracy in Mexico only as it intersected with another more pressing interest. Mere opportunism, though, is an oversimplified explanation, as many in the minority felt that the lack of full democracy in Mexico was needed to explain their chief concerns regarding corruption, drug trafficking, or labor rights.[7] Another factor limiting the minority's effectiveness and size was the limited and mixed support provided by outside groups—

NGOs, Mexican opposition parties, intellectuals. While not essential, other cases in which the United States has shifted to a more active pro-democracy stance (e.g., in South Africa and Haiti) have had greater external impetus and support. The previous chapters record times over the fifteen-year period when some in the Mexican opposition or intellectual community actively discouraged or castigated U.S. officials for statements critical of the government and other times when the minority actively campaigned for a more vocal U.S. policy to the confusion of U.S. officials.[8] These many limiting factors were even more relevant as it became clear that democracy in Mexico was never a "do or die" issue for anyone in the minority.

What could not be fully explored in this work was the extent of private discussions between U.S. and Mexican officials regarding democracy and political reform. Officials, particularly in the Clinton administration, emphasized that they said more in private than in public and that this was the more likely way to get results from the Mexican government. The picture that emerges from interviews is that what private conversations did take place relied heavily on the motivation and interest of particular administration officials rather than as the result of a deliberate policy initiative. Many officials said they were constrained in what they said in private as well, still not wanting to appear too critical. Ultimately, it must be recognized that any private dialogue to advance democracy will have serious limitations when not back by an equally strong public policy. To the government, the United States risks sending mixed signals about the strength and seriousness of its interest in political change. To the opposition parties and civil society, the United States risks appearing at best indifferent, at worst, an obstacle to serious democratic change.

While the overall pattern of U.S. relations with Mexico over democracy has been relatively predictable to date, this is not to say there has been no change. Particularly in the face of a series of more public crises in Mexico in the 1990s, the Clinton administration moved to broaden pro-democracy assistance and made more upfront statements on human rights. Even under the PRI, U.S. officials met more publicly and frequently with a range of Mexican political actors. As one PRD official described it: "The Mexican government doesn't like them [the opposition] meeting with the U.S. but they don't say anything."[9] Ambassador Gavin confirmed that meeting with the opposition, which drew strong criticism in the 1980s, has now become accepted activity.[10] The evolution of formal relations is a credit to all the principal actors: the Mexican government, the United States, the Mexican opposition, and NGO communities. In May 1997, this culminated in a historic move by President Clinton to meet publicly with the leaders of all three major Mexican political parties in Mexico City. The meeting did not cause so much as a ripple in United States–Mexico relations.

This is not to say that formal relations over democracy have become regular or that their impact is clear. As evidence that such meetings under the PRI were not yet pro forma, the U.S. government sought to preempt conflict over the 1997 Clinton meeting with the opposition by deliberately not informing the Mexican government until setting up the meeting.[11] Mexican human rights leaders still do not feel they have the ease and regularity of relations with the U.S. government that they enjoy with other nations.[12] Nor is it apparent just what the change in formal relations means for U.S. policy. While they may meet more often with U.S. officials, a number of Mexican human rights and opposition leaders are careful to point out that, they "don't think it makes any difference in U.S. policy."[13] Why did U.S. officials perceive themselves so constrained in their public stance toward democracy? Why did so many U.S. officials for so many years believe they should not speak out regarding Mexico when they did so toward other countries?

Probing the Constraint on Public Criticism

Officials across the three U.S. administrations were asked if and why they believed that the United States should not publicly criticize or confront Mexico on anti-democratic practices. Such a belief was found across administrations and widely across different departments, although it was stronger within the State Department. Such a constraint against public criticism has been termed a belief here, not because it has some ideological origin, but because it had become so assumed and taken for granted that it took on the characteristic of an article of faith. U.S. policy seemed to operate more like a computer default setting in which assumptions about how the United States should treat internal politics in Mexico were so shared that they rarely required debate. U.S. officials repeatedly stressed they did not struggle over whether to take specific pro-democracy actions or critical statements toward Mexico; the question rarely came up.

The roots or assumptions regarding why U.S. officials felt they should not publicly criticize or confront Mexico were similar across parties and administrations. Surprisingly, one of the assumptions was not that speaking out against undemocratic practices in Mexico would undermine Mexican stability. That is because U.S. officials did not perceive pro-democracy actions, particularly the first level of actions, be it public diplomacy/criticism/pressure, significant enough to affect Mexican stability.[14] The overall objective of U.S. policy toward Mexico may be to safeguard stability, but this was not perceived as a particular constraint to undertaking initial actions to encourage democratic reform. Rather, U.S. officials held three more pragmatic assumptions about the impact of such actions on the bilateral agenda; many of these assumptions may be similar among other geostrategic states:

1. *Negative Impact on Bilateral Relations.* With the multitude and importance of ties between the United States and Mexico over issues such as drugs, immigration, and foreign policy, U.S. officials frequently believed that public criticism of democracy in Mexico would impede bilateral cooperation in resolving more important items on the agenda. "The cost you pay for being openly, publicly critical is you risk harming interests in other areas,"[15] explained Ambassador Negroponte. Interestingly, U.S. officials did not identify specific retaliatory actions they feared or a specific experience the United States had. Rather, it was a more generalized assumption that negative comments would contribute to tense relations; tense relations would make it more difficult to get resolution on other bilateral concerns. This perceived negative impact on bilateral relations can be seen to stem from the widening of the bilateral agenda characteristic of all geostrategic states. In the case of Mexico, its foreign policy importance to the United States expanded during the Good Neighbor policy/World War II and from then on into the Cold War.

2. *Possibility of a Counterproductive Reaction.* Given historic Mexican sensitivities to U.S. interference and nationalist sentiments, U.S. officials commonly believed that public criticism would backfire in Mexico if it were seen as pressure from the United States. U.S. officials argued that the Mexican government would have more room to maneuver for political change if approached behind the scenes, without the appearance of overt U.S. pressure. Given the past history of U.S. intervention, the sensitivities in the United States—Mexico case have their own unique character. The concern about a negative counterreaction, however, is likely to be found in other geostrategic states in which sensitivity to U.S. influence is strong.

3. *Desire to Safeguard the Mexican President and His Reforms.* U.S. officials also believed they should avoid criticism of Mexican politics in order not to undermine particular Mexican presidents who were leading U.S.-desired reforms or suffering economic troubles. This assumption has more contemporary rather than historic roots, beginning with President De la Madrid. Former Assistant Secretary of State Elliot Abrams noted: "We rarely criticized Mexican human rights performance publicly. The overall attitude was De la Madrid was more like what we wanted."[16] The desire to protect and reward grew stronger in the Salinas years, and continued into the Zedillo *sexenio.* Interestingly, this desire to support a particular Mexican presidency seems to have taken precedence over supporting the Mexican system (or PRI party) against instability or supporting it toward greater governability.

To those experienced in United States–Mexico relations, these assumptions are not surprising.[17] What is more interesting is how each assumption supports the same "approach to political calculation," to use Alexander George's term, to avoid public criticism and public acts to support democratic change. Embedded historic assumptions regarding safeguarding U.S. interests (assumption #1) and the sensitive Mexican reaction (assumption #2) were powerfully reinforced in the mid-1980s by a contemporary rationale to support economic reform-minded presidents (assumption #3).

Reexamining U.S. Policy

A key problem with policymaking based on embedded assumptions about U.S. interests is that events and trends that challenge those assumptions often go unrecognized. In a changing Mexico and an international environment more supportive of democracy, is it possible that U.S. support for democracy might not have been so counterproductive or repudiated? Might there be ways that U.S. interests would be advanced by a more out-front U.S. policy, even if opposed by the ruling party?

There was little evidence that U.S. officials drew lessons from assessing the Mexican reaction to key events and growing sensitivity to international opinion. This could have occurred, for example, in the wake of the positive experience of supporting international observers to the 1994 Mexican presidential elections where the Mexicans did not react as negatively as U.S. officials expected.[18] Conversely, the 1986 hearings held by Senator Jesse Helms (R-NC), considered the high point of U.S. criticism, did not cause substantial or long-term discord in United States–Mexico relations, according to U.S. officials,[19] and both countries soon reached a new debt agreement. This is not to say that the hearings had a positive effect, but rather that the negative fallout was not as great as the underlying assumption would have predicted. A number of authors note that Mexican administrations, particularly that of Carlos Salinas, may have taken certain steps toward political liberalization in response to, or in anticipation of, U.S. congressional or press criticism.[20]

While trends and events that challenge prevailing assumptions often go unrecognized, events that appear to reinforce these assumptions are often accepted without a second look. When the Mexican government publicly complains of U.S. "intervention"—be it over a U.S. action, statement, or even a non-binding congressional resolution—it reinforces the assumption that there will be a negative counterreaction (assumption #2) or negative impact on bilateral relations (assumption #1), whether or not that counter-reaction or impact on bilateral relations comes to pass. The history of the 1980–1995 period does not, in fact, record a specific negative counterreaction or impact on bilateral relations over the question of pro-democracy actions. Vocal Mexican government protestations, however, were effective enough to reinforce these assumptions. Such a tempest ensued over congressional testimony of Secretary of State Madeline Albright in June 1998 in which she stated the United States was "pressing" for a peaceful settlement in Chiapas. Diplomatic conflict erupted over whether *pressing* in English meant *pressuring*, which the Mexican government condemned as unwanted U.S. interference. While this tempest ensued over words, not actions, the controversy likely reinforced the assumption among U.S. diplomats that there would be a negative counterreaction should the United States try more forcefully to push Mexico toward a peace settlement. Human Rights Watch argues, however, that the Mexican government protestations were more a means for deflecting attention away from the issues of human rights abuses and stalled negotiations in Chiapas at the hearings.[21] By not questioning or reexamining the assumptions driving the U.S. approach to democracy in Mexico, U.S. officials were less able to gauge and adjust to how those assumptions might be changing over time. Some, such as Mexican pollster Miguel Basañez, have argued that the Mexican government manipulated and fed U.S. taboos: "It's a myth ... [T]he idea of a fervent nationalism and anti-Americanism has been exploited by the Mexican government to enhance its negotiating position with the U.S. It has been a weapon used by the Mexican government time and again, but it is not supported by the facts."[22]

Implications for Internal (U.S.) Policymaking

Also striking is the impact that this shared agreement of external silence to political infractions in Mexico might have had on internal (U.S.) policymaking and analysis. U.S. officials widely operated under the belief that negative political information was not to be used publicly and was not needed to respond to the daily demands of bilateral relations. The question is what constraint this may have had on how the United States collected information and understood complex Mexican political developments.

This study turned up widespread complaints on the quality of U.S. intelligence on Mexico from all three administrations. Clinton administration officials in the first administration declined to order a new intelligence assessment of Mexico on the assumption that they wouldn't get anything they could really use. NSC official Richard Feinberg argued that the lack of solid information on Mexico extended to the U.S. Embassy in Mexico as well.[23] U.S. officials openly admit they were caught off guard by nearly every recent major political event in Mexico, prominently, the Chiapas rebellion, the existence of guerrilla forces in Guerrero and Oaxaca, the peso crisis in 1995, and widespread drug corruption.

To be certain, there are complaints everywhere that it has become harder to predict and analyze foreign intelligence developments. Highly paid Wall Street analysts missed the Mexican financial crises; reports on the existence of guerrilla forces in Chiapas were reported lightly in the Mexican press, but few picked up on them. Nonetheless, there is a question of whether so strong an internal prohibition against presenting negative facts about Mexican politics added an additional constraint to U.S. understanding of Mexican developments.

A number of examples can be recalled. Tim Carlsgaard, deputy staff director of the Senate Select Committee on Intelligence, argued that the United States was caught off guard by Chiapas because it wasn't looking for the information in the first place. He emphasized that U.S. intelligence efforts in Mexico are focused more on the activities of others—be it Russians, East Germans, Cubans—than on Mexicans. He maintained: "The last thing you want is too much of a U.S. presence trying to find out what is going on. It would look like we're involved."[24] Internal analysis was sometimes constrained out of concern that something might be leaked externally or offend the Mexicans. This was true in 1994 when the State Department nixed an analysis of potential alternative political scenarios for the outcome of the Mexican presidential elections for fear it might get out publicly. CIA Director John M. Deutch was sufficiently worried about the quality of U.S. intelligence on Mexico in 1995 to include it, for the first time, as one of the agency's strategic priorities. In 1995, though, a far-reaching assessment of Mexico's internal turmoil was ordered but eventually forgotten.

U.S. officials interviewed maintained that they often discounted, or never saw, information that challenged the public portrayal of a reforming Mexico. A DEA regional director maintained, "A lot of this information has been out there, in the bowels of the system. But it has been ignored because people don't want to believe it, the extent of corruption."[25] On corruption linked to President Salinas, another official simply stated: "We didn't ask."[26] Former Assistant Secretary of State Bernard Aronson recalls that during his tenure "I never heard of Raul Salinas [the Mexican president's brother linked to drug corruption and political assassination]."[27] These internal (U.S.) policy implications are particularly problematic, as they undermined the ability of the U.S. government to analyze and respond to evolving political developments in Mexico that affect a broad range of U.S. interests.

The "don't look, don't tell" approach toward Mexico policy also masked a deeper issue that officials sought to avoid. Specifically, the U.S. government wasn't sure exactly how it viewed or wanted to treat evolving Mexican internal politics even if it were to take a more active stance. Nearly all interviewees stressed that the United States desired, over the long run, competitive party politics and a democratic system in Mexico. While few would argue with this long-term goal, what does this translate to in terms of day-to-day U.S. policy? Elliot Abrams reflected: "We didn't know what we should do beyond platitudes.... We never came to any kind of consensus on what we thought had to happen in Mexico other than it had to be a freer society. We were confused about what we could do to prod them to move in the right direction."[28] With a full and complex bilateral agenda, diplomats argue, such difficult political questions easily fell to the low end of U.S. priorities.[29]

Does It Matter?

Does it matter that the United States was unsure of what its policy toward the evolving Mexican democracy should be and constrained its public criticism and actions toward Mexico? Would Mexico be any more democratic today any sooner if the U.S. position had been different? Academic literature is replete with references to the relatively minor role that external actors have played in democratic transitions. It also stresses cases where U.S. involvement has been clearly negative.[30] Many U.S. officials understandably felt the wisest course was to steer clear of Mexican internal politics to avoid disturbing the neighbors, particularly if they seemed headed in the reformist direction anyway.

Others argue that the United States looms too large in Mexican life to rationalize away that it is a neutral actor, claiming that the hands-off, positive-only U.S. approach has served to undercut the Mexican opposition and reduce external pressure for meaningful political reform.[31] It is the lack of more sustained reform through the 1980s and 1990s with the worsening of drug-related corruption, some argue, that make today's key problems in Mexico much more difficult to resolve. Sergio Aguayo has argued that the lack of U.S. support has been a major factor in slowing down the pace of change in Mexico:

> I believe that the PRI's capacity to survive has been greatly enhanced by the support of the international community, and in particular the United States. Neither the amount and timeliness of the financial aid provided, nor the massive indifference toward Mexico's pro-democracy movements have any precedent or comparison in the world's recent history.[32]

The "what if" question—where would Mexico be if U.S. policy had been different—is impossible to answer and well beyond the scope of this work. It is interesting, however, that a number of key U.S. officials from the Reagan and Bush administrations believe they perceived the constraints to a more direct U.S. policy supporting democracy in Mexico greater than they were and, in retrospect, wish they had pushed more forcefully earlier for greater democratic reforms.[33] This is only a matter of degree, however, for few U.S. officials feel there was great potential for a starkly different policy.

What motivates a rethinking of the past "keep-quiet" approach is the concern that the United States failed to recognize or address the growing link between undemocratic politics and emerging problems of drug-related corruption and weakened judicial and law enforcement systems in Mexico in the 1980s and 1990s. These troubling developments directly affect the new Mexican government's ability to govern effectively and progress democratically. They have also injected a political dimension to a host of emerging U.S. interests with Mexico from drugs to financial management to trade. It is the growing political dimension of United States–Mexico relations combined with growing pluralism in Mexico itself that have been the two driving forces of change in U.S. relations with Mexico over democracy since 1995. These two trends will now accelerate and deepen under the new Fox government.

Future Prospects

While in the recent past, U.S. officials could be lulled into thinking that keeping political items off the agenda facilitated progress on the bilateral agenda, this has become increasingly harder to argue. Political issues now affect in profound ways each of the U.S. top interests with Mexico: trade (e.g., labor rights, judicial enforcement), drug policy (e.g., corruption, weak judicial systems, law enforcement, civil/military relations, human rights), immigration (e.g., civil and human rights, law enforcement), and financial management and stability (e.g., democratic/executive accountability, political stability). The United States and Mexico are embarking on unprecedented U.S. training and technical support to the Mexican armed forces to combat drug trafficking. This new relationship will inevitably tie the United States more closely to the political performance of the Mexican government and military, like it or not. Mexico also has growing political concerns with the United States in the treatment of immigrants, harsh border policies of the Immigration and Naturalization Service, drug certification policy, and the death penalty.

With the increased prominence of political concerns, a more open international environment and greater political pluralism in Mexico come the greater difficulty in maintaining the cold wall of silence to political infractions in both countries. The administration nearly ruptured it in the case of the 1995 peso crisis. In cases of events of international prominence, such as the Chiapas uprising and Acteal massacre, more open U.S. concern can be seen about human rights conditions. The occasional rupturing of the ban against public criticism appears even more likely if the locus of bureaucratic power continues to shift from the State Department to the line agencies as it had begun to do under Secretary of State Christopher.

The new democratic government in Mexico will make it easier for the United States to directly broach political topics with the government. The growing strength of opposition parties and citizens groups, combined with a more vocal press compel the United States to revise the status quo. As former NSC official Richard Feinberg characterized it, with the change in Mexican politics, "it becomes possible for the United States to make Mexico more consistent with the rest of Latin America policy."[34]

Even though external dynamics may propel democracy more often onto the bilateral agenda, U.S. officials might indeed see less of a need to reexamine the beliefs and assumptions that have governed U.S. policy for so long. Important political changes already took place without a strong U.S. role. In July 1997 midterm elections, the PRI conceded victory to a slim majority of opposition parties in the Chamber of Deputies and recognized Cuáuhtemoc Cárdenas from the PRD as the first elected mayor of Mexico City. The greatest barrier to political change in Mexico—the PRI's lock-hold on the presidency and government apparatus—will effectively begin to be dismantled in December of 2000. The United States will likely not want to rock the boat of a new Fox government by questioning their difficult process of deconstructing PRI rule.

Where change will be emerging is not through the "front door" of directly confronting past assumptions and developing a more open, comprehensive policy toward political relations with Mexico. Rather, it is through the "back door" of slowly and fitfully changing bureaucratic patterns to deal more directly with the political dimension of specific United States–Mexico interests and respond to changes within Mexico. Important change was emerging in the human rights area even under the PRI. As both nations have more public human rights concerns with each other, they have initiated bilateral talks, although still outside the regular binational meetings framework.

Recent events continue to remind us of the minefields present as the United States tries to avoid confronting its political concerns with Mexico. In May 1998, U.S. Treasury officials arrested Mexican, Venezuelan, and Colombian officials in connection with a two-year money laundering sting, Operation Casablanca. The indictments included three top Mexican banks and more than one hundred bankers, some lured over the border for arrest. While the United States had apparently informed the Mexican government in 1996 of the investigation, they did not seek Mexican consent in the arrests. Underneath the understandable affront to Mexican national sovereignty lay another sensitive issue, namely, that U.S. Treasury and Justice officials at least were not willing to trust the protection of sensitive law enforcement information to the Mexican government, a government with which the U.S. publicly claimed to have no political concerns. This case, which the United States tried to patch up afterwards, could very well repeat itself without more open political cooperation and attention to the very political differences that constrain cooperation.

The challenge for more productive United States–Mexico relations under a democratic Mexico will not be in how successfully the United States avoids raising the question of democracy or how skillfully it avoids disturbing the neighbors. The challenge will be in creating fresh approaches to bilateral relations that more comprehensively respond to the increasing political dimension of these relations and challenge old stereotypes of how things "must" be between the two countries.

Appendix:
List of Interviews*

Elliot Abrams, U.S. Assistant Secretary of State for Human Rights and Humanitarian Affairs, 1981–1985; U.S. Assistant Secretary of State for Inter-American Affairs, 1985–1989; interview: 4 October 1996

Marie Claire Acosta, Director, Mexican Commission for the Defense and Promotion of Human Rights; interview: 14 March 1996

Sergio Aguayo Quezada, Director, Civic Alliance; Mexican political analyst; interview: 9 July 1997

Adolfo Aguilar Zinzer, Mexican political analyst; Director, *Fundación Lazaro Cárdenas*; interview: 22 July 1992

Richard V. Allen, National Security Advisor, 1981–1982; telephone interview: 10 July 1996

Bernard Aronson, U.S. Assistant Secretary of State for Inter-American Affairs, 1985–1989; interview: 1 July 1997

David Beall, Deputy Chief of Mission, U.S. Embassy, Mexico City, 1993–1995; interview: 7 January 1997

Matthew Benson, legislative assistant to Representative David Bonior (D-MI), September 1991–February 1994; interview: 18 March 1997

Ambassador Morris Busby, Deputy Chief of Mission, U.S. Embassy, Mexico City, March 1984–January 1987; telephone interview: 11 September 1996

Santiago Canton, Director for Latin America and the Caribbean, National Democratic Institute for International Affairs (NDI); interview: 20 February 1996

Jorge Castañeda, Mexican political analyst/author; interview: 29 September 1995

Lucy Conger, journalist, Mexico City; interview: 7 July 1998

* Titles refer to professional position at the time of the interview. Dates are provided for previous positions of interviewees when that position was related to U.S.–Mexican relations and the subject of the book.

Ambassador T. Frank Crigler, Country Director for Mexico, U.S. State Department, 1981–1983; telephone interview: 29 August 1996

Art Danart, Director, Agency for International Development (USAID) Office, U.S. Embassy, Mexico City; interview: 14 November 1995

Matt Dippell, program officer for Mexico, NDI; interview: 20 February 1996

Sara Donnelly, program assistant, USAID, U.S. Embassy, Mexico City; interview: 14 November 1995

Mark Falcoff, professional staff member, Senate Foreign Relations Committee 1985–1986; senior advisor to the Kissinger Commission; fellow, American Enterprise Institute; telephone interview: 19 July 1996

Georges Fauriol, fellow, Center for Strategic and International Studies (CSIS); discussion: 29 February 1996

Richard Feinberg, Senior Director for Inter-American Affairs, National Security Council, 1993–1996; interview: 8 May 1996

Dan Fisk, majority staff member, Senate Foreign Relations Committee, aide to Senator Jesse Helms; telephone interview: 23 August 1996

Kim Flower, Director for Latin American Affairs, National Security Council, January 1986–June 1987; interview: 26 June 1996

John Gavin, U.S. Ambassador to Mexico, 1981–1986; telephone interview: 30 December 1996

Dennis Hayes, Country Director for Mexico, U.S. State Department, 1993–1995; interview: 22 December 1995

George High, Deputy Chief of Mission, U.S. Embassy, Mexico City, 1982–1983; Country Director for Mexico, U.S. State Department, 1983–1985; interview: 8 June 1996

Dick Howard, Country Director for Mexico, U.S. State Department, 1989–1992; interview: 19 January 1996

Phillip Hughes, Latin America advisor in the Office of Vice President 1981–1985; Director for Latin American Affairs, National Security Council, August 1985–April 1986; Deputy Assistant Secretary for Political-Military Affairs, U.S. State Department, April 1986–1987; interview: 9 July 1996

Ambassador Julius Katz, lead negotiator for North American Free Trade Agreement (NAFTA); Deputy U.S. Trade Representative, 1989–1993; interview: 20 May 1997

Jared Kotler, associate for Mexico, Washington Office on Latin America (WOLA); interview: 7 August 1995

Ann MacDonald, Acting Director, USAID Latin America and Caribbean region; interview: 19 January 1996

Jamie McCormick, Assistant Staff Director, Subcommittee on Domestic and International Monetary Policy, House Banking, Housing, and Urban Affairs Committee; interview: 29 August 1996.

Joseph Manzo, political officer, U.S. Embassy, Mexico City, 1986–1988 and 1994–1997; interview: 8 July 1997

Paul Meek, Vice President for Programs, Parlimentary Human Rights Foundation; interview: 17 January 1996

Johanna Mendelson, senior advisor, USAID Office of Democratic Transition Initiatives; interview: 1 March 1996

Constantine Menges, Central Intelligence Agency (CIA) Analyst for Latin America, 1982–1983; Latin America specialist on National Security Council, 1983–1986; interviews: 17 July 1996 and 9 October 1996

Mexican government representative, interview (background only): 8 August 1996

Augustin Navarro, Secretary for International Relations, Mexican National Action Party (PAN); interview: 13 March 1996

Ambassador John Negroponte, U.S. Ambassador to Mexico, 1989–1993; Deputy Assistant to the President for National Security Affairs, 1987–1989; interview: 30 May 1997

Janice O'Connell, minority staff member, Senate Foreign Relations Committee, aide to Senator Christopher Dodd (D-CT); interview: 8 July 1996

Eric Olson, senior associate for Mexico, Washington Office on Latin America; discussions: 11 November 1995 and 16 November 1999

Norma Parker, Assistant Administrator, USAID Latin America and Caribbean Bureau; interview: 1 March 1996

Richardo Pascoe, Fundación Democracia y Debate, Mexico City; aide to Cuáuhtemoc Cárdenas; interview: 14 March 1996

Scott Paul, legislative assistant to Rep. David Bonior (D-MI), Citizen's Trade Campaign, 1991–1992; interview: 6 September 1997

Douglas Payne, political analyst, Freedom House, New York; telephone interview: 27 August 1996

Janine Perfit, program officer for Mexico, International Republican Institute for International Affairs (IRI), 1987–1994; interviews: 24 October 1995 and 22 January 1996

William Perry, staff member, Senate Foreign Relations, 1985–1986; specialist on Latin America, National Security Council, 1986–1987; interview: 16 February 1996

Rafael Reygadas, member of Civic Alliance, Director of Service, Development and Peace (SEDEPAC), Mexico City; interview: 14 March 1996

Cecilia Romero Castillo, General Secretary of Regional Directive Committee, National Action Party (PAN); interview: 10 July 1997

John Sammis, economic officer, Office of Mexican Affairs, U.S. State Department; telephone interview: 3 July 1996

Ivan Schlager, Minority Staff Director, Senate Commerce, Science and Technology Committee, aide to Senator Ernest Hollings (D-SC), interview: 4 February 1997

Jesus Gonzales Schmall, member of Democratic Forum, Mexico City; Senator and PAN Secretary for International Relations, 1982–1987; interview: 12 March 1996

Jeffrey Shafer, U.S. Assistant Secretary of the Treasury for International Affairs, 1993–1995; Treasury Undersecretary for International Affairs, 1996–1997; interview: 31 January 1997

Michael Shifter, Director for Democracy and Human Rights, Inter-American Dialogue; senior program officer for Latin America and the Caribbean, National Endowment for Democracy (NED), January 1993- March 1994; interview: 1 May 1996

Barry Sklar, Democratic staff member, Senate Foreign Relations Committee, 1980–1991; interview: 7 July 1996

Edward Smith, economic officer, Office of Mexican Affairs, U.S. State Department, 1994–1995; telephone interview: 9 July 1996

Joel Solomen, Research Director for the Americas, Human Rights Watch; discussion (background only): 16 November 1999

Dr. Alejandro Solvarzo, Secretary for International Relations, National Revolutionary Party (PRI); interview: 13 March 1996

Bill Spencer, Deputy Director, Washington Office on Latin America; former foreign policy aide, Rep. Joe Kennedy (D-MA) 1992–1994; discussion: 29 June 1995

John St. John, Country Director for Mexico, U.S. State Department, 1987–1989; telephone interview: 28 June 1996

Ambassador Paul V. Taylor, Deputy Assistant Secretary of State for Mexico, 1987–1988; telephone interview (background only): 23 July 1996

Yvonne Thayer, policy planning staff, U.S. State Department; discussion (background only): 21 April 1996

Jane Thiery, professional staff member, House Foreign Affairs Committee, Subcommittee on Western Hemisphere Affairs, April 1994–December 1994; interview: 3 December 1996

Catherine Thorup, USAID, former member of Binational Commission on U.S.-Mexican-Relations; interview (background only): 3 May 1996

Michael Treisman, legislative assistant for Foreign Policy, Rep. Barney Frank (D-MA); telephone interview: 27 August 1996

Arturo Valenzuela, Deputy Assistant Secretary of State for Mexico, January 1994-August 1996; interview (background only): 31 October 1996

Jim Wagner, political officer, Office of Mexican Affairs, U.S. State Department 1996–1997; interview: 2 November 1995

Howard Wiarda, professor, National Defense University and University of Massachusetts at Amherst; interview: 8 February 1996

Theodore Wilkinson, political officer, U.S. Embassy, Mexico City, 1991–1994 and 1981–1984; telephone interview: 16 December 1996

Daniel Zelikow, Deputy Assistant Secretary of the Treasury for the Americas, Asia, and Africa; head of U.S. Interagency Task Force on Mexican Peso Crisis, 1995; interview: 29 January 1997

Robert Zoellick, Deputy Chief of Staff, Assistant to the President 1992–1993; Counselor to the U.S. State Department with the Rank of Undersecretary,

Notes

Preface

1. Samuel P. Huntington, *The Third Wave: Democratization in the Late Twentieth Century* (Norman: University of Oklahoma Press, 1991), 93–94.
2. Larry Diamond, *Protecting Democracy in the 1990s: Actors and Instruments, Issues and Imperatives.* A report to the Carnegie Corporation of New York, December 1995, 15.
3. *Freedom in the World: 1994–95* (New York: Freedom House, 1995), Mexico brief, 1.
4. Richard E. Neustadt, *Presidential Power: The Politics of Leadership* (New York: Wiley, 1960), 139.

Chapter 1

1. Ronald Reagan, "Promoting Democracy and Peace," Address to the British Parliament, *American Foreign Policy Current Documents: 1982* (Washington, DC: U.S. State Department, 8 June 1982), 18.
2. Elizabeth Cohn, *Idealpolitik in U.S. Foreign Policy: The Reagan Administration and U.S. Promotion of Democracy* (Ph.D. dissertation: American University, 1995).
3. Thomas Carothers, *In the Name of Democracy: U.S. Policy Toward Latin America in the Reagan Years* (Berkeley: University of California Press, 1991), 238.
4. As quoted in David W. Dent, *U.S.–Latin American Policymaking: A Reference Handbook* (Westport, CT: Greenwood Press, 1995), xiv.
5. Abraham Lowenthal, "Learning from History," in Abraham Lowenthal, ed., *Exporting Democracy: The United States and Latin America* (Baltimore: Johns Hopkins University Press, 1991), 399.
6. Lorenzo Meyer, "Mexico: The Exception and the Rule," in Lowenthal, ed., *Exporting Democracy*, 228.
7. *Ibid.*
8. Alexander L. George, "The 'Operational Code': A Neglected Approach

to the Study of Political Leaders and Decision-Making," *International Studies Quarterly*, 12, 2 (1969): 190–222; Nathan Leites, *A Study of Bolshevism* (Glencoe, IL: The Free Press, 1953).

9. George, "The 'Operational Code,' "220.
10. *Ibid.*, 191.
11. Josefina Zoraida Vásquez and Lorenzo Meyer, *The United States and Mexico* (Chicago: University of Chicago Press, 1985), 163.
12. This includes Cuba policy and Mexican opposition to U.S. military interventions in Guatemala and the Dominican Republic.
13. Sergio Aquayo Quezada, "The Uses, Abuses, and Challenges of Mexican National Security: 1946–1990," in Bruce Michael Bagley and Sergio Aguayo Quezada, eds., *Mexico: In Search of Security* (Miami: University of Miami, North-South Center, 1993), 98.
14. Jorge Domínguez, "Introduction," in Jorge Domingue, ed., *Mexico's Political Economy: Challenge at Home and Abroad* (Beverly Hills, CA: Sage Publications, 1982), 13–14.
15. Robert A. Pastor and Jorge G. Castañeda, *Limits to Friendship: The United States and Mexico* (New York: Vintage Books, 1989), 10.

Chapter 2

1. Bruce Michael Bagley, "Interdependence and U.S. Policy toward Mexico in the 1980s," in Riordan Roett, ed., *Mexico and the United States: Managing the Relationship* (Boulder, CO: Westview Press, 1988), 227; and Lorenzo Meyer, "Mexico: The Exception and the Rule," in Abraham Lowenthal, ed., *Exporting Democracy: The United States and Latin America* (Baltimore: Johns Hopkins University Press, 1991).
2. Wayne Cornelius, "Las Relacciones de Estados Unidos Con México: Fuentes de Su Deterioro: 1986–87," *Foro Internaciónal XXIX*, 2 (1988): 213.
3. Susan Kaufman Purcell, "Mexico–U.S. Relations: Big Initiatives Cause Big Problems," *Foreign Affairs* 60, no. 2 (Winter 1981/82): 380.
4. "Enders Plans for Freedom and Free Enterprise in the Caribbean," *Latin American Newsletters*, 19 June 1981: 1.
5. Purcell, "Mexico–U.S. Relations," 380.
6. Philip Hughes, interview with the author, 7 September 1996.
7. T. Frank Crigler, telephone interview with the author, 29 August 1996.
8. This is confirmed by Carlos Gonzales Gutíerrez, *México en el Congreso Estadounidense: Coaliciones y Alineamientos (1981–1986)* (México D.F.: El Colegio de México, 1987).
9. U.S. State Department, Bureau of Public Affairs, *Realism, Strength, Negotiation: Key Foreign Policy Statements of the Reagan Administration* (Washington, DC: U.S. State Department, Bureau of Public Affairs, 1984), 121.
10. Juan J. Walte, "Actor-Diplomat John Gavin: Our Man in Mexico," *United Press International*, 23 April 1981: 1.
11. U.S. State Department, "Mexican–Nicaraguan Relations: Can Mexico Moderate the Sandinistas?" classified memorandum, Washington, DC, 12 August 1981, 1–2, from the files of the National Security Archives, George Washington University, Washington, DC.

12. Lou Cannon, "Reagan Is Conciliatory in Foreign Policy Statements," *Washington Post*, 18 March 1980: A4.
13. Constantine Menges, "Radicalism Abroad," *New York Times*, 11 June 1980: 31.
14. John Sammis, telephone interview with the author, 3 July 1996.
15. Bob Woodward, *Veil: The Secret Wars of the CIA: 1981–1987* (New York: Pocket Books, 1988), 95.
16. Frank Horton, "Mexico, The Way of Iran?" *Journal of Intelligence and Counterintelligence* 1, no. 2 (1986): 91–92.
17. Crigler interview, 29 August 1996.
18. *Ibid.*
19. Constantine Menges, interview with the author, 9 October 1996.
20. Horton, "Mexico, The Way of Iran?" 96.
21. Crigler interview, 29 August 1996.
22. George Lardner, Jr., "Senators Question Gavin on Credentials for Mexican Post," *Washington Post*, 23 April 1981: A10.
23. *Ibid.*
24. Menges interview, 17 July 1996.
25. Elliot Abrams, interview with the author, 4 October 1996.
26. *Ibid.*
27. Crigler interview, 29 August 1996.
28. Howard Wiarda, interview with the author, 8 February 1996.
29. *Ibid.*
30. Kim Flower, interview with the author, 26 June 1996.
31. U.S. Department of State, American Consulate Monterrey, "The Partido Accion Nacional (PAN): History and Platform," Department of State Airgram, unclassified, Monterrey, Mexico, 29 September 1981, 6.
32. Abrams interview, 4 October 1996.
33. Crigler interview, 29 August 1996.
34. George High, interview with the author, 8 June 1996.
35. Georges Fauriol, discussion with the author, 29 February 1996.
36. Menges interview, 10 September 1996.
37. Crigler interview, 29 August 1996.
38. *Ibid.*
39. Edward Cowan, "Loans and Credits for Aiding Mexico Are Mapped by U.S.," *New York Times*, 21 August 1982: 1.
40. Alan Riding, *Distant Neighbors: A Portrait of the Mexicans* (New York: Vintage Books, 1985), 325.
41. *Ibid.*, 326.
42. High interview, 8 June 1996.
43. Cathryn Lynn Thorup, "Managing Extreme Interdependence: Alternative Institutional Arrangements for U.S. Policymaking toward Mexico: 1976–1988," Ph.D. dissertation, Harvard University, 1992, 323.
44. High interview, 8 June 1996.
45. Ambassador John Gavin, telephone interview with the author, 30 December 1996.
46. Jesus Gonzales Schmall, interview with the author, 12 March 1996.
47. Marie Claire Acosta, interview with the author, 14 March 1996.
48. Crigler interview, 29 August 1996.
49. High interview, 8 June 1996.

50. Robert Pastor and Jorge Castañeda, *Limits to Friendship: The United States and Mexico* (New York: Vintage Books, 1989), 81.
51. High interview, 8 June 1996.
52. Pastor and Castañeda, *Limits to Friendship*, 81.
53. David Gardner, "Mexico and the U.S. — a Gulf of Misunderstanding," *Financial Times*, 6 June 1984: 6.
54. U.S. Department of State, "Mexico-Gen. Gorman Congressional Testimony," telegram, unclassified, Washington, DC, 27 February 1984, contained in the National Security Archives, Iran-Contra Collection, File 01399, George Washington University, 2.
55. This compilation of events relies heavily on the accounts of Woodward in *Veil*, which is based on extensive interviews with CIA Director Casey and other intelligence officials, and Horton, in "Mexico, The Way of Iran?"
56. Horton, "Mexico, The Way of Iran?" 94.
57. Woodward, *Veil*, 388.
58. *Ibid.*, 389.
59. Jack Anderson and Dale Van Atta, "The Mexican Time Bomb," *Penthouse*, May 1987: 42.
60. Philip Taubman, "Analyst Said to Have Quit in C.I.A. Dispute," *New York Times*, 27 September 1984: A1.
61. Alfonso Chardy, "The Case of Mexico: From Alliance, to Pressure, to Distrust," *Miami Herald*, 27 December 1987: B1.
62. Constantine C. Menges, *Inside the National Security Council: The True Story of the Making and Unmaking of Reagan's Foreign Policy* (New York: Simon and Schuster, 1988), 118–119.
63. *Ibid.*, 119.
64. Jack Anderson, "Mexico Makes Its Presidents Millionaires," *Washington Post*, 15 May 1984: C15.
65. High interview, 8 June 1996.
66. "Mexicans File Protest against Press Report on Leader's Finances," *Washington Post*, 29 May 1984: A12.
67. "U.S. Graft Charges Protested," *Facts on File*, 1 June 1984: 398, G2.
68. Hughes interview, 7 September 1996.
69. High interview, 8 June 1996.
70. Gardner, "Mexico and the U.S.," 6.
71. Laura Lopez, "Talk from a Neighbor: Mexico's President Presses the U.S. on Central America," *Time*, 28 May 1984: 60.
72. Richard V. Allen, telephone interview with the author, 10 July 1996.
73. *Ibid.*
74. *Ibid.*
75. Schmall interview, 12 March 1996.
76. Sammis interview, 3 July 1996.
77. *Ibid.*
78. Ambassador Morris Busby, telephone interview with the author, 11 September 1996.
79. Pastor and Castañeda, *Limits to Friendship*, 81.
80. Schmall interview, 12 March 1996.
81. Abrams interview, 4 October 1996.
82. Crigler interview, 29 August 1996.

Chapter 3

1. Ambassador Morris Busby, telelphone interview with the author, 11 September 1996.
2. Lorenzo Meyer, "Mexico: The Exception and the Rule," in Abraham Lowenthal, ed., *Exporting Democracy: The United States and Latin America* (Baltimore: Johns Hopkins University Press, 1991), 228.
3. Busby interview, 11 September 1996.
4. Marjorie Miller and Juan M. Vasquez, "DEA Agent, Pilot's Bodies Positively Identified," *Los Angeles Times*, 8 March 1985: 3.
5. Elliot Abrams, interview with the author, 4 October 1996.
6. Ambassador Gavin later claimed that the rationale was much broader: to pressure the Mexican government toward criminal prosecution, including the prosecution of drug traffickers. George Russell, "Slowdown on the Border," *Time*, 4 March 1985: 8.
7. Carlos Gonzáles Gutiérrez, "El Papel del Congreso Estadounidense en las Relacciones Bilaterales," in Gerardo Bueno, ed., *México-Estados Unidos 1986* (México D.F.: El Colegio de México, 1987), 235.
8. William Perry, interview with the author, 16 February 1996.
9. Carlos Ramíerez, *Operación Gavin: México en la Diplomacia de Reagan* (México, D.F.: Sociedad Cooperativa, August 1987), 119.
10. Ramíerez, *Operacíon Gavin*, 122. Citations include *La Jornada*, 4 September 1985; the *Houston Post*, 21 August 1985; and *El Excelsior*, 16 May 1986.
11. Ramíerez, *Operación Gavin*, 11.
12. Robert J. McCartney, "U.S.–Mexican Ties Warm a Little: Officials Seek to Ease Tensions after Drug-Trafficking Disputes," *Washington Post*, 1 June 1985: A25.
13. George High, interview with the author, 8 June 1996.
14. Philip Hughes, interview with the author, 9 July 1996, and Busby interview, 11 September 1996.
15. Busby interview, 11 September 1996.
16. High interview, 8 June 1996.
17. Busby interview, 11 September 1996. The PAN candidate was likely Manuel Rosas.
18. *Ibid.*
19. *Ibid.*
20. Joel Brinkley, "Mexico and the Narcotics Traffic: Growing Strain in U.S. Relations," *New York Times*, 20 October 1986: A1.
21. Robert J. McCartney, "Mexico's Ruling Party Pressed; Rightists Offer Unprecedented Regional Electoral Challenge," *Washington Post*, 31 May 1985: A25.
22. Lucy Conger, interview with the author, 7 July 1998.
23. Frank del Olmo, "Mexico's Ruling PRI Can't Win for Losing," *Los Angeles Times*, 11 July 1985, Part 2: 5.
24. Conger interview, 7 July 1998.
25. Blanca Torres, "La Visíon Estadounidense de las Elecciones de 1985: ¿Presíon de Coyuntura o Preoccupación de Largo Plazo?" in Gabriel Székely, ed., *México-Estados Unidos, 1985* (México, D.F.: El Colegio de México, 1986), 59.

26. *Congressional Record–Extension of Remarks*, 99th Congress, 2d sess., Vol. 131, no. 105, 31 July 1985: E 3660.

27. Suzanne Bilello, "La Prensa Extranjera y las Elecciones en Chihuahua, Julio de 1986," in Gerardo Bueno, ed., *México-Estados Unidos, 1986* (México, D.F.: El Colegio de México, 1987), 163.

28. Vincent J. Schodolski and George de Lama, "Reagan, Mexican OK Drug Summit," *Chicago Tribune*, 4 January 1986; and Dennis Volman, "Mexico Meeting Spawns Both Hope and Concern," *Christian Science Monitor*, 6 January 1986.

29. Hughes interview, 9 July 1996.

30. Dan Williams, "An Angry Mexico Calls U.S. Aide's Remarks Slander," *Los Angeles Times*, 15 May 1986: 1.

31. Kim Flower, interview with the author, 26 June 1996.

32. U.S. State Department, Bureau of Public Affairs, "Background on Mexico," *U.S. Department of State: Background Notes* (Washington, DC, March 1986).

33. Senate Committee on Foreign Relations, Subcommittee on Western Hemisphere Affairs, *Situation in Mexico*, 99th Congress, 2nd sess., S. Hrg. 99–942, 13 May 1986, 17 and 26 June 1986, 3.

34. Dan Williams, "An Angry Mexico," *Los Angeles Times*, 15 May 1986: 1.

35. Senate Committee, *Situation in Mexico*, 94.

36. *Ibid.*, 6.

37. *Ibid.*, 43.

38. *Ibid.*, 41.

39. Abrams interview, 4 October 1996.

40. Senate Committee, *Situation in Mexico*, 25.

41. *Ibid.*, 91.

42. *Congressional Record*, 99th Congress, 2d sess., Vol. 132, no. 84, 19 June 1986: 7934.

43. Abrams interview, 4 October 1996.

44. Wayne Cornelius, "Mexico's Delayed Democratization," *Foreign Policy* 95 (Summer 1994): 71.

45. Robert A. Pastor and Jorge G. Castañeda, *Limits to Friendship: The United States and Mexico* (New York: Vintage Books, 1989), 72.

46. Joanne Omang, "Administration Reviewing Disjointed Policy on Mexico," *Washington Post*, 4 June 1986: A1.

47. Jim Lehrer, television broadcast, *McNeil-Lehrer Report*, 18 June 1986.

48. Abrams interview, 4 October 1996.

49. Omang, "Administration Reviewing Disjointed Policy," A1.

50. Abrams interview, 4 October 1996. Reagan was reported to have endorsed the hearings on May 14, 1986, and on May 15, a State Department spokesman said the hearings constituted a balanced review of the Department's position; see Cathryn Lynn Thorup, "Managing Extreme Interdependence: Alternative Institutional Arrangements for U.S. Policymaking toward Mexico: 1976–1988" (Ph.D. diss., Harvard University, 1992), 152.

51. Abrams interview, 4 October 1996.

52. Senate Committee, *Situation in Mexico*, 45.

53. Perry interview, 16 February 1996.

54. Thorup, "Managing Extreme Interdependence," 311–312.

55. Perry interview, 16 February 1996.

56. Thorup, "Managing Extreme Interdependence," 156.

57. *Congressional Record*, 99th Congress, 2d sess., Vol. 132, no. 84, 26 June 1986: S 8735.

58. Sidney Weintraub, *A Marriage of Convenience: Relations between the United States and Mexico* (New York: Oxford University Press, 1990), 46.

59. *Congressional Record*, 99th Congress, 2d sess., Vol. 132, no. 84, 6 August 1986: S 10618.

60. Jesus Gonzales Schmall, interview with the author, 12 March 1996.

61. Flower interview, 26 June 1996.

62. *Congressional Record*, 6 August 1986: S 10618.

63. Janice O'Connell, interview with the author, 7 August 1996.

64. Barry Sklar, interview with the author, 11 July 1996.

65. *Ibid.*

66. Juan L. Gonzáles, "El Viajo de Miguel de la Madrid a Washington," *Carta de Politica Exterior Mexicana* 6, no. 3 (July–September 1986): 24.

67. Gonzáles Gutierrez, "El Papel del Congreso Estadounidense," 243.

68. Pastor and Castañeda, *Limits to Friendship*, 75.

69. Alfonso Chardy, "The Case of Mexico: From Alliance, to Pressure, to Distrust," *Miami Herald*, 27 December 1987: B1.

70. The National Security Archives, *Sample Documents Related to Latin America* (Washington, DC: The National Security Archives, August 1986), 12.

71. Flower interview, 26 June 1996.

72. Pico Iyer, "Shaking Hands, Not Fists," *Time*, 25 August 1986: 30.

73. "Reagan Praises Mexico for Economic Struggle, Drug War," *Reuters Ltd.*, 14 August, 1986: 1.

74. Ronald Reagan, *Weekly Compilation of Presidential Documents*, Vol. 22, 1113 (Washington: Government Printing Office, 14 August 1986).

75. Mario Ojeda, "La Doble Agenda México-Estados Unidos," in *México-Estados Unidos 1986*, 30.

76. High interview, 8 June 1996.

77. *Ibid.*

78. Ramíerez, *Operacíon Gavin*, 208.

79. Thorup, "Managing Extreme Interdependence," 326.

80. Dan Williams, "Envoy to Mexico Juggles Local, Washington Pressures," *Los Angeles Times*, 22 May 1987: 17.

81. Abrams interview, 4 October 1996.

82. Williams, "Envoy to Mexico," 17.

83. John St. John, telephone interview with the author, 28 June 1996.

84. Williams, "Envoy to Mexico," 17.

85. *Ibid.*

86. Constantine Menges, *Inside the National Security Council: The True Story of the Making and Unmaking of the Reagan Foreign Policy* (New York: Simon and Schuster, 1988), 305.

87. This statement is based on interviews with Abrams, High, Flower, Hughes, and St. John.

88. Joel Brinkley, "Mexico? Did Someone Mention Mexico?" *New York Times*, 28 October 1986: 1B.

89. Abrams interview, 4 October 1996.

90. Larry Smith (D-FL) sponsored a successful amendment in the House to cut $1 million in anti-narcotics aid to Mexico pending the successful resolution

of the Camarena and Cortez cases. There was no companion Senate measure, and the amendment died.

91. There is some disagreement among sources over when the review process started. Mexico Country Director John St. John recalled the review was "pretty much a done deal by mid-1987," while the official document calling for the review (National Security Decision Directive-291) is dated December 16, 1987.

92. The Defense Department was principally concerned with problems on the United States–Mexico border, responses to a scenario of Mexican instability, and developments in Panama.

93. This description of the document relies on an interview with Mexico Country Director John St. John on June 28, 1996, and on an administration source as reported in Thorup, "Managing Extreme Interdependence."

94. Thorup, "Managing Extreme Interdependence," 237.

95. St. John interview, 28 June 1996.

96. Janine Perfit, interview with the author, 22 January 1996.

97. *Ibid.*

98. Beth Sims, *Foreign Support for the Mexican Democratization Process: Focus on the U.S. Agency for International Development and the National Endowment for Democracy*, Discussion Paper #2 (Albuquerque: Resource Center Press, 1995), 2.

99. Flower interview, 26 June 1996.

100. Ken Flynn, "Regional News," *United Press International*, 28 April 1988: 1.

101. Abrams interview, 4 October 1996.

102. St. John interview, 28 June 1996.

103. Abrams interview, 4 October 1996.

104. *Ibid.*

105. St. John interview, 28 June 1996.

106. Abrams interview, 4 October 1996.

107. U.S. State Department, "ARA Press Guidance," Document 9271, Ronald Reagan Presidential Library, Country File CO104.

108. Abrams interview, 4 October 1996.

109. *Ibid.*

110. St. John interview, 28 June 1996.

111. Abrams interview, 4 October 1996.

112. St. John interview, 28 June 1996.

113. Laurence Whitehead, "Mexico and the 'Hegemony' of the United States: Past, Present, and Future," in Riordan Roett, ed., *Mexico's External Relations in the 1990s* (Boulder, CO: Lynne Rienner Publishers, 1991), 246.

114. Ricardo Pascoe, interview with the author, 14 March 1996.

115. Schmall interview, 12 March 1996.

116. T. Frank Crigler, telephone interview with the author, 29 August 1996.

117. St. John interview, 28 June 1996.

118. Crigler interview, 29 August 1996.

119. Abrams interview, 4 October 1996.

120. St. John interview, 28 June 1996.

121. High interview, 8 June 1996.

122. Constantine Menges, interview with the author, 17 July 1996.

123. Hughes interview, 9 July 1996.

124. Interviews supporting this claim include those with Ambassador John

Gavin, telephone interview with the author, 30 December 1996; Busby interview, 11 September 1996; and Abrams interview, 4 October 1996.

125. Abrams interview, 4 October 1996.
126. Marie Claire Acosta, interview with the author, 14 March 1996.
127. High interview, 8 June 1996.

Chapter 4

1. Héctor Aguilar Camín and Lorenzo Meyer, *In the Shadow of the Mexican Revolution, Contemporary Mexican History: 1910–1989* (Austin: University of Texas Press, 1993), 237.
2. Dick Howard, interview with the author, 19 January 1996.
3. U.S. State Department, "Visit of Mexican President Salinas," *Department of State Bulletin*, December 1989: 1.
4. Georges Fauriol, discussion with the author, 29 February 1996.
5. Walter Astié-Burgos, *El Águila Bicéfala: Las Relaciones México–Estados Unidos a Través de la Experiencia Diplomática* (México, D.F.: Ariel-Divulgación, April 1995), 378, translation.
6. Robert Zoellick, interview with the author, 12 June 1997.
7. *Ibid.*
8. William Orme, Jr., *Continental Shift: Free Trade and the New North America* (Washington, DC: Washington Post Company, 1993), 222.
9. Bernard Aronson, interview with the author, 1 July 1996.
10. Aguilar and Meyer, *In the Shadow of the Mexican Revolution*, 236.
11. John Bailey, *Governing Mexico: The Statecraft of Crisis Management* (New York: St. Martin's Press, 1988); and Lorenzo Meyer, "Democratization of the PRI: Mission Impossible?" in Wayne Cornelius, Judith Gentleman, and Peter Smith, eds., *Mexico's Alternative Political Futures* (La Jolla: Center for U.S.–Mexican Studies, 1989).
12. Wayne A. Cornelius, Judith Gentleman, and Peter H. Smith, eds., *Mexico's Alternative Political Futures* (La Jolla: Center for U.S.–Mexican Studies, 1989), 33.
13. Aronson interview, 1 July 1997.
14. Senate Committee on Foreign Relations, *Hearing on the Nomination of James Baker to Secretary of State*, 101st Congress, 1st sess., 17 and 18 January 1989, 13.
15. Ken Silverstein and Alexander Cockburn, "Who Broke Mexico? The Killers and the Killing," *The Nation*, 6 March 1995: 309.
16. Denise Dresser, "Exporting Conflict," in Abraham Lowenthal and Katrina Burgess, eds., *The California-Mexico Connection* (Stanford: Stanford University Press, 1993), 90.
17. Manuel Garcia y Griego, "New Presidents; More Controversy for U.S. and Mexico, a Short Honeymoon," *Los Angeles Times*, 13 February 1989: 23.
18. "New U.S. Envoy Seeks to Ease Mexico Fears on Intervention," *San Diego Union-Tribune*, 4 July 1989: A-3.
19. Jack Nelson, "CIA Chief Warns of 'Coup-Plotting' in Latin America," *Los Angeles Times*, 9 February 1989: 1.
20. Larry Rohter, "Mexico Puts Signs from Bush in the Worst Light," *New York Times*, 19 February 1989: 2.

21. Ambassador John Negroponte, interview with the author, 30 May 1997.
22. *Ibid.*
23. *Ibid.*
24. Marie Claire Acosta, interview with the author, 14 March 1996.
25. Senate Committee on Appropriations, Subcommittee on Foreign Opera-
    tions, *Hearing on FY 90 Foreign Operations Bill,* 101st Congress, 1st sess., 15
    March 1989, 40.
26. Beth Sims, *Foreign Support for the Mexican Democratization Process: Focus
    on the U.S. Agency for International Development and the National Endow-
    ment for Democracy* (Albuquerque, NM: Resource Center Press, 1993), 10.
27. Stephen D. Morris, "Political Reformism in Mexico: Salinas at the Brink,"
    Journal of Interamerican Studies and World Affairs 34, no. 1 (Spring 1992):
    31.
28. Denise Dresser, *Neopopulist Solutions to Neoliberal Problems: Mexico's
    National Solidarity Program* (La Jolla: Center for U.S.–Mexican Studies,
    1991), 3.
29. "Mexico Seeks to Build a New Era of Cooperation: Q&A Gustavo Petricioli,
    Mexico's Ambassador," *San Diego Union-Tribune,* 16 July 1989: C-6.
30. *Department of State Bulletin,* December 1989, 79.
31. Robert Pastor, "Post-Revolutionary Mexico: The Salinas Opening," *Journal
    of Interamerican Studies and World Affairs* 33, no. 4 (Fall 1990): 16.
32. *State Department Bulletin,* December 1989, 76.
33. William Orme, Jr., *Understanding NAFTA: Mexico, Free Trade, and the New
    North America* (Austin: University of Texas Press, 1996), 31.
34. Andrew Reding, "Mexico: The Crumbling of the 'Perfect Dictatorship,'"
    World Policy Journal 8, no. 2 (Spring 1991): 262.
35. *A Policy of Impunity* (Washington, DC: Human Rights Watch, 1990), 1.
36. William Branigin, "Human-Rights Group Attacks Mexico's Record," *Wash-
    ington Post,* 12 June 1990: A33.
37. Ellen Lutz, "Human Rights Concerns in Mexico," *Current History* 92, no.
    571 (1993): 79.
38. Denise Dresser, "Treading Lightly and without a Stick: International Actors
    and the Promotion of Democracy in Mexico" (paper presented at the XIX
    International Congress of the Latin American Studies Association, Wash-
    ington, DC, 30 September 1995).
39. Sergio Aguayo, interview with the author, 9 July 1997.
40. Negroponte interview, 30 May 1997.
41. Ambassador Julius Katz, interview with the author, 20 May 1997.
42. Charlotte Saikowski, "Where the Candidates Stand on Foreign Policy,"
    Christian Science Monitor, 17 October 1988: 1.
43. Charles Lane, Tim Padgett, and Douglas Waller, "Tough Sell for Salinas,"
    Newsweek, 3 December 1990: 39.
44. Mark Uhlig, "Mexico's Salinas Rains on His Own Parade, *New York Times,*
    25 November 1990: 3.
45. P. Muñoz, C. Ochoa, R. Benítez, and D. Estévez, "México Rechaza Condi-
    ciones Políticas en el ALC; Solo Negociaremos Comercio e Inversíon:
    Solana," *El Financiero,* 8 November 1990: 1.
46. Dolía Estévez, "Inexpertos Funcionarios Mexicanos Complican, en el Con-
    greso de EU, el Debate Sobre el ALC," *El Financiero,* 29 November 1990: 16.
47. Judith Gentleman and Voytek Zubek, "International Integration and

Democratic Development: The Cases of Poland and Mexico," *Journal of Interamerican Studies and World Affairs* 34, no. 1 (Spring 1992): 79.

48. Peter H. Smith, "The Political Impact of Free Trade on Mexico," *Journal of Interamerican Studies and World Affairs* 34, no. 1 (Spring 1992): 4.
49. Gentleman and Zubek, "International Integration," 81.
50. M. Delal Baer, "Salinas' Achilles' Heel," *Christian Science Monitor*, 5 December 1990: 19.
51. M. Delal Baer, "Mexican Elections: Shadow over the Summit," *Washington Post*, 30 November 1990: A29.
52. Dresser, "Treading Lightly," 26.
53. "The Man behind the Mask," *Time*, 19 November 1990: 74.
54. "The Cloud over Reform in Mexico," *New York Times*, 17 November 1990: 6A.
55. Reymundo Riva Palacio, "'A Nivel Privado,' CSG y Bush Podrían Hablar de la Reforma Política Mexicana: Casa Blanca," *El Financiero*, 27 November 1990: 28.
56. Reymundo Riva Palacio, "Raspaldo en EU, George Bush Tuvo Ayer un Gran Día en Agualeguas y Monterrey," *El Financiero*, 27 November 1990: 30.
57. Aronson interview, 1 July 1997.
58. Riva Palacio, "A 'Nivel Privado,'" 28.
59. Gentleman and Zubek, "International Integration," 81.
60. Linda Robinson and Jane Bussey, "Can 'Salinastroika' Work?" *U.S. News and World Report*, 3 December 1990: 51.
61. R. Riva Palacio, "Por la Relación CSG-Bush, Mexico y EU Atraviesan un 'Momento Mágico,'" *El Financiero*, 28 November 1990: 35.
62. U.S. State Department, "President Bush's Upcoming Visit to Mexico," Foreign Press Center Briefing, 21 November 1990, 52.
63. U.S. State Department, "President Bush's Upcoming Visit," 52.
64. Jorge Chabat, "Mexico's Foreign Policy in 1990: Electoral Sovereignty and Integration with the United States," *Journal of Interamerican Studies and World Affairs* 33, no. 4 (Winter 1991): 21.
65. Ambassador Julius Katz pointed out that oil was the most sensitive political issue of the talks, but that the Mexicans had agreed early on to U.S. insistence that oil be included in the agreement. The United States agreed that this would be kept secret, with a secret negotiating task force to conduct the talks. Katz interview, 20 May 1997.
66. Aronson interview, 1 July 1997.
67. *Ibid.*
68. Ivan Schlager, interview with the author, 2 April 1997.
69. Cathryn Thorup, "The Politics of Free Trade and the Dynamics of Cross-Border Coalitions in U.S.–Mexican Relations," *Colombia Journal of World Business* 26, no. 11 (Summer 1991): 18.
70. Gentleman and Zubek, "International Integration," 79.
71. "Mexico Rejects Calls for Election Observers," *Reuters*, 4 December 1990: 1.
72. Aronson interview, 1 July 1997.
73. Thorup, "The Politics of Free Trade," 16.
74. Senate Committee on Finance, *Hearing on the U.S.–Mexico Free Trade Agreement*, 101st Congress, 1st sess., S. Hrg. 102–75, 6 and 20 February 1991, 8.
75. Scott Paul, interview with the author, 9 June 1997.

76. *Ibid.*
77. Katz interview, 20 May 1997.
78. House Committee on Banking, Housing and Urban Affairs, Subcommittee on International Development, *Hearing on Proposed U.S.–Mexico Free Trade Agreement,* 102nd Congress, 1st sess., 16 April 1991, 4.
79. "Salinas on the Road; Promoting the FTA," *IBC USA: Mexico Service,* 24 April 1991: 2.
80. *Ibid.,* 3.
81. Bernard W. Aronson, Assistant Secretary of State for Inter-American Affairs, "Statement before the Subcommittee on Western Hemisphere and Peace Corps Affairs of the Senate Foreign Relations Committee," *Department of State Dispatch* (Washington, DC: U.S. Department of State, 29 April 1991), 23.
82. "North American Free Trade Agreement: Letter to Congress, May 1, 1991," *U.S. Department of State Dispatch,* 6 June 1991.
83. Thorup, "The Politics of Free Trade," 20.
84. Katz interview, 20 May 1997.
85. Pamela Constable, "Congress Warming to Free Trade Pact," *Boston Globe,* 22 May 1991: 3.
86. *Congressional Record,* 102d Congress, 2d sess., 1991, Vol. 137, no. 105: S 6550.
87. *Ibid.*
88. *Ibid.,* H3517.
89. Carlos Puig, "Conclusión de Negroponte: con el Tratado de Libre Comercio, México Quedaría a Disposición de Washington," *El Proceso,* 13 May 1991: 7.
90. Robert Pastor in Christopher Marquis, "Mexico's Political Status Still Haunts Free-Trade Talks," *Orange County Register,* 25 May 1991: A1.
91. Michael Wilson, *Political Reform in Mexico: Salinas' Other Revolution* (Washington, DC: The Heritage Foundation, 11 October 1991), 52.
92. As reported in Dresser, "Treading Lightly and without a Big Stick," 26.
93. "U.S. Urged to Send Observers to Mexico Election," *Reuters,* 6 August 1991: 19.
94. Ricardo Alemán Alemán, *Guanajuato-Espejismo Electoral* (México, D.F.: La Jornada Ediciones, 1993), 93.
95. *Country Reports on Human Rights Practices for 1991: Mexico* (Washington, DC: U.S. Congress, Joint Committee Print, 102nd Congress, 2nd sess., February 1992), 664.
96. Tom Barry, Harry Browne, and Beth Sims, *The Great Divide: The Challenge of U.S.–Mexico Relations in the 1990s* (New York: Grove Press, 1994), 401.
97. Gentleman and Zubek, "International Integration," 83.
98. Katz interview, 20 May 1997.
99. Zoellick interview, 12 June 1997.
100. Andrew Reding, "Reaction to Cries of Election Fraud Clouds Mexico's Reform Commitment," *San Diego Union-Tribune,* 24 October 1991: 8.
101. "Human Rights in Mexico," Testimony of Holly Burkhalter before the House of Representatives, Foreign Affairs Subcommittees on Western Hemisphere Affairs and Human Rights and International Organizations, Washington, DC, 16 October 1991, 7.
102. Ernest Hollings, "Reform Mexico First," *Foreign Policy* 93 (1993–1994): 91–103.
103. Schlager, interview, 4 February 1997.
104. Dresser, "Treading Lightly," 14.

105. Senate Committee on Finance, *Hearing on North American Trade Agreement*, 103rd Congress, 1st sess., 22 April 1993, 44.
106. Rosa Rojas, "Cartas a Salinas y Carla Hills Contra el Fraude en Michoacán," *La Jornada*, 26 July 1992: 8.
107. Zoellick interview, 12 June 1997.
108. Negroponte interview, 30 May 1997.
109. Zoellick interview, 12 June 1997.
110. Ambassador Negroponte recalled that the administration "didn't worry that much during my tenure about stability in Mexico." Negroponte interview, 30 May 1997.
111. Aronson interview, 1 July 1997.
112. Howard interview, 19 January 1996.
113. Aronson interview, 1 July 1997.
114. Gentleman and Zubek, "International Integration": 61.

Chapter 5

1. Damian Fraser, "Mexican Glee at Clinton's NAFTA Stance—Salinas Believes the Cloud over the Free Trade Pact Has Been Lifted," *Financial Times*, 7 October 1992: 5.
2. Jorge G. Castañeda, "The Clouding Political Horizon," *Current History* 92 (February 1993): 66.
3. Tom Barry, Harry Browne, and Beth Sims, *The Great Divide: The Challenge of U.S.–Mexico Relations in the 1990s* (New York: Grove Press, 1993), 370.
4. Richard Feinberg, interview with the author, 8 May 1996.
5. Tim Golden, "U.S. and Mexico Spar over Limits of Intervention," *New York Times*, 1 December 1993: 3.
6. U.S. Department of State, "Fact Sheet: U.S. National Interests and Cooperation with Mexico," *U.S. Department of State Dispatch* 4, Washington, DC, 17 May 1993, 354.
7. Scott Paul, interview with the author, 9 June 1997.
8. Janice O'Connell, interview with the author, 8 July 1996.
9. Paul interview, 9 June 1997.
10. Matt Benson, interview with the author, 18 March 1997.
11. Ambassador Julius Katz, interview with the author, 20 May 1997.
12. Jorge Castañeda, interview with the author, 29 September 1995.
13. Ricardo Pascoe, interview with the author, 14 March 1996.
14. Denise Dresser, "Mr. Salinas Goes to Washington" (paper delivered at the Research Conference, "Crossing National Borders: Invasion or Involvement?" Colombia University, New York, NY, 6 December 1991), 11–14.
15. O'Connell interview, 8 July 1996.
16. U.S. Department of State, "NAFTA: Embracing Change," *Department of State Dispatch* 4, no. 37 (13 September 1993): 1.
17. Simon Tisdall, "Clinton Turns Belatedly to NAFTA's Aid," *Manchester Guardian*, 15 September 1993: 9.
18. Miguel Ángel Valverde, *The Institutional Setting of the NAFTA Debate in the United States* (Mexico City: Centro de Investigación y Docencia Económicas, 1997), 19.
19. Golden, "U.S. and Mexico Spar," 3.

20. Mary McGrory, "The Human Rights Trade-off," *Washington Post*, 18 November 1993: A2.
21. *Ibid.*
22. Golden, "U.S. and Mexico Spar," 3.
23. Todd Robberson, "In Mexico, Gore Stresses Goal of Democracy," *Washington Post*, 2 December 1993: A37.
24. Georges Fauriol, discussion with the author, 29 February 1996.
25. Marie Claire Acosta, interview with the author, 14 March 1996.
26. "News Conference Concerning NAFTA with Various Anti-NAFTA Groups," National Press Club, Washington, DC, 18 November 1993, 1.
27. Denise Dresser, "Treading Lightly and without a Stick: International Actors and the Promotion of Democracy in Mexico" (paper presented at the XVIII International Congress of the Latin American Studies Association, Atlanta, Georgia, 11 March 1994, draft mimeograph), 36.

Chapter 6

1. K. Larry Storrs, "Mexican Difficulties in 1994: Uprising in Chiapas, Assassination of Colosio," *Congressional Research Service Issue Brief* (Washington, DC: Congressional Research Service, June 21, 1994), 2.
2. Andrés Oppenheimer, *Bordering on Chaos: Guerrillas, Stockbrokers, Politicians and Mexico's Road to Prosperity* (Boston: Little, Brown, and Company, 1996), 31.
3. Richard Feinberg, interview with the author, 8 May 1996.
4. As quoted in Oppenheimer, *Bordering on Chaos*, 31.
5. *Ibid.*
6. Theodore Wilkinson, telephone interview with the author, 16 December 1996.
7. U.S. State Department, "Press Briefing," Washington, DC, 25 January 1994, 1.
8. House Committee on Foreign Affairs, Subcommittee on Western Hemisphere Affairs, *Mexico: The Uprising in Chiapas and Democratization in Mexico*, 103rd Congress, 2d sess., 2 February 1994, 1.
9. *Ibid.*
10. Bill Spencer, discussion with the author, 29 June 1995.
11. *Ibid.*
12. Denise Dresser, "Treading Lightly and without a Stick: International Actors and the Promotion of Democracy in Mexico" (paper presented at the XVII International Congress of the Latin American Studies Association, Atlanta, Georgia, 11 March 1994), 35.
13. House Committee, *Mexico: The Uprising in Chiapas*, 15–16.
14. *Ibid.*, 25.
15. *Ibid.*, 29.
16. *Ibid.*, 30.
17. *Ibid.*, 43–44.
18. *Ibid.*, 13.
19. *Ibid.*, 104.
20. Jorge Castañeda, interview by David Welna, *National Public Radio, Morning Edition*, Public Broadcasting System, 2 February 1994.

21. House Committee, *Mexico: The Uprising in Chiapas*, 102–3.
22. Dresser, "Treading Lightly," 34.
23. Jim Wagner, interview with the author, 2 November 1995.
24. Ann MacDonald, interview with the author, 19 January 1996.
25. Other observers questioned the invitation of Peru as a democratic nation to the summit.
26. Feinberg interview, 8 May 1996.
27. "Miami Congressional Workshop Features Heated Discussions on Haiti, NAFTA and Cuba," *Business Wire*, Miami Chamber of Commerce, 14 January 1994: 1.
28. House Committee, *Mexico: The Uprising in Chiapas*, 10.
29. Michael Shifter, interview with the author, 1 May 1996.
30. Norma Parker, interview with the author, 1 March 1996.
31. Santiago Canton, interview with the author, 20 February 1996.
32. John Goshko, "Clinton Strongly Affirms Confidence in Stability of Mexican Government," *Washington Post*, 25 March 1994: A14.
33. *Ibid.*
34. Human Rights Watch/Americas, *Mexico at the Crossroads: Political Rights and the 1994 Presidential and Congressional Elections*, Vol. VI, no. 9 (Washington, DC: Human Rights Watch, August 1994): 22.
35. U.S. Department of State, "Daily Press Briefing," Washington, DC, 6 May 1996, 7.
36. Human Rights Watch/Americas, *Mexico at the Crossroads*, 23.
37. "Jones: Trabajaría EU Con Gobierno de Oposición," *El Porvenir*, 7 April 1994: 1.
38. John MacCormack and Carmina Danini, "Mexico Importing Riot-Control Vehicles," *San Antonio Express-News*, 27 April 1994: 1.
39. Human Rights Watch/Americas, *Mexico at the Crossroads*, 24.
40. Representative David Bonior, "Remarks by Congressman David E. Bonior," press conference, U.S. House of Representatives, Washington, DC, 17 May 1994, 1.
41. House Committee on Foreign Affairs, Subcommittee on Western Hemisphere Affairs, "Opening Statement of Chairman Robert C. Torricelli: Hearing on Electoral Reform in Mexico," Washington, DC, 20 April 1994, 2.
42. This account was provided by an anonymous participant.
43. Tim Golden, "Christopher Presses Mexico to Insure Its Election Is Fair," *New York Times*, 10 May 1994: A2.
44. U.S. State Department, "Secretary Christopher: A New Consensus of the Americas," *State Department Dispatch*, Washington, DC, 9 July 1994: 3.
45. Golden, "Christopher Presses Mexico," A3.
46. Juanita Darling and Doyle McManus, "U.S. Cautions Mexico against Election Fraud," *Los Angeles Times*, Washington edition, 10 May 1994: 7.
47. Golden, "Christopher Presses Mexico," A2.
48. Jared Kotler, *The Clinton Administration and the Mexican Elections* (Albuquerque, NM: Resource Center Press, December 1994), 9.
49. Adolfo Aguilar Zinzer, interview with the author, 22 July 1992.
50. Jane Thiery, interview with the author, 3 December 1996.
51. Representative David Bonior, "Bonior and Torricelli Introduce Resolution Supporting Democratic Reforms in Mexico," press release, Washington, DC, 17 May 1996, 1.

52. *Ibid.*
53. Thiery interview, 3 December 1996.
54. "Declaración Politica," Poder Legislativo Federal, Camara de Diputados, México D.F., 23 May 1994, 1 (author translation).
55. U.S. Senate, Letter to Secretary of State Warren Christopher, Washington, DC, 28 June 1994.
56. Canton interview, 20 February 1996.
57. Parker interview, 1 March 1996.
58. Joanna Mendelson, interview with the author, 1 March 1996.
59. Parker interview, 1 March 1996.
60. Parker and Mendelson interviews, 1 March 1996.
61. Parker interview, 1 March 1996.
62. Janine Perfit, interview with the author, 22 January 1996.
63. Canton interview, 20 February 1996.
64. M. Delal Baer, "Observing the Mexican Observers," *Wall Street Journal*, 3 June 1994: A15.
65. Ricardo Pascoe, interview with the author, 14 March 1996.
66. Richard Seld, "Mexico's TV Debate Lets the Public Join In," *Christian Science Monitor*, 20 May 1994: 14.
67. The following details were provided by an anonymous interviewee.
68. Letter from Speaker Gingrich and House Republicans to President William J. Clinton, Washington, DC, 4 August 1994.
69. Jim Cason and David Brooks, "Alertan a Clinton Sobre una Eventual Coalición PRI-PRD," *La Jornada*, 20 August 1994: 30.
70. Based on a confidential cable two weeks before the election. Oppenheimer, *Bordering on Chaos*, 161.
71. Pascoe interview, 14 March 1996.
72. Thiery interview, 3 December 1996.
73. House Committee on Foreign Affairs, Subcommittee on Western Hemisphere Affairs, "Opening Statement of Robert Torricelli at Markup of H. Con. Res. 250, Electoral Reform in Mexico," Washington, DC, 14 July 1994, 2.
74. "Boletín de Prensa," Embassy of Mexico, Washington, DC, 3 August 1994.
75. Thiery interview, 3 December 1996.
76. Oppenheimer, *Bordering on Chaos*, 160.
77. U.S. State Department, Letter from Wendy Sherman, Assistant Secretary of State for Legislative Affairs to Senator Ben Nighthorse Campbell, 19 July 1994, 3.
78. House Committee, *Mexico: The Uprising in Chiapas*, 13.
79. Jerry Hagstrom, "Mexican Revolution?" *National Journal*, 23 July 1994: 1738.
80. "How Clean in Mexico?" *New York Times*, 20 August 1994: A19.
81. Perfit interview, 22 January 1996.
82. As quoted in Kotler, *The Clinton Administration and the Mexican Elections*, 21.
83. Canton interview, 20 February 1996.
84. Kotler, *The Clinton Administration and the Mexican Elections*, i.
85. *Ibid.*, 6.
86. Office of the President, Office of the Press Secretary, "Statement by the Press Secretary: Mexican Presidential Elections," Washington, DC, 24 August 1994, 1.

87. U.S. Embassy, "Statement by U.S. Ambassador James R. Jones," undated (August 1994).
88. Mendleson and Parker interviews, 1 March 1996.
89. National Democratic Institute for International Affairs (NDI) and International Republican Institute (IRI), "Preliminary Statement by the IRI/NDI International Delegation to the August 21 Mexican Elections," Washington, DC, 23 August 1996, mimeographed, 2.
90. *Ibid.*, 5.
91. Kotler, *The Clinton Administration and the Mexican Elections*, 16.
92. Feinberg interview, 8 May 1996.
93. *Ibid.*
94. Shifter interview, 1 May 1996.
95. *Ibid.*
96. MacDonald interview, 19 January 1996.
97. *Ibid.*
98. Sara Donnelly, interview with the author, 14 November 1995.
99. Art Danart, interview with the author, 14 November 1995.
100. Key political appointees played important roles: Arturo Valenzuela at the State Department, Norma Parker and Joanna Mendelson at USAID, and Ambassador Jones.
101. Canton interview, 20 February 1996.
102. David Beall, interview with the author, 7 January 1997.

Chapter 7

1. Stephan Haggard and Robert R. Kaufman, *The Political Economy of Democratic Transitions* (Princeton, NJ: Princeton University Press, 1995), 305.
2. Edward Smith, telephone interview with the author, 9 August 1996.
3. Rogelio Ramierez de la O., "The Mexican Peso Crisis and Recession of 1994–95: Preventable Then, Avoidable in the Future?" in Riordan Roett, ed., *The Mexican Peso Crisis: International Perspectives* (Boulder: Lynne Rienner Publishers, 1996), 11.
4. Manuel Pastor, Jr., "Pesos, Policies, and Predictions: Why the Crisis—and Why the Surprise?" in Carol Wise, ed., *The Post-NAFTA Political Economy: Mexico and the Western Hemisphere* (Baltimore: Johns Hopkins University Press, 1999), 2.
5. Nora Lustig, "The Mexican Peso Crisis: The Foreseeable and the Surprise," *Brookings Discussion Papers in International Economics* (June 1995): 11.
6. Manuel Pastor, Jr., "Pesos, Policies, and Predictions," 19. This conclusion also builds on the work of Pastor and Wise, "The Origins and Sustainability of Mexico's Free Trade Policy."
7. See Denise Dresser, "Mexico: The Decline of Dominant Party Rule," in Abraham F. Lowenthal and Jorge Domínguez, eds., *Challenges to Democratic Governance in Latin America* (Baltimore: Johns Hopkins University Press, 1996).
8. Andrés Oppenheimer, *Bordering on Chaos: Guerrillas, Stockbrokers, Politicians, and Mexico's Road to Prosperity* (Boston: Little, Brown, and Company, 1996), 217–218.

9. Anthony De Palma, "Mexican President Outlines Rescue Plan," *New York Times*, 30 December 1994: D1.

10. "Clinton Bypasses Hill on Peso Rescue," *Washington Post*, 1 February 1995: A1.

11. Office of the President, "Statement with Congressional Leaders on the Economic Situation in Mexico," press release, 12 January 1995.

12. "Democratic Leader Seeks Mexico Conditions," *Reuter European Business Report*, 17 January 1995: 1.

13. *Ibid.*

14. "The Mexican Peso Crisis; Critics Fear Plunge in Currency Likely to Turn Country into an Export Machine," *Star Tribune* (Detroit), 24 January 1995, Metro section: 1.

15. David Sanger, "Mexico Crisis Seen Spurring Flow of Aliens," *New York Times*, 18 January 1995: 3.

16. U.S. House, "Opposition to Loan Guarantees to Mexico," *Federal News Service*, news conference, 18 January 1995, 1.

17. *Ibid.*

18. Sanger, "Mexico Crisis," *New York Times*, 18 January 1995: 3.

19. Janice O'Connell, interview with the author, 8 July 1996.

20. U.S. House/Senate staff, "Commitments (Additions to draft of 1/14/95)," unofficial draft congressional document, undated.

21. Dan Fisk, notes of meeting, 16 January 1995.

22. Dan Fisk, telephone interview with the author, 23 August 1996.

23. Fisk notes of meeting, 16 January 1995.

24. Jeffrey Shafer, interview with the author, 31 January 1997.

25. Fisk, notes of meeting, 16 January 1995.

26. U.S. Senate, Committee on Foreign Relations, *Mexico's Economic Situation and the U.S. Efforts to Stabilize the Peso*, Hearing before the Senate Committee on Foreign Relations, 104th Congress, 1st sess., 26 January 1995, 57.

27. Dan Fisk, memorandum to Senator Jesse Helms, 17 January 1995, 1.

28. James A. Leach, letter to the Honorable Robert E. Rubin, 17 January 1996, 4.

29. "Talks on Aid Drawing Ire in Mexico; Zedillo Is Pressed to Detail U.S. Terms," *Washington Post*, 28 January 1995: A22.

30. Matt Benson, interview with the author, 18 March 1997.

31. U.S. House/Senate staff, "H.R.____," discussion draft, 30 January, 2:30 p.m., 5.

32. Jamie McCormick, telephone interview with the author, 29 August 1996.

33. Benson interview, 18 March 1977.

34. Michael Treisman, telephone interview with the author, 27 August 1996.

35. U.S. House/Senate staff, "H.R.____," discussion draft, 24 January 1995, 9 A.M., 17.

36. As quoted in Riordan Roett, ed., *The Mexican Peso Crisis: International Perspectives* (Boulder, CO: Lynne Rienner Publishers, 1996), 36.

37. Sanger, "Mexico Crisis," 3.

38. U.S. Senate, *Mexico's Economic Situation*, 26 January 1995, 57.

39. White House, "Mexico Fact Sheet," undated.

40. U.S. Senate, Committee on Foreign Relations, "Prepared Statement of Ernest Hollings," Hearing before Senate Foreign Relations Committee, 104th Congress, 1st sess., 26 January 1996, 1.

41. Denise Dresser, "Post-NAFTA Politics in Mexico: Uneasy, Uncertain, Unpredictable," in Carol Wise, ed., *The Post-NAFTA Political Economy: Mexico and the Western Hemisphere*, 43.
42. "Talks on Aid Drawing Ire," A22.
43. George Graham, "Mexican Rescue: Bitter Legacy of Battle to Bail Out Mexico," *Financial Times*, 16 February 1995: 4.
44. McCormick interview, 29 August 1996.
45. *Ibid.*
46. U.S. House/Senate staff, "H.R.____," discussion draft, 30 January 1995, 2:30 P.M., 17.
47. *Ibid.*, 24–25.
48. *Ibid.*, 5.
49. Shafer interview, 31 January 1997.
50. *Ibid.*
51. McCormick interview, 29 August 1996.
52. *Ibid.*
53. Graham, "Mexican Rescue," 4.
54. Oppenheimer, *Bordering on Chaos*, 218–219.
55. *Ibid.*
56. Shafer interview, 31 January 1997.
57. *Ibid.*
58. McCormick interview, 29 August 1996.
59. U.S. Senate, Committee on Banking, Housing, and Urban Affairs, *The Mexican Peso Crisis*, Hearings before the Committee on Banking, Housing, and Urban Affairs, 104th Congress, 1st sess., Report to the Senate Banking Committee, 24 May 1995, 474.
60. U.S. House, *Economic Support for Mexico*, 7 March 1995, 6.
61. *Ibid.*, 7.
62. *Ibid.*, 10.
63. U. S. Senate, *The Mexican Peso Crisis*, 386.
64. *Ibid.*, 350.
65. Oppenheimer, *Bordering on Chaos*, 268.
66. Wayne Cornelius, "Between the Center, the Periphery, and a Hard Place" (comments at the XX International Congress of the Latin American Studies Association, Guadalajara, Mexico, 19 April 1997).
67. U.S. State Department, *Mexico: Human Rights Practices: 1995* (Washington, DC, March 1996), 2.
68. Dennis Hayes, interview with the author, 22 December 1995.
69. U.S. House, *Economic Support for Mexico*, 11.
70. Dresser, "Post-NAFTA Politics," 7–8.
71. Haggard and Kaufman, *Political Economy of Democratic Transitions*, 268.
72. David Sanger, "Upbeat White House Visit for the President of Mexico," *New York Times*, 11 October 1995: A10.
73. U.S. Senate, Committee on Finance, *Nominations of Joseph H. Gale, Darcy E. Bradbury, Jeffrey R. Shafer, David Lipton, Melissa T. Skolfield, and David Williams*, Hearing before the Senate Finance Committee, 104th Congress, 1st sess., 30 November 1995, 18–19.

Chapter 8

1. Dennis Hayes, interview with the author, 22 December 1995.
2. Exceptions include statements around the Chiapas conflict and murder of DEA agent Camarena.
3. T. Frank Crigler, telephone interview with the author, 29 August 1996.
4. Hayes interview, 22 December 1995.
5. *Freedom in the World,* various issues from 1980 to 1998–1999, Freedom House, NY.
6. An exception being a group of political appointees around CIA Director Casey in the early 1980s.
7. What was found surprisingly among some in the minority was a similar belief against public criticism of Mexican politics. This partly explains why the mention of Mexican internal politics faded once the pressing vote or policy conflict passed.
8. Active encouragement included that by PAN officials in the 1980s and Mexican intellectuals during the NAFTA debate. There was active discouragement of U.S. action during the same NAFTA period and towards congressional resolutions in the 1990s by some nongovernmental organizations and Mexican opposition leaders.
9. Ricardo Pascoe, interview with the author, 14 March 1996.
10. Ambassador John Gavin, telephone interview with the author, 30 December 1996.
11. Joseph Manzo, interview with the author, 8 July 1997.
12. Marie Claire Acosta, interview with the author, 14 March 1996.
13. Acosta interview, 14 March 1996. Similar comments were made by Sergio Aguayo, interview with the author, 9 July 1997, and Ricardo Pascoe, interview with the author, 14 March 1996.
14. The exception being 1988, when officials such as Elliot Abrams maintained that the United States might have destabilized the government by saying the election was stolen.
15. John Negroponte, interview with the author, 30 May 1997.
16. Elliot Abrams, interview with the author, 4 October 1996.
17. The first two of these assumptions appear commonly in academic literature. See Robert Pastor, "Post-Revolutionary Mexico: The Salinas Opening," *Journal of Interamerican Studies and World Affairs* 32, no. 3 (Fall 1990): 19.
18. Norma Parker, interview with the author, 1 March 1996.
19. Abrams interview, 4 October 1996.
20. As noted in Chapter 4, Mexican analysts have pointed to the Salinas administration's decision to appoint a Human Rights Commission and to replace governors elected in San Luis Potosí and Guanajuato in response to fraud charges.
21. *Systematic Injustice: Torture, "Disappearance," and Extrajudicial Execution in Mexico* (Washington, DC: Human Rights Watch, January 1999, 116.
22. Quoted in Andres Oppenheimer, *Bordering on Chaos: Guerrillas, Stockbrokers, Politicians, and Mexico's Road to Prosperity* (Boston, MA: Little, Brown, and Company, 1996), 10.
23. Richard Feinberg, interview with the author, 8 May 1996.
24. Jerry Hagstrom, "Mexican Revolution?," *National Journal,* 23 July 1994: 1742.

25. Tim Golden, "Misreading Mexico: How Washington Stumbled—A Special Report: Mexico and Drugs; Was U.S. Napping?" *New York Times,* 11 July 1997: 1.
26. Hayes interview, 22 December 1995.
27. Bernard Aronson, interview with the author, 1 July 1997.
28. Abrams interview, 4 October 1996.
29. George High, interview with the author, 8 June 1996.
30. Abraham Lowenthal, ed., *Exporting Democracy: The United States and Latin America* (Baltimore: Johns Hopkins University Press, 1991), 400.
31. Judith Gentleman and Voytek Zubek, "International Integration and Democratic Development: The Cases of Poland and Mexico," *Journal of Interamerican Studies and World Affairs* 34, no. 1 (Spring 1992): 83.
32. Sergio Aguayo, "Mexico in the United States Press, 1946–1997" (paper presented to the conference on "Press Coverage of Mexico and the United States," National Press Club, Washington, DC, 3 October 1997), 21.
33. Abrams interview, 4 October 1996, and Aronson interview, 1 July 1997.
34. Feinberg interview, 8 May 1996.

Bibliography

Books, Articles, Dissertations, and Papers

Aguayo, Sergio. "Mexico in the United States Press, 1946–1997." Paper delivered at the conference "Press Coverage of Mexico and the United States," National Press Club, Washington, DC, 3 October 1997.

Aguilar, Héctor Camín, and Lorenzo Meyer. *In the Shadow of the Mexican Revolution.* Austin: University of Texas Press, 1993.

Alemán Alemán, Ricardo. *Guanajuato-Espejismo Electoral.* México, D.F.: La Jornada Ediciones, 1993.

Amnesty International. *Mexico: Torture with Impunity.* New York: Amnesty International Publications, September 1991.

Anderson, Jack, and Dale Van Atta. "The Mexican Time Bomb." *Penthouse,* May 1987: 42.

Astié-Burgos, Walter. *El Águila Bicéfala: Las Relaciones México–Estados Unidos a Través de la Experiencia Diplomática.* México, D.F.: Ariel-Divulgación, April 1995.

Baer, M. Delal, and Sidney Weintraub. *The NAFTA Debate: Grappling with Unconventional Trade Issues.* Boulder, CO: Lynne Rienner Publishers, 1992.

Bagley, Bruce Michael. "Interdependence and U.S. Policy toward Mexico in the 1980s," in Riordan Roett, ed., *Mexico and the United States: Managing the Relationship.* Boulder, CO: Westview Press, 1988.

Bagley, Bruce Michael, and Sergio Aguayo Quezada, eds. *Mexico: In Search of Security.* Miami, FL: University of Miami, North-South Center, 1993.

Bailey, John. *Governing Mexico: The Statecraft of Crisis Management.* New York: St. Martin's Press, 1988.

Bailey, John, and Arturo Valenzuela. "The Shape of the Future." *Journal of Democracy* 8, no. 4 (October 1999): 41–57.

Barry, Tom, Harry Browne, and Beth Sims. *The Great Divide: the Challenge of U.S.-Mexico Relations in the 1990s.* New York: Grove Press, 1994.

Bilello, Suzanne. "La Prensa Extranjera y las Elecciones en Chihuahua, Julio de 1986," in Gerardo Bueno, ed., *México–Estados Unidos, 1986*, México, D.F.: El Colegio de México, 1987, 163.

Brinkley, Douglas. "Democratic Enlargement: The Clinton Doctrine." *Foreign Policy* 10 (Spring 1997): 111–127.

Bueno, Gerardo M., ed. *Mexico–Estados Unidos, 1986*. Mexico, D.F.: El Colegio de México, 1987.

Camín, Héctor Aguilar, and Lorenzo Meyer. *In the Shadow of the Mexican Revolution: Contemporary Mexican History: 1910–1989*. Austin: University of Texas Press, 1993.

Carothers, Thomas. "Democracy Promotion under Clinton." *The Washington Quarterly* 18, no. 4 (Autumn 1995): 13–25.

———. *In the Name of Democracy: U.S. Policy toward Latin America in the Reagan Years*. Berkeley: University of California Press, 1991.

Castañeda, Jorge G. "The Clouding Political Horizon." *Current History* 92 (February 1993): 64–70.

———. "Salinas's International Relations Gamble." *Journal of International Affairs* 43, no. 2 (Winter 1990): 407–422.

Centeno, Miguel Angel. *Democracy within Reason: Technocratic Revolution in Mexico*. University Park: Pennsylvania State University Press, 1994.

Chabat, Jorge. "Mexico's Foreign Policy in 1990: Electoral Sovereignty and Integration with the United States." *Journal of Interamerican Studies and World Affairs* 33, no. 4 (Winter 1991): 1–25.

Cohn, Elizabeth. "Idealpolitik in U.S. Foreign Policy: The Reagan Administration and the U.S. Promotion of Democracy." Ph.D. dissertation, American University, 1995.

Cook, Maria Lorena, Kevin J. Middlebrook, and Juan Molinar Horcasitas, eds. *The Politics of Economic Restructuring; State-Society Relations and Regime Change in Mexico*. San Diego: Center for U.S.–Mexican Studies, 1994.

Cornelius, Wayne. "Las Relacciones de Estados Unidos Con México: Fuentes de Su Deterioro: 1986–87." *Foro Internaciónal* XXIX, 2 (1988): 213.

———. "Between the Center, the Periphery, and a Hard Place." Comments delivered at the Twentieth International Conference of the Latin American Studies Association, Guadalajara, Mexico, 19 April 1997.

Cornelius, Wayne, Ann Craig, and Jonathon Fox. *Transforming State-Society Relations in Mexico: The National Solidarity Strategy*. San Diego: Center for U.S.–Mexican Studies, 1994.

Cornelius, Wayne, Judith Gentleman, and Peter H. Smith, eds. *Mexico's Alternative Political Futures*. La Jolla: Center for U.S.–Mexican Studies, 1989.

Dent, David W. *U.S.–Latin American Policymaking: A Reference Handbook*. Westport, CT: Greenwood Press, 1995.

Diamond, Larry. *Promoting Democracy in the 1990s: Actors and Instruments, Issues and Imperatives*. A report to the Carnegie Corporation of New York, December 1995.

Diamond, Larry, Juan J. Linz, and Seymour Martin Lipset, eds. *Democracy in Developing Countries: Volume 4, Latin America.* Boulder, CO: Lynne Rienner Publishers, 1989.

———. *Politics in Developing Countries: Comparing Experiences with Democracy.* Boulder, CO: Lynne Rienner Publishers, 1995.

Domínguez, Jorge I. "Introduction," in Jorge Domínguez, ed., *Mexico's Political Economy: Challenge at Home and Abroad.* Beverly Hills, CA: Sage Publications, 1982, 13–14.

———. *Mexico's Political Economy: Challenges at Home and Abroad.* Beverly Hills, CA: Sage Publications, 1982.

Dornbush, Rudiger, and Alejandro Werner. "Mexico: Stabilization, Reform, and No Growth." *Brookings Papers on Economic Activity* 1 (1994): 253–315.

Dresser, Denise. "Mr. Salinas Goes to Washington." Paper delivered at the conference "Crossing National Borders: Invasion or Involvement," Columbia University, New York, NY, 6 December 1991.

———. *Neopopulist Solutions to Neoliberal Problems: Mexico's National Solidarity Program.* La Jolla: Center for U.S.–Mexican Studies, 1991.

———. "Treading Lightly and without a Big Stick: International Actors and the Promotion of Democracy in Mexico." Paper presented the Nineteenth International Conference of the Latin American Studies Association, Washington, DC, 30 September 1995.

———. "Exporting Conflict," in Abraham Lowenthal and Katrina Burgess, eds., *The California-Mexico Connection.* Stanford: Stanford University Press, 1993, 90.

———. "Mexico: The Decline of Dominant Party Rule," in Abraham F. Lowenthal and Jorge Domínguez, eds., *Challenges to Democratic Governance in Latin America.* Baltimore: Johns Hopkins University Press, 1996.

———. "Post-NAFTA Politics in Mexico: Uneasy, Uncertain, Unpredictable," in Carol Wise, ed., *The Post-NAFTA Political Economy: Mexico and the Western Hemisphere,* University Park: Pennsylvania State University Press, 1993, 43.

"Enders Plans for Freedom and Free Enterprise in the Caribbean." *Latin American Newsletters,* 19 June 1981: 1.

Farer, Tom, ed. *Beyond Sovereignity: Collectively Defending Democracy in the Americas.* Baltimore: Johns Hopkins University Press, 1996.

Fauriol, Georges. "The Shadow of Latin American Affairs." *Foreign Affairs* 69, no. 1 (1989/90): 116–134.

Freedom in the World, various issues from 1980 to 1998–1999. Freedom House, NY.

Garfinkle, Adam. *The Devil and Uncle Sam: A User's Guide to the Friendly Tyrants Dilemma.* New Brunswick, NJ: Transactions Publishers, 1992.

Gentleman, Judith, and Voytek Zubek. "International Integration and Democratic Development: The Cases of Poland and Mexico." *Journal of Interamerican Studies and World Affairs* 34, no. 1 (Spring 1992): 59–97.

George, Alexander. "The 'Operational Code': A Neglected Approach to the Study of Political Leaders and Decision-Making." *International Studies Quarterly* 13, no. 2 (June 1989): 190–222.

Goldman, Ralph, and William Douglas. *Promoting Democracy: Opportunities and Issues.* New York: Praeger Publishers, 1988.

Gonzáles, Juan J. "El Viaje de Miguel de la Madrid a Washington." *Cartas de Politica Exterior Mexicana* 6, no. 3 (July-September 1986): 22–34.

Gonzáles, Juan J., Yolanda Muñoz, Georgina Núñez, and Priscila Sosa. "El Impacto de Las Audiencias Helms en la Relación Bilateral." *Cartas de Politica Exterior Mexicana* 6, no. 2 (April–June 1986): 5–19.

Guitíerrez, Carlos Gonzales. *Mexico en el Congreso Estadounidense: Coaliciones y Alineamientos (1981–1986).* México D.F.: El Colegio de México, 1987.

———. "El Papel del Congreso Estadounidense en las Relacciones Bilaterales," in Gerardo Bueno, ed. *Mexico-Estados Unidos 1986.* México D.F.: El Colegio de México, 1987.

Haggard, Stephan, and Robert R. Kaufman, *The Political Economy of Democratic Transitions.* Princeton, NJ: Princeton University Press, 1995, 305.

Hagstrom, Jerry. "Mexican Revolution?" *National Journal* (23 July 1994): 1738–1742.

Hollings, Ernest. "Reform Mexico First." *Foreign Policy* 93 (1993–1994).

Horton, Frank. "Mexico, The Way of Iran?" *Journal of Intelligence and Counterintelligence* 1, no. 2 (1986): 91–92.

Hunt, Michael H. *Ideology and U.S. Foreign Policy.* New Haven, CT: Yale University Press, 1987.

Huntington, Samuel P. *The Third Wave: Democratization in the Late Twentieth Century.* Norman: University of Oklahoma Press, 1991.

Implausible Deniability: State Responsibility for Rural Violence in Mexico. Washington, DC: Human Rights Watch, April 1997.

Kotler, Jared. *The Clinton Administration and the Mexican Elections.* Albuquerque, NM: Resource Center Press, December 1994.

Krasner, Stephan D. *Defending the National Interest: Raw Materials Investments and U.S. Foreign Policy.* Princeton, NJ: Princeton University Press, 1978.

Leites, Nathan. *A Study of Bolshevism.* Glencoe, IL: The Free Press, 1953.

Linz, Juan J. *The Breakdown of Democratic Regimes: Crisis, Breakdown and Reequilibration.* Baltimore: Johns Hopkins University Press, 1978.

Lowenthal, Abraham, ed. *Exporting Democracy: The United States and Latin America.* Baltimore: Johns Hopkins University Press, 1991, 399.

Lowenthal, Abraham, and Katrina Burgess, eds. *The California-Mexico Connection.* Stanford, CA: Stanford University Press, 1993.

Lustig, Nora. "The Mexican Peso Crisis: The Foreseeable and the Surprise." *Brookings Discussion Papers in International Economics* (June 1995): 11–32.

Lutz, Ellen. "Human Rights Concerns in Mexico," *Current History* 92, no. 571 (1993): 79.

Maxwell, Kenneth. "The Thorns of the Portuguese Revolution." *Foreign Affairs* 54, no. 2 (January 1976): 250–270.

Menges, Constantine C. *Inside the National Security Council: The True Story of the Making and Unmaking of Reagan's Foreign Policy.* New York: Simon and Schuster, 1988.

———. *Mexican Actions in Central America: Time for a Positive Change.* Washington, DC: American Enterprise Institute, Studies in International Policy, 1989.

Mexico at the Crossroads: Political Rights and the 1994 Presidential and Congressional Elections. Washington, DC: Human Rights Watch/Americas Watch, August 1994.

Meyer, Lorenzo. *La Segunda Muerte de la Revolución Mexicana.* México, D.F.: Cal y Arena, 1992.

———. "The United States and Mexico: The Historical Structure of their Conflict." *Journal of International Affairs* 43, 2 (Winter 1990): 251–271.

Meyer, Lorenzo. "Mexico: The Exception and the Rule," in Abraham Lowenthal, ed., *Exporting Democracy: The United States and Latin America.* Baltimore: Johns Hopkins University Press, 1991, 228.

———. "Democratization of the PRI: Mission Impossible?" in Wayne Cornelius, Judith Gentleman, and Peter Smith, eds., *Mexico's Alternative Political Futures.* La Jolla: Center for U.S.-Mexican Studies, 1989.

Morris, Stephan D. "Political Reformism in Mexico: Salinas at the Brink." *Journal of Interamerican Studies and World Affairs* 34, no. 1 (Spring 1992): 27–57.

Muravchik, Joshua. *Exporting Democracy: Fulfilling America's Destiny.* Washington, DC: American Enterprise Institute, 1991.

National Democratic Institute for International Affairs and International Republican Institute for International Affairs. "Preliminary Statement by the IRI/NDI International Delegation to the August 21 Mexican Elections." Washington, DC, 23 August 1996, mimeograph.

Oppenheimer, Andrés. *Bordering on Chaos: Guerrillas, Stockbrokers, Politicians, and Mexico's Road to Prosperity.* Boston: Little, Brown, 1996.

Orme, William, Jr. *Continental Shift: Free Trade and the New North America.* Washington, DC: Washington Post Company, 1993.

Osgood, Robert. *Ideals and Self-Interest in America's Foreign Relations: The Great Transformation of the Twentieth Century.* Chicago: University of Chicago Press, 1953.

Packenham, Robert A. *Liberal America and the Third World: Political Development Ideas in Foreign Aid and Social Science.* Princeton, NJ: Princeton University Press, 1973.

Pastor, Manuel, Jr. "Mexican Trade Liberalization and NAFTA." *Latin American Research Review* 29, no. 3 (1994): 153–173.

Pastor, Manuel, Jr., and Carol Wise. "The Origins and Sustainability of Mexico's Free Trade Policy." *International Organization* 48, no. 3 (1994): 459–489.

Pastor, Robert. "Post-Revolutionary Mexico: The Salinas Opening." *Journal of Interamerican Studies and World Affairs* 33, no. 4 (Fall 1990): 1–16.

Pastor, Robert, and Jorge G. Castañeda. *Limits to Friendship: The United States and Mexico.* New York: Vintage Books, 1991.

Pastor, Robert, and Rafael Fernandez de Castro, eds. *The Controversial Pivot: The U.S. Congress and North America.* Washington, DC: Brookings Institution Press, 1999.

A Policy of Impunity. Washington, DC: Human Rights Watch, 1990, 1.

Pridham, Geoffrey, ed. *Encouraging Democracy: The International Context of Regime Transition in Southern Europe.* Leicester, England: Leicester University Press, 1991.

Purcell, Susan Kaufman. "Mexico-U.S. Relations: Big Initiatives Cause Big Problems." *Foreign Affairs* 60, no. 2 (Winter 1981/82).

Ramíerez, Carlos. *Operación Gavin: México en la Diplomacia de Reagan.* México, D.F.: Sociedad Cooperativa, August 1987.

Reding, Andrew. "Mexico: The Crumbling of the 'Perfect Dictatorship.'" *World Policy Journal* 8, no.2 (Spring 1991): 255–283.

Riding, Alan. *Distant Neighbors: A Portrait of the Mexicans.* New York: Vintage Books, 1985.

Roett, Riordan, ed. *The Mexican Peso Crisis: International Perspectives.* Boulder, CO: Lynne Rienner Publishers, 1996.

———. *Mexico's External Relations in the 1990s.* Boulder, CO: Lynne Rienner Publishers, 1991.

———. *Political and Economic Liberalization in Mexico: At a Critical Juncture?* Boulder, CO: Lynne Rienner Publishers, 1993.

Sample Documents Related to Latin America. Washington, DC: National Security Archives, August 1986.

Sims, Beth. *Foreign Support for the Mexican Democratization Process: Focus on the U.S. Agency for International Development and the National Endowment for Democracy.* Albuquerque, NM: Resource Center Press, 1993.

Smith, Peter H. "The Political Impact of Free Trade on Mexico." *Journal of Interamerican Studies and World Affairs* 34, no. 1 (Spring 1992): 1–25.

Smith, Tony. *America's Mission: The United States and the Worldwide Struggle for Democracy.* Princeton, NJ: Princeton University Press, 1994.

Systematic Injustice: Torture, "Disppearance," and Extrajudicial Execution in Mexico. Washington, DC: Human Rights Watch, January 1999.

Thorup, Cathryn Lynn. "Managing Extreme Interdependence: Alternative Institutional Arrangements for U.S. Policymaking toward Mexico: 1976–1988." Ph.D. dissertation, Harvard University, 1992.

———. "México-EU: La Democratización y la Agenda Bilateral." *Nexos* 14 (June 1990): 57–60.

———. "The Politics of Free Trade and the Dynamics of Cross-Border Coalitions in U.S.-Mexican Relations." *Columbia Journal of World Business* 26, no. 11 (Summer 1991): 12–25.

Torres, Blanca. "La Visíon Estadounidense de las Elecciones de 1985: ¿Presíon de

Coyuntura o Preoccupación de Largo Plazo?" in Gabriel Székely, ed., *México–Estados Unidos, 1985*. México, D.F.: El Colegio de México, 1986, 59.

Valverde, Miguel Ángel. *The Institutional Setting of the NAFTA Debate in the United States*. Mexico City: Centro de Investigación y Docencia Económicas, 1997.

Vásquez, Josefina Zoraida, and Lorenzo Meyer. *The United States and Mexico*. Chicago: University of Chicago Press, 1985, 163.

Weintraub, Sidney. *A Marriage of Convenience: Relations between Mexico and the United States*. New York: Oxford University Press, 1990.

Whitehead, Laurence. "International Aspects of Democratization." In Guillermo O'Donnell, Philippe Schmitter, and Laurence Whitehead, eds. *Transitions from Authoritarian Rule: Comparative Perspectives*. Baltimore: Johns Hopkins University Press, 1986.

———. "Mexico and the 'Hegemony' of the United States: Past, Present, and Future," in Riordan Roett, ed., *Mexico's External Relations in the 1990s*. Boulder, CO: Lynne Rienner Publishers, 1991, 246.

Wiarda, Howard. "Mexico: The Unraveling of a Corporatist Regime?" *Journal of Interamerican Studies and World Affairs* 30, no. 4 (Winter 1988–89): 1–28.

———. *Cracks in the Consensus: Debating the Democracy Agenda in U.S. Foreign Policy*. New York: Praeger Publishers, 1997.

Wilson, Michael. *Political Reform in Mexico: Salinas' Other Revolution*. Washington, DC: The Heritage Foundation, 11 October 1991.

Wise, Carol, ed. *The Post-NAFTA Political Economy: Mexico and the Western Hemisphere*. University Park: Pennsylvania State University Press, 1998.

Woodward, Bob. *Veil: The Secret Wars of the CIA: 1981–1987*. New York: Pocket Books, 1988.

Zoellick, Robert. Presentation to a meeting of SAIS-Georgetown Mexico Study Group, Washington, DC, 23 February, 1996.

Periodicals, Newspapers, Radio and TV Broadcasts

Chicago Tribune, 15 May 1985–21 December 1986.

Christian Science Monitor, 6 January 1986–5 December 1990.

Financial Times, 6 June 1984–16 February 1995.

El Financiero, 8 August 1990–28 November 1990.

El Porvenir, 7 April 1994.

La Jornada, 26 July 1992–4 September 1995.

Los Angeles Times, 11 July 1985–13 February 1989.

McNeil-Lehrer Report, 18 June 1986.

Miami Herald, 27 December 1987–14 July 1994.

Newsweek, 3 December 1990.

New York Times, 11 June 1980–18 January 1995.

Notimex, 8 February 1988.

Orange County Register, 25 May 1991–17 June 1992.

Proceso, 13 May 1991.

Reuters, 14 August 1986–17 January 1995.

San Antonio Express-News, 27 April 1994.

San Diego Union-Tribune, 4 July 1989–24 October 1991.

Time, 28 May 1984–19 November 1990.

United Press International, 23 April 1981–28 April 1988.

Wall Street Journal, 3 June 1994.

Washington Post, 18 March 1980–1 February 1995.

Washington Times, 14 February 1995.

U.S. and Mexican Government Documents

Congressional Record. 99th Congress, 2d sess., 1986, Vol. 132: S 7934.

———. 102d Congress, 2d sess., 1991, Vol. 132: S 8753–S 10618.

———. 102d Congress, 2d sess., 1991, Vol. 137: S 6550, H 3517.

Congressional Record–Extension of Remarks, 99th Congress, 2d sess., Vol. 131, no. 105, 31 July 1985: E 3660.

———. 102d Congress, 2d sess., 1991, Vol. 131, no. 105: E 3660.

Congressional Research Service. See Storrs, K. Larry.

D'Amato, Senator Alfonse. *Report on the Mexican Economic Crisis.* Report presented to the Senate Banking Committee, Washington, DC, 29 June 1995.

Embassy of Mexico. "Boletín de Prensa." Washington, DC, 3 August 1994.

Office of the President. "Statement with Congressional Leaders on the Economic Situation in Mexico." Washington, DC, 12 January 1995.

Office of the President, Office of the Press Secretary. "Statement by the Press Secretary: Mexican Presidential Elections." Washington, DC, 24 August 1994.

Poder Legislativo Federal, Camara de Diputados. "Declaración Politica." México, D.F., 23 May 1994.

Reagan, Ronald. "Promoting Democracy and Peace: Address to the British Parliament." *American Foreign Policy Current Documents: 1982.* Washington, DC: U.S. State Department, 8 June 1982.

———. *Public Papers of the Presidents of the United States.* 22 Weekly Compilation of Presidential Documents, doc. nos. 1090 and 1113, 14 August 1986.

Storrs, K. Larry. "Mexican Difficulties in 1994: Uprising in Chiapas, Assassination of Colosio." *Congressional Research Service Issue Brief.* Congressional Research Service, Washington, DC, 21 June 1994.

U.S. Department of State, American Consulate Monterrey. "The Partido Accion Nacional (PAN): History and Platform." Department of State Airgram, unclassified, Monterrey, Mexico, 29 September 1981, 6.

U.S. Department of State. "Bernard W. Aronson, Assistant Secretary of State for Interamerican Affairs. Statement before the Subcommittee on Western Hemisphere and Peace Corps Affairs of the Senate Foreign Relations Committee." *Department of State Dispatch.* Washington, DC, 29 April 1991.

———. *Country Reports on Human Rights Practices: Mexico.* Reports submitted to the Committee on Foreign Relations, U.S. Senate and Committee on International Relations, U.S. House of Representatives, Washington, DC, 1980–1996.

———. "Fact Sheet: Cooperation with Mexico: In Our National Interest." Washington, DC, 18 May 1994.

———. "Fact Sheet: U.S. National Interests and Cooperation with Mexico." *U.S. Department of State Dispatch* 4, no. 17, May 1993.

———. Letter from Wendy Sherman to Senator Ben Nighthorse Campbell, 19 July 1994.

———. "Mexico–Gen. Gorman Congressional Testimony." Telegram, unclassified. Washington, DC, 27 February 1984. As contained in the National Security Archives, Iran-Contra Collection, File 01399, George Washington University, Washington, DC.

———. "NAFTA: Embracing Change." *Department of State Dispatch* 4, no. 37. Washington, DC, 13 September 1993, 1.

———. "North American Free Trade Agreement: Letter to Congress, 1 May 1991." *U.S. Department of State Dispatch.* Washington, DC, June 1991.

———. "President Bush's Upcoming Visit to Mexico." Foreign Press Center Briefing, Washington, DC, 21 November 1990.

———. "Press Briefing." Washington, DC, 25 January 1994.

———. "Secretary Christopher: A New Consensus of the Americas." *State Department Dispatch.* Washington, DC, 9 July 1994, 3.

———. "Statement of Warren Christopher before the House Banking and Financial Services Committee." Washington, DC, 25 January 1995.

———. "Visit of Mexican President Salinas." *Department of State Bulletin.* Washington, DC, December 1989.

U.S. Department of State, Bureau of Intelligence and Research. "Mexican-Nicaraguan Relations: Can Mexico Moderate the Sandinistas?" Classified memorandum, Report 195-AR. Washington, DC, 12 August 1981.

U.S. Department of State, Bureau of Public Affairs. "Background on Mexico." *U.S. Department of State: Background Notes.* U.S. Department of State, Washington, DC, March 1986.

———. *Realism, Strength, Negotiation: Key Foreign Policy Statements of the Reagan Administration.* U.S. Department of State, Washington, DC, May 1984.

U.S. Embassy, Mexico City. "Statement by U.S. Ambassador James R. Jones." Undated (August 1994).

U.S. General Accounting Office. *Mexico's Financial Crisis: Origins, Awareness, Assistance, and Initial Efforts to Recover.* GAO/GGD-96–56, U.S. General Accounting Office, Washington, DC, February 1996.

U.S. House. "Remarks by Congressman David E. Bonior." Press conference, Washington, DC, 17 May 1994.

U.S. House Committee on Banking, Housing and Urban Affairs, Subcommittee on International Development. *Hearing on Proposed U.S.–Mexico Free Trade Agreement,* 102nd Congress, 1st sess., 16 April 1991.

U.S. House Committee on Foreign Affairs, Subcommittee on Western Hemisphere Affairs. *Mexico: The Uprising in Chiapas and Democratization in Mexico: Hearings before the Subcommittee on the Western Hemisphere,* 103rd Congress, 2d sess., 2 February 1994.

———. "Opening Statement of the Honorable Robert Torricelli at Markup of H.Con.Res. 250, Electoral Reform in Mexico." Washington, DC, 14 July 1994.

U.S. House Committee on International Relations. *Economic Support for Mexico.* 104th Congress, 1st sess., 7 March 1995.

———. *Hearing on Economic Support for Mexico: Hearing before the Committee on International Relations.* 104th Congress, 1st sess., 7 March 1995.

U.S. House/Senate staff. "H.R.____," 104th Congress, 1st sess., 23–30 January, discussion drafts.

U.S. Senate Committee on Appropriations, Subcommittee on Foreign Operations. *Hearing on FY 90 Foreign Operations Bill.* 101st Congress, 1st sess., 15 March 1989.

U.S. Senate Committee on Banking, Housing, and Urban Affairs. *The Mexican Peso Crisis and the Administration's Proposed Loan Guarantee Package to Mexico: Hearings before the Committee on Banking, Housing, and Urban Affairs.* 104th Congress, 1st sess., 31 January, 9 March, 10 March, 24 May, and 14 July 1995.

U.S. Senate Committee on Finance. *Hearing on the U.S.-Mexico Free Trade Agreement.* 102nd Congress, 1st sess., 6 and 20 February 1991.

———. *Nominations of Joseph H. Gale, Darcy E. Bradbury, Jeffrey R. Shafer, David Lipton, Melissa T. Skolfield, and David C. Williams: Hearing before the Committee on Finance.* 104th Congress, 1st sess., 30 November 1995.

U.S. Senate Committee on Foreign Relations. *Hearing on the Nomination of James Baker to Secretary of State.* 101st Congress, 1st sess., 17 and 18 January 1989.

———. *Mexico's Economic Situation and U.S. Efforts to Stabilize the Peso: Hearing before the Committee on Foreign Relations.* 104th Congress, 1st sess., 26 January 1995.

U.S. Senate Committee on Foreign Relations, Subcommittee on Western Hemisphere Affairs. *Situation in Mexico: Hearings before the Subcommittee on Western Hemisphere Affairs,* 99th Congress, 2d sess., 13 May, 17 and 26 June 1986.

U.S. Senate. Letter to Secretary of State Warren Christopher. Washington, DC, 28 June 1994.

Index